A Day in the Life

By

Ray Burton

ISBN: 1-4033-2790-4

This book is printed on acid free paper.

1stBooks - rev. 05/15/02

Trust in the Lord with all your heart and lean not on your own understanding. In all your ways acknowledge HIM and HE will make your paths straight.

—Proverbs 3:5-6

I dedicate this book to my mother, Mary Burton, the Black Pearl, for her warmth and unending love throughout my life. Mom, I cherish the ground you walk on.

(I just hope she doesn't read this book)

A world of thanks to the following: The Saturn Corporation and all the team members who supported me in my first endeavor; to the staff of the Local UAW 1853 Wheel Magazine; to the cities of Nashville, Detroit, Chattanooga, Atlanta, Kentucky; to WJRS in Russellville Ky; to Orion Media, Black Expressions, Concord Productions, Writer's World Magazine, Barnes & Noble; to all the superb review houses who gave *If I Ruled the World* soaring reviews. Thank you all...you made it happen.

Special shout-outs: to my second set of parents Nollie and Fannie, thanks for everything; to Aunt Peggy who owns and operates the Shear Ritz Hair Salon in Detroit; Team member Ginger Parham for her responsive support; to Rose Jones for her collaboration in the cover design.

To the following Book Clubs: "Women of Leisure", "'Bout Town", "Inner Expressions", "What's Good To Read?", and "Lady Readers". I'd like to say thanks to all you lovely... ladies for having me, you stimulate the mind. Let's do it again—soon! We have a lot to talk about!

To my team of precious readers: Lanae and Dana Burton, Regina Johnson, Bobbie Nix, Cheryl Smith, Susan Riddle, Ann Soule, Zumi Carvalho, Diane Koch, Will Smith, Stephanie Jackson, you guys provide a tremendous service. I tip my hat to you.

To my Chief Editor-in-charge: Krystal Burton, who keeps me on my toes.

A big hug and kiss: to Bobbie Nix. This beautiful lady took the ball and literally ran with it! Bobbie, I can't say enough about you. Thanks, girl, I *really* mean it.

...it came in short, two second intervals, a dark foreboding of coming disaster, shattering my joyous mood instantly, rudely, almost maliciously. The sensation that I was about to get the shock of my life made everything distinct and slow as I turned my head around. I stared at it. I could hear it clearly—too clearly; in fact, it was a sound that I had come to hate.

Not ten feet from where I was standing, it sat there, on a cherrywood and marble pedestal, beckoning me from the sofa.

...it was the sound of my telephone ringing...

Chapter 1

I left my apartment at seven-thirty, wearing my usual attire: denim blue jeans, white silk shirt, and black Italian-cut boots. Even though the sky carried a veil of darkness, a black velvet swirl inoculated in its backdrop, a pair of heavily-tinted Versace's rested on the brow of my nose, giving me a casual, nonchalant look. Nestled firmly in my left palm was a small leather pouch which contained my ID, keys, money and credit cards. I hated to place anything in my jeans; it takes away from that smooth, contoured look I strive to achieve.

Instead of taking my car, I walked east for a few blocks, crossing Fourteenth Avenue and going to Vanborne Street, where I caught a cab. I told the driver to take me to Palmer Estates, then settled back on the seat, thinking about the evening to come, and of my recently acquired client.

His name was Alvin Harris, and he was quite wealthy. A house in Palmer Estates, he had to be. I had met him a week ago at a club located twenty miles outside of Detroit, near Sterling Heights. We'd caught each other in the midst of a glance, just a simple glance and nothing more, but I knew undoubtedly how much could be communicated by a look. We talked a few times over the phone and a date was made. This date. Which was new for me, the people I usually encountered on a first date met me at a predetermined location. But this time I decided to stray away from my usual strict routine. He seemed so different, so sophisticated. I wanted to see what the man was all about.

I could still picture his face sitting in the club. He was tall, virile and strong, with skin like burnished copper. His deep-set eyes were soft and kind, and the laugh lines around them betrayed the fact he had a sense of fun and adventure. His short black hair was trimmed immaculately, with a touch of gray feathering the temples. His nails were manicured and his teeth perfect, bright and white as snow. There was a quiet, confident nature about him, and although he said he was forty-four, he came off as much younger, yet refined and full

1

of wonder. He was wearing a dark blue double-breasted Armani suit with a red silk tie. The man was in there, I'll give him that.

I could tell he liked me. He seemed smitten from the moment he laid eyes on me, seeing at once that I was not only prepossessing but I appeared sincere and discreet, which I am. He invited me to sit down and we talked, covering a wide range of subjects, and he was surprised and pleased that there was nothing he couldn't discuss with me. Movies, politics, the theater, cars, and especially music: how Luther Vandross had the silkiest voice in the business, how rap was overcrowding the entire music industry, why you had to find an oldies but goodies club like the one we were sitting in to dodge that shit.

We drank Dom Perignon and I laughed delightedly at his jokes, which were quite decent. When he turned serious, his nostrils flared when he did, I was immensely interested in everything he had to say. The man was intelligent. At some point during his words, our hands touched, and his knee brushed against mine, and by the time the night had ended, he was so ravenous and horny it seemed as if he were panting. But nothing happened. Oh, he wanted it to, believe me. But I didn't want to appear easy, and even though I knew I'd be walking away from a small fortune, I decided to hold my ground. Besides, there was a certain professionalism I had to keep.

The cab pulled to a red light. I stared out of my window. I couldn't keep my mind off the evening to come. I had to pinch myself. Shit, just thinking about this man was making me wonder about my limitations; was there anything I couldn't do? I found a grin creeping a bit at the corner of my mouth. Slow *down*, I said to myself, you can't let yourself become too cocky. And besides, you may have your work cut out for you. He might not be all that easy, and you may have to spend all evening trying to get him up, let alone getting him off. I've had my share of disappointments, clients that presented the perfect package and turned out to be the hardest, stubbornness lays in the world. This was especially true of Arabs. They were very appealing to look at but as a whole, they were extremely disappointing. Rich, yes. But arduous lays. I hope this wasn't the case with Alvin Harris. I *really* hope not. I was a little tired.

Massive pillars flanked the gates. When the cab drove up, lights flashed on, holding the driver in a harsh white glare. A figure loomed in the background, then a man stepped out from the lights. The guy was massive—about six four, two fifty, with nose-tackle shoulders. He was attired in a sand-colored suit with a green tie and carrying a long black Mag-lite flashlight in one hand, a clipboard in the other; a silver-plated Smith and Wesson rested in a holster on his hip. He stared at the cab for several seconds. Then he walked up and peered inside.

His voice was flat as he shined the light in the interior of the cab. "My name is Ron Ingram, security. Can I help you, please?"

The driver craned his head over his shoulder, directing the man to me.

I rolled my window down halfway then I assumed what I hoped was my politest expression. "I'm here to see a Mister Alvin Harris."

The man looked comfortable, yet there was no reply for a moment. Apparently he was checking out things, making sure everything was on the up and up. Then the man's head, with it's neatly trimmed gray hair, bowed. "Would you sign this, please?"

There was a blank space to sign on the bottom of the clipboard. I signed my name with a flick of my wrist, then returned the clipboard and the pen to the man. I noticed there was a flat hump across the bridge of his nose that suggested it had been broken more than once. I also caught a slight paunch that tailoring had done a good job of camouflaging.

"Follow the drive to the main residence," the man instructed at the driver. "When you drop your passenger off, come back the same way, please."

The gates swung open, and when the cab passed through, the driver saw a reflection in his rearview mirror, with the gates closing behind him. "Some place, huh?" he said.

"Some," I agreed.

The asphalt pathway wound through groves of maples and oaks, the headlights picking up the vivid colors of the leaves. It wasn't until I came over a rise, leaving lots of space between my back and the seat cushion, that I caught so much as a glimpse of the house. It was a great sprawling structure, ablaze with light. Standing magnificently, the center section had wings extending from either end, all of it three stories high. The drive was circular in front of the house, and to one side was an area in which to park vehicles. The cab pulled to a stop alongside a titanium-colored XK8 convertible Jaguar.

I paid the fare and gave the driver a little something extra, for luck. When I got out, I gave the house a good once over. To my left was a courtyard planted with privet-hedged rose gardens and precisely cut flower beds. Large conifers, some pruned in the spare, graceful Japanese style were also situated in the area. Then, in front, were looser plantings of fern and ground cover and crushed rock walkways, which lined the low-growing lilies. From what I could tell, judging by a wooden arbor positioned off to the side, the display extended to the rear of the home.

I could only shake my head.

As the cab pulled away I took a deep breath. This was it. A date with the rich and handsome Alvin Harris. I exhaled slowly and smiled, again experiencing a surge of confidence attributed to my good looks. I proceeded up the walkway. Artfully placed spotlights allowed just enough illumination for a safe passage. As I made my way, all around me, wafting in the air, botanic perfume blended in wonderful, strange combinations. The results were pleasing, to say the least.

Strolling pass a collection of miniature conifers which had been trimmed surgically, and a boxwood knot garden as intricate as any maze I'd ever seen, I climbed three steps and rung the doorbell. Almost instantly, I adjusted my expression to a professional one. Seconds later, another light from out of nowhere appeared, seemingly setting the stage. My pulse was racing now. I had to force myself to keep still. Slowly, silently, I heard the locks being disengaged. *God be with me*, I uttered, resisting the urge to cross myself.

The front door opened. To my surprise, a woman stood in the archway. She was slim and quite attractive, approximately five-feet two and looked to weigh no more than a hundred and twenty pounds. Her dark hair came to just above her shoulders. She was wearing a pair of blue denim jeans a shade darker than mine. The white blazer she had on as well as the salmon-colored blouse underneath were smartly tailored. Full lips on a pleasant smile added additional beauty to her features.

For a moment, I thought I'd gone to the wrong house. But then the woman's face lit up in an inviting expression. "Hi. I'm Denise,

Alvin's sister. You must be Terry Allens. Please, come on in." Her voice was soft and southern, and her demeanor seemed cultured.

"Thank you." I stepped past the woman and she closed the door. From the foyer, I checked the place out. It was laid. The drapes, the hardwood flooring, the furniture which sat on it—everything about the place screamed money. To my right, a white Baby Grand piano sat royally, looking as if it should be showcased in glass.

"May I offer you something to drink?" the woman asked, heading over to where dark bottles and glasses and an ice bucket were sitting on a bar cart. Without waiting for a reply she turned and I was handed a glass of red wine. My mouth was dry so I immediately took a sip. I'm not a great lover of wine but this was good. It carried a gentle tang of cinnamon. The woman extended a hand, palm upward, to a black leather sofa. I took a seat, still glancing around. Other than the sofa and loveseat, the rest of the room was furnished in antiques, mostly French provincial, I presumed.

"Alvin will be down in a second or so," the woman said inside of a sigh, crossing back to the bar cart. "Never mind me, I was just leaving."

I nodded my head.

Using tongs, the woman refilled her glass with ice then poured herself another glass of wine. She added a lemon slice from a diced fruit tray positioned on the cart. She took a sip as she turned to face me. It seemed she read my mind. "I know it's strange, but I find lemon slices really makes this type of wine taste better." She stepped over to me and smiled. "Care to try it?"

I shook my head. "No, thanks, I'm afraid I'm not very adventurous."

"Really now." She took a seat next to me and sipped her drink. "You, not adventurous? I find that kind of hard to believe."

I wet my lips with my wine. "Well, I'm here to confess, I'm not. I'm really a square. I like simple things, and doing simple things with down-to-earth people." I looked at her directly. "Know what I mean?"

She smiled, almost seductively. "Yes, yes, I do." She shifted in her seat, and slid closer to me. With delicate fingers, she stroked her hair back from her face and stated, almost wondrously, "You're very…how should I say…easy to look at, Terry. I see why my brother is attracted to you."

Slowly, involuntarily, I grinned back. I shifted my weight comfortably on the sofa, refusing to drop my gaze on her. "I thank you for the compliment. You're quite a dish yourself, Denise."

She scrunched her mouth, giving me a chance to take note of her full, succulent lips. They were nice I had to admit; they looked very rewarding, to say the least. She stared at me, hard, and fell into a short period of silence, then she said, "Can I ask you something, Terry…I mean, I don't mean to pry?"

I arched my right eyebrow, knowing what was on her mind. "You're going to ask me *why*, am I right?"

Abruptly she turned her head. It was a start of embarrassment. Turning to me, she said, "Yes, but I'm not here to judge you—in any way. It's just I'm…I'm a bit confused. You're so attractive and all…"

It was roundabout flattery, and I didn't mind it a bit. I ate it up, in fact. "I do what I do because it's fulfilling, it satisfies a need. To tell you the honest truth, at times, under certain conditions, I love it." I leaned back into the folds of the sofa. "Surely you can't blame me for loving what I do? I mean, how many people can honestly say they really love what they do?"

Her face blank, she replied, "Not many, I guess. It's just…with your looks…" The corners of her jaw bunched.

My voice was studiously neutral as I said, "Are you saying I'm too good for your brother, Denise? Let me know if I'm out of line but is this what I'm hearing?"

At that she appeared stiff, awkward. She was frowning hard, deep in thought. What she was thinking made her look sick. "No, that's not what I'm saying at all," she breathed to herself. "I *love* Alvin. I'm not saying anything like that…"

"Then, what is it?" I finished.

For a moment she stared at me, as frankly as one could. Her mouth was tight and I bet she could have screamed at me at the top of her lungs, *Yes, you are too good for my brother!* But her expression was closed; she was eager to leave. Carefully, she said, "I think I'll take off now, before I make a fool of myself." She looked away.

I cupped my hands over hers and gripped them tightly. "Denise, you're not making a fool of yourself, you're just curious, and there's nothing wrong with that. And if I seem smug, it's just that I get asked this question all the time." I squeezed her hands tighter. "Really, it's okay."

With those words, she was momentarily frozen. Then she shook herself in what I perceived as disgust. Did she feel threatened by what she wanted to ask, or was it by something she was thinking? Or feeling? Was it because of her brother, his choice in life? Or was it because of some shortcoming on her part as a woman? *Hell, I* thought, *it was probably all these things.*

Finally, after gazing at me as straight as she could, she shrugged her shoulders in total disinterest, and said, "You and Alvin have a nice time." She now wore a smile, and it was unconstrained as her earlier dismay as she shook a reproving finger at me. "For the record, Terry, you should consider yourself special, it isn't everyday that my brother invites people into his home."

In response, I shot a glance at her and murmured, "Well, thank you. I'd like to think of myself as special, especially after what it took to get in here."

She made no effort to conceal her fondness for me. "You are."

There was a certain tingling in the air and instead of her leaving right away, we continued with our little introductory chat. I could tell this isn't what she wanted. She tried to keep a vapid smile on her face and nod at appropriate times while her mind toyed with her own reserves. I looked into her eyes. There were so many other things she wanted to explore, to ask, but inquiring about them at the moment proved to be difficult for her, and I guess there just wasn't enough time. I kept a direct gaze on her, and it was impossible to concentrate. The woman took my breath away. Her startling features, the pouting lips, the high cheekbones, everything about her face could hold its own in any company, and she had the most exquisite eyes, a shade I had never seen before.

She giggled suddenly, nearly laughed as she rose from the sofa. She placed her glass on the bar cart and headed for the door. She turned and smiled at me. A second later, however, as she gazed deep into my eyes, I could sense something happening within her, like her emotions turning, until she was nearly close to tears. She opened the

7

door and stepped through. The door closed quietly behind her. I smiled. Something was definitely on her mind, and she was going to have a bitch of a time trying to get some sleep.

I finished my wine and set the glass down on the coffee table. I leaned back on the sofa and crossed my legs, thinking about Alvin's sister, and of the evening to come…and then of Alvin Harris…the star of the evening. I was going to have this man—tonight! I suddenly imagined myself a collector of rare artifacts, about to add another fine piece to my compilation. Maybe I was wrong to think of myself in this manner, but at the moment it's what I felt.

It wasn't long before the moment presented itself.

The star of the evening descended a set of spiraling stairs, his bare feet padding softly as he floated down. Handsome, composed, majestic and regal, wearing a red silk robe with matching pajama bottoms, his chest chiseled and outlined beautifully, he came towards me. The silk flowing around his limbs picked up the contrast of the room, giving off glimpses of light and dark as he moved. With the face of a model and with one of the most gracious smiles I'd ever seen, he stood over me.

"Well, hello, Terry," he announced in a voice that reverberated throughout the room, "I hope I didn't keep you."

For a second, and a second only, I was at a loss for words. I could only stare into his brown eyes. He *was* a good-looking man. Hell, this may not be so bad I thought. Hell, I might even enjoy it. But strictly for the money, of course. "No, Mister Harris, you didn't keep me. Besides, your sister and I had a nice chat."

He smiled charmingly. "Nothing negative about me, I hope."

I raised a hand. "Oh no, on the contrary, there were some great things said on your behalf, on both ends."

He remained cool, in perfect form as he walked over to the bar cart where he prepared himself a shot of Remy-Martin over ice. He brought the glass to his mouth and took a small swallow. He set the glass down and then took a seat next to me. In a smooth gesture, he reached into the outer pocket of his robe and pulled out an envelope. He handed it to me. "A thousand, right?"

He looked at me as if the money didn't mean a thing to him. Apparently, with his wealth, it didn't.

However, it did to me.

The envelope wasn't sealed and because of its bulkiness I decided to count the money. It totaled three thousand dollars, all in hundred dollar bills. I looked at him, a little taken back. "There's three grand in here, Mister Harris?" I inquired earnestly, with a smile.

"Yes, Terry, I know this."

"Explanation?"

"I want you to spend the night."

Strengthening myself mentally, I forced my mind from the money to ask in a husky whisper, "That's a little presumptuous on your part, don't you think?"

His voice came back, exceptionally deep. "Not at all. I believe in laying the cards out on the table and telling it like it is. Besides, Terry, I think you're beautiful, and I didn't want nothing...not anything...to destroy the romantic illusion to come by asking you to stay."

I digested his words, and afterwards, could only nod. They sounded *so* good. I might even use them in the future, on another client I thought. I reached out and touched him because he wanted me to, trailing my fingers across the smoothness of his cheek. His skin was warm to the touch and scented with some fragrance that was earthy and all male.

Expectedly, he smiled and showed his appreciation with a kiss on my lips. His lips were slightly moist, soft and firm. He pulled back and beckoned lightly in my ear, "Take off your clothes and let me see you."

Though I was a little nervous, and felt something wet and soggy churn in the pit of my stomach I, nevertheless, rose to my feet, thinking this was business, with a bonus, hopefully. I stared into his eyes, my hips eye-level with his gaze. Ordinarily when I undress on a working date I do it casually, without a lot of fanfare. But this man, devastatingly handsome with captive, yearning eyes—and filthy rich—threw a wrench into my plans. I couldn't afford to lose him as a client. No fucking way.

A highly-saturated striptease was in order.

Turning to face him, I arched my back as I removed my shirt, which slid off gracefully. I turned to place the shirt on the other side of the sofa. I turned back to face him. I take great care of my body and knew it looked *damn* good, so I took my time, letting him see

9

what a real chest looked like. It was perfect. A chest that had caused clients to slobber over, causing them to inwardly stare and gape—as Alvin Harris was now.

"Beautiful," he remarked. "Simply beautiful. Please, Terry, please go on." A tongue flicked out, re-wetting his lips.

After removing my footwear, I unbuckled my belt and slid my jeans over my hips and stepped out of them. I added the jeans next to my shirt. Dressed only in black silk underwear, I stood up straight, showing the perfection of my flesh. I could tell from his fastened gaze that I was making a great impression. I knew I would. And just to rub it in a little, I did a leisurely three-sixty.

His voice fell to a soft whisper. "Damn, you certainly are breathtaking."

I blushed, purposely. "Thank you."

More breathless calls of encouragement followed, then, kind of timidly, as if to see if I were real, he reached a hand to my stomach. With a slow hand, he stroked my six-pack. His touch was nice, non-intrusive. I could deal with it. In fact, I encouraged his touch, and began a slow turn, letting his hand drift over my faintly-oiled body. He gasped just under his breath. I liked that. It felt great to hear a handsome and sophisticated client like Alvin Harris watching and admiring me as he was doing now. The way his hand reached, hesitated, caressed—the way his body tensed, then shuddered and relaxed—I was driving him crazy. Hunger and desire had come to unravel his once subtle features. There was pleasure in his eyes, and I had to admit, in mine, as well; in fact my chest was swelling with the fierceness of it.

With an admirable display of control, I modeled for him for a few minutes more, until he couldn't take it. I knew he was ready. I could see it in his eyes, amongst other places.

In a voice that was low and thick, the way a man's became when he was fully aroused, he said, "Let's take this to the bedroom."

We did.

The evening went off with no hitches; he was everything I could hope for. He was easy to do, easy to please. He wasn't into anything real kinky; mostly he wanted to be held. A simple intimacy that seemed to be missing from his life. So I utilized all my experience and gave him the closeness he desired, caressing him gently with firm hands and feathery touches. I must have done my job very well.

I left the next morning with five grand.

In the early morning hours following the affair with Alvin Harris, I was awakened from a profound and dreamless sleep by a nagging and persistent ringing at the door of my apartment. The ringing of the doorbell startled me almost as much as the angle of sunlight coming in through my bedroom window. I turned on a bedside light, illuminating a copy of *Sister 2 Sister* and a digital clock which read seven-thirty. I am not a morning person so I was pissed. After knuckling my eyes, I groped for my bathrobe, a faded, well-worn checkered thing, and stumbled hurriedly to the door. I checked the peephole and smiled. It was Regina Cook.

I flung the door open and hugged her tightly. We embraced for a few seconds, drawing a certain need from each other. She pulled away with a bright smile, pleading hunger pangs. The girl could cook her ass off, so hey, no problem. We had eggs and bacon and she did her thing and whipped up a mean batch of waffles. The girl should have been a cook, I shit you not. She poured a small amount of orange juice into my glass, filled it to the brim with cranberry juice, and handed it to me. That was my favorite. I guess I am a little adventurous, after all.

Regina drank her coffee and went on about her boyfriend. In the harsh morning light, I thought to myself, without makeup, she bore little resemblance to the dazzling creature on stage. Regina was a stripper, a damn good one. And nobody, I mean *nobody* could touch her. Her act was sexually charged, intense. But at times, it seemed, at least in the last few months, she was losing her edge. Although her tits had been through a series of three enhancements, she was, unquestionably, slipping a notch in her appearance. I could see the competitive edge also slipping in her eyes, as well as in her attitude. And her once smooth complexion had also withered a bit.

But her condition wasn't from age, like me, she was only twenty-six. No, her early decline was a product of stress, maybe something even deeper. Nevertheless, she could still turn a few heads, for her tits, if nothing else. But no matter how the girl looked, she was cool, my girl. She had three boys: seven, nine and four—three badass kids.

I believe this was the reason for her desiccated, world-weary look. Those little heathens raised all kinds of hell. I joked and told her she should shipped them off to their father. She said she was going to. She wouldn't. She'd talk a good game but she loved her kids to death. Regina was a typical mother, one who loved their kids no matter what. She believed in them, and had every right to do so...they were hers. But she definitely deserved better in life.

This included that sleaze ball boyfriend of hers, Derrick Collins. But like her kids, good old Derrick could do no wrong. Which was ironic, Regina was a strong black woman, a woman who spoke her mind and did it vehemently, without the head moving thing, so when she told me she had hooked up with Derrick Collins, I was like *get the fuck outta here!*

She shook her head in reply, a little shocked herself.

At first she thought him beneath her. He was, for openers, a good three inches shorter than she was. And she disliked the goatee he wore; the flashing rings on each finger; the too-baggy trousers; the bulky clothing period, which was designer name stuff right down to his Timberlands. She also hated the loud gold teeth wedged in the front of his mouth. On top of all of this, the fool had done some jail time.

But apparently he had game, and his flattery won her over. Starved for praise and a bit vain, she believed him all too eagerly when he told her she was the best-looking thing he had ever laid eyes on. He made her feel relaxed, too, much less guilty about being a stripper and having three kids with no man around. He was a slick one. The man knew all the right things to say, telling her that if she stuck with him he'd put her on a stairway to stardom. Which was all bullshit. How and why she fell for it, I couldn't begin to tell you.

Though I got to believe he was good in bed. I'd known Regina for nearly seventeen years, since we were nine. And in these years she never had anything good to say about the men in her life, at least sexual. She claimed all she ever had were duds—men who promised to her curl her toenails, but failing to deliver. Even her first and only husband had failed to bring her relief. On her wedding night she'd told me, he tried desperately to bring her to orgasm. After his failure to do so, he told her she was helpless, "lying there like a bump on a log," and thereafter sought only to please himself. The marriage ended about four years ago leaving her with the three boys.

I remembered Regina crying her heart out the day her divorce became final.

They were tears of joy.

"So, Terry," Regina said with a sly look in her eyes, "how was the date?"

Looking directly into her eyes over the rim of my glass, I smiled back at her. "I don't kiss and tell."

"Please, nigga, cut me some slack," she laughed.

I continued to smile. My gaze on her was direct—and piercing, as if it could pass straight through her eyes and mind to something beyond. "It was cool. I made my ends."

"I *know* that." She looked at me strangely, and her face had a probing expression. "So tell me, was it wood or coochie?"

I shifted in my seat. "Wood."

"Really! So who was it, you never did tell me?" she prodded on impulse. She raised an eyebrow.

The look she gave me took me by surprise. I instinctively felt she knew I had found a real winner. She was one of those few people who could read me—one of the few with whom it was possible to have a down-to-earth friendship and not have anything you say surface later to reek havoc. For that precise reason, I said, "Alvin Harris."

"Alvin Harris!" she shouted. There was a genuine awe in her tone. "You fucked Alvin Harris!"

I met her eyes. They were focused on me hard, not harshly, but direct and eager. After a pause, I uttered, "Yes, and why are you so surprised? Did you think him out of my league?"

"Yes...I mean, no...I don't know..." she whispered, abandoning the pretense that she was still shakened by what she'd learned. "...I mean, Alvin Harris. That man is rich, baby! He owns half the real estate in Detroit! How in the hell did you ever get next to him?"

She looked at me incredulously, as if I had performed some prodigious feat. I guess, in a way, I had. "I met him at Alters. We had a few drinks, we talked, exchanged numbers, and ended up in bed."

13

She nodded as though she understood. "Man, I bet that was wild." She looked up with widened eyes. "Is he hung?"

I chuckled mildly. I found her eagerness both humorous and flattering. Slowly, I replied, "He's okay. I mean, he's ample."

At that, she laughed. "He must be hung like a fuckin' horse, cause your ass is blushing like a peach!"

If it would have been anyone else with a comment like that I would have pulled a veil of coolness over me. I'm a person who considers himself professional, in control. But Regina's friendly manner defused the frank pressure of putting on airs. She went on laughing; I went on blushing. After a few minutes she settled down and looked at me intently.

"Terry," she started slowly, "how…how do you get all these beautiful people—the finest men—the prettiest women." In spite of herself, she smiled with fascination.

I grinned, then went silent for a moment, seemingly relapsing into seriousness; then said easily, "I just tell people what they want to hear. I flatter them, stroke their fragile egos, make them forget about their troubles," smoothly, I sang a quick Luther Vandross line, "if only for one ni-i-i-i-ght."

The results sent Regina in a convulsive fit of laughter. She brought a hand to her chest and shook her head. She then gave me a stern look. "But how, Terry? What do you say? How do you grab their attention?" She became more animated as she spoke, bright with curiosity. "What line do you use? How do you get them in bed like you do?"

I shook my head. "I don't get them into bed. On the contrary, *they do*. I just encourage the fantasy. All people, young and old, rich or poor, pretty or not so pretty, straight or gay, share a common factor: they have needs." I made a deliberate effort not to be candid. "I simply try to find out through conversations and body gesticulations what these people want, and if they have the money or can help me in other ways, I offer them a service." I shrugged, and then as if I were speaking into the air added, "It really doesn't take a lot of brainwork."

"Yeah, but I bet it takes a lot of dick work," she chuckled easily.

"Oh, it does," I agreed wholeheartedly. "It most certainly does. And my clients don't want to hear shit about headaches, or not feeling well because of some twenty-four hour flu, or me not being in the mood. All they want to do is to drop their money and see me drop my pants. 'All right, you son-of-a-bitch, get it up, dammit. I've paid my money and now it's time for you to release the pressure'."

Regina laughed loudly then looked at me as though my simple words counted as wisdom. A gleam shone in her face. "Okay, I'll buy the...supply and demand theory, but people don't always come out and say let's go some place and screw our brains out, do they?"

"For the most part, they do," I said frankly. "Once they find out I'm a provider of sexual fantasies they want to get it on as soon as possible. In me, like most providers, they see a way of tipping out on the mates for an illicit tryst, flirting on the edge with a person who does it for a living. It's all exciting to them. Hell, sometimes they get themselves so worked up—all I have to do is touch them. But as far as the men goes, it's pretty cut and dry. Men are ready to go at the drop of a dime. *However*, the women, well now, that's another cup of tea entirely. You women are special, and I have to be oh-so-skillful. And it starts with something as simple as a kiss, the first sign of affection."

Regina tilted her head. "A kiss?"

I nodded. "A kiss." I wet my lips as I shifted in my seat. "A woman generally makes up her mind whether or not she's going to be a client based on much she likes the way I kiss. So it has to be exceptional, in every way...an intricate balance of pressure, control, tongue technique and moisture. I have to give serious attention to every detail, but not with just my lips and tongue. No, that's just the beginning. My hands have to be involved...placed just so...in her hair, the back of her neck, tracing her jaw line, caressing her shoulders. I have to be an expert in every way, reading her emotions, and varying my intensity and pressure, never allowing her to anticipate what sensation is coming next, and I have to kiss her like I have all the time in the world...like I have the entire night to taunt and tease." I sat back and crossed my legs. "The foreplay power of kissing is quite a delicious surprise, if one has the patience."

Regina agreed with a slow bowing of her head, then, for a long while, she went silent, apparently giving thought to what I had just said. Then she shivered and wrapped her arms about her body. After a few more seconds she looked up and smiled—throwing me her one hundred and ten percent thumbs-up approval. Then, once again, she went silent as she stared at me. A note of sadness finally entered her voice, "After doing what you do, for all these years, do you ever feel cheap?" She held her breath, kicking herself for asking this same question over and over again.

I didn't mind, however. Sometimes I like to talk about it; it helps. I replied with a verbal shrug, "No, not really, not anymore. I've learned to disassociate myself from my profession. As with your dancing, you have to distant yourself from reality, otherwise you'll go crazy thinking about what you're doing for a living. What we do is service the public with a fantasy, nothing else."

Timidly, like a small animal coming out of a burrow after a storm, she nodded her head and began to smile. She seemed relieved by my words. I guess I had spoken critically of her profession, as if I had the right to do so—and nothing terrible had happened. That really pleased her for her expression turned soft and reassuring. In the minutes that followed she drank her coffee—in her own world.

Then, to keep the conversation safe for a while, Regina and I talked about the weather, about politics, about books and movies, our families...anything other than our professions. No, for the moment, we decided to leave the fantasy world at just that.

Chapter 2

I used the abating, time-consuming drive to Ann Arbor Michigan to organize my thoughts and plan the next few hours. I had an eight o'clock appointment that evening and needed to air out my head. I ran a palm over the waves in my hair. Could all this really be happening to me? Am I really a whore? It seemed only yesterday that I was a bartender at a popular nightclub counting my tips at the end of the night, and here I am now, pushing a black convertible SL500 Benz. I am truly blessed, and I guess I should be grateful. It seemed I had everything: a laid apartment, a fat-ass bank account, a change of clothes for nearly everyday of the year, and looks that could carry me for at least another decade or so.

I guess, in all actuality, I *had* to be blessed. At that I laughed, a low and throaty chuckle, as a fanciful, sort of conceited notion hit me. I knew I was a handsome man; my assurance said as much. Other men and women looked at me with hungry eyes; my manner said that, too. There was a kind of electricity in their eyes, a subtle tingle. I could see it glowing in the expression of nearly everyone I came into contact with, whether cool or intense, desperate or confident. And there's no kidding myself, I felt the contagion of it, the pull of their gazes, the inner longing just below the surface. But I try not to come off too cocky or presumptuous; it's not my style. Yet a tiny, barely microscopic feeling lingers inside me that suggests I *am* a cut above the rest. I guess you can call it confidence. I mean, I'm certainly not intimidated by any individual out there.

I shook my head; it was wrong to think like this; sometimes I'm as vain as a strutting peacock.

I adjusted the rearview mirror and stared at my image. I'd been at this game for nearly seven years now. In the beginning I accepted what I did, my new lifestyle, and enjoyed the luxury of buying anything I wanted. But now I feel a deep sense of loneliness. At times it feels like obligation, drudgery to be done again and again. Sometimes I have to ask myself am I real or am I just a gigolo prince who appears for a shining moment to please everyone and then

17

vanishes? My looks and performances charms everyone utterly, and they all feel an enormous sense of freedom to be themselves with me. But who was I coming home to at night? Who was fulfilling my fucking fantasies? Hell, I was a man like other men—I have needs!

Years ago, right after high school, I'd decided I was not a natural man, not whole. It wasn't anything sexual, I mean I loved women. I was not gay! No, there was something else. Something was left out of me, some natural nesting instinct, and I'd felt frustrated over this. I tried to block this frustration by following the traditional route after graduating, but going to college and doing the cramming-for-finals thing had always seemed to be an effort. I thought about selling drugs, or becoming a street hustler, even working a nine-to-five. But that wasn't me. No way. I needed another outlet.

I guess I found it.

But it isn't enough, not for me. I feel blah, and it wears on me heavily some time. On days when I'm especially melancholy, my mind stirs, things tumble in my head like building blocks. That's when I begin constructing tables of organization of my emotion, from different standpoints: frustration, desire, envy, ambition, disappointment. I divide and subdivide these parts and try to give reasons and degrees of why I feel like I do. I gather and collect them and then placed them on what I call my Clarification Chart. I go through each one, my exercise, I call it, and by the time I finish my spirits are boosted. I usually rank pretty high, finding an explanation for nearly every reason—but my elation only lasts for a while.

I know it's because of my chosen profession.

Frequently, I wonder what happens to used, homely whores with decimated figures and missing teeth when they grow old—who takes care of them? Are these the same individuals I see who are public drunkards, with gravely, masculine voices quarreling with each other loudly on sidewalks in warm weather? As always, when I think like this, I'll ask myself if I could hang on to my looks and be able to do what I do for the rest of my life would I really want to do it. A resounding *Hell No!* would surface, regardless of what inducements were offered.

But for the time being I have to accept what I do for a living. I have to come to grips that I was the object of people's affection, their outlet for hidden and suppressed desires...people, who for the most part, were lonely and needed some added spice in their lives. I guess, at least while I could, I would be there for them, wearing a smile that would be breezy and complacently obliging.

I shook my head and drove faster on the expressway, which was totally out of character for me. I'm usually relaxed when I drive, listening to Sade, with her depressing-ass songs. I mean, can't that girl ever sing anything upbeat for a change? But I listen to her anyway. Her voice is like a sedative, so mellow. I think it keeps me stable. No, it's more therapeutic than anything; her voice purges the system, discarding the vestiges of guilt and regret, not to mention shame.

With that, I popped open my console and retrieved a Sade CD. It was entitled *Promise*. I slid it inside my deck and selected track three, my favorite: *War of the Hearts*, and hit play. Then I reached for the pair of sunglasses lying atop the dash and slipped them on. Like oozing honey Sade began to play.

With the wind cutting in my face in all directions, and with the soothing, therapeutic music in my ears, I settled back in the seat. I tipped my head against the headrest as if inviting the breeze to play lover and caress my face. It felt nice, as did the afternoon sun on my neck and arms. I allowed myself to drift into a half-alert state, where the conscious and subconscious were one. Let me tell you, if you haven't been there, you haven't lived.

And if you have been there, you know exactly what I'm talking about.

Vera Armstrong was a tall woman in her middle thirties, on the lean side. Her caramel complexion was flawless and seemed to glow, and her rare gray eyes were winners. For a woman her age, her body was nothing short of perfection. Her breasts were not large, but they were round and full. Her ribcage was tiny, as was her waistline, and her hips were round. Broad where a woman should be broad. All in all, an exceptional woman to be acquainted with.

Vera was the wife of the well-known Mel Armstrong, the president and chief executive officer of Armstrong Automotive Group, a chain of well-established and very profitable dealerships scattered throughout the tri-county area. He was a powerfully built man, and at the age of fifty-three, remarkably fit. His appearance and the knowledge of his power intimidated men and fascinated women.

Over the years Mel Armstrong's money had grown to an impressive sum. And so had his greed. He'd acquired a reputation for spending huge amounts of money to make more. His desire for money—not only the outward trappings of wealth, but money in and of itself—mounted to a physical craving. It became his practice to entertain any and all clients who could push him further into monetary bliss. He was a shrewd business man, but he was also hot-headed, thus making him a man to avoid.

Because of this Vera and I had to practice extreme caution during our meetings. I'd chosen a quaint little place in Novi, fifty miles from her home. It was a low-key tavern that served excellent steaks and had pretty decent drinks. We were seated near the back, Vera's choice, and had a good view of the parking lot. We ordered a couple of glasses of white wine then glanced over our menus. I peered at Vera from a cornered eye. The woman looked magnificent, sitting there in a beige and white Ralph Lauren ensemble. She knew how to put the inner workings of a woman together, and knew the right people for everything: hair, nails, makeup. And it seemed she didn't have a single qualm about spending her husband's money to obtain the look she was after.

In fact, she devoted a great deal of her time to shopping, keeping pace with the latest trends in fashion, and adapting them to what was right for her. I guess that included any other extracurricular items; it was also clear she didn't show any qualms about spending money on me. And I didn't mind cause I must say, the woman treated me *right*. But it wasn't a decision by necessity. According to her, her husband was quite the stallion in bed. But apparently his outstanding performances drifted outside of their marriage. She had heard rumors about a "fuck party" at some hotel involving her husband, but wasn't sure whether to believe it, or whether getting bent out of shape over it would do her more harm than good. I guess she figured any woman who is married to a powerful and successful man has to deal with the possibility of this happening.

But that didn't mean she had to take the shit lying down.

I had met Vera at a play, a splendid rendition of Lorraine Hansberry's *A Raisin in the Sun* was debuting at the Fisher Theatre.

We bumped into each other during intermission. I was by myself and so was she. We connected instantly; our personalities locked with an almost audible click. There was something about her. The innocence and the vulnerability in her face and eyes moved me. I was captivated. Although everything about her appearance bespoke class, and she seemed so well-preserved, she could barely conceal a tremor of excitement as she flashed the most dazzling smile I had ever seen. Yes, the woman had won me over.

I could detect the same emotion in her as her eyes caught mine, though I did catch her attention drifting over my crotch a few times.

We left without seeing the conclusion of the play. Hell, we both figured it would be back next year anyway. We had a light dinner in an inconspicuous little spot in Southfield. We traveled in separate cars. We ate and talked. And that's when she went to work, very quickly, as if to get the preliminaries out of the way—asking probing questions—learning the history of my life. I was frank, and told her everything, even about my profession, though I did hold back a few key things. But I figured it didn't really make a difference, at least not at the moment.

She told me about herself, her problems as she called it, and found me to be an attentive listener who seemed terribly interested in what she had to say. I could tell she was comfortable in my presence, and as we talked, her burdens seemed to be transferred from her weaknesses to her strengths. During the conversation I read between the lines and then saw the bottom line: she saw a way of having her cake and eating it too.

At last, with great reluctance, she rose to go. She hated to leave the pleasant mood, as did I. What a lovely moment it had been I thought. In just that short time, she had aroused both my intellect and my interest, but mainly, my lust. The woman had torn down all my defensive instincts and put a fever in my blood. It was a new feeling for me, and I wasn't sure I was comfortable with it. But it felt so *damn* good! I gave her my cell phone number and we both left the restaurant. Before I had made it home I received a call.

It was Vera.

A date was made. I was soon to find that I had never known a woman with a hunger as intense as Vera's. As for her, after the initial shock and uneasiness, she soon convinced herself that this, after two dates, must be what screwing is all about. She felt it had to be.

That was three years ago, and we've been seeing each other on a regular basis every since. Sometimes money was involved, sometimes not; mostly not.

"Vera," I whispered lightly, hunching forward and touching her hand, "you okay?"

For an instant, ferocity came over her face. She clenched one eye closed and a murderous scowl emerged. Then, as if by magic, she glanced at me and her mood changed immediately. Her expression relaxed into a warm smile as she glared at me. *He was my sweet revenge*, I could hear her saying. Apparently she still carried a thing for her husband. Nobody could change expressions like that. And apparently her husband still loved her, but showed his love with a relationship that was kind and friendly. But the kindness he illustrated was not tenderness; it was not love.

And she was disgusted with herself, with her inability to deal with this.

"Yes, I'm fine, Terry," she replied. "Just fine."

"Is there anything you'd like to talk about?" I asked sincerely, with a purring smile. "You know I'm here for you."

She took an abrupt sip from her glass, then stared at me. I guess she saw the smile that so many clients regarded as sexy as a slap in her face. She knew, too well, how many times I used it to get my money. A hint of annoyance showed in her face as she snapped, "Tell me this, Terry, why do men fuck around? I mean, why get married just to keep fucking around?"

I stared back at her, and she rolled her eyes with a determined, beckoning look, twisting her wedding ring round and round on her finger. "Not all men mess around, Vera," I tried to explain as subtly as I could. "There are a few good men out there with morals."

"Bull-*fuckin'*-shit." She spoke with more harshness than I had expected from her. "All men fuck around, it's their nature...in their blood. They act as though they have to be knee deep in every woman out there—driven by the same ancient needs." She took another hard pull from her glass and slammed it roughly on the table. She shook her head with a mixture of anger and exasperation. "Time and tide waits for no woman," she protested with narrowing eyes, "but it seems they always wait for men." Her eyes started to blur and two red spots surfaced on each of her cheeks.

"That's a reasonable assumption on things as any," I whispered. "But time has been extremely gracious to you." I reached a hand to hers. "You look beautiful tonight, Vera...a wondrous vision of beauty."

I must have said the wrong thing, pushed the wrong button, for she sat up in her seat as if she were ready to spit acid. "Cut the shit, Terry, I don't need that soothing, passive crap right now." She threw me a look that might have been an insult.

I settled back in my seat. "Then what do you need?"

"What do I need?" she hissed like a serpent. "You wanna know what I need?" Her expression was more than vicious—it was positively bloodthirsty. "What I need is your big dick to keep me satisfied—not some pacifying compliment!" She was becoming more tense by the second. Her breathing was clearly labored. Her voice dropped dramatically. "You sit there as smug as a bug—fucking your way through life without a care in the world. You don't give a shit about who you're with—just as long as you're getting paid, am I right, Terry? For you it's all about money, right? Is this where you find your satisfaction?" She tried to summon more indignation, but it eluded her.

For a moment I chose to remain silent, while the words slammed through me like a sledgehammer. The words hurt, deeply, and my nerves jangled like badly tuned strings, and my pulse refused to slow down. *You don't know me!* I wanted to scream. With so much adrenaline in my veins, I wanted to get up from the table and leave. But everything seemed to leak away as I stared at Vera. Reality for her, had become like sand, trickling through her fingers. Her marriage, her life, for that matter, was a sham. It was like a festering wound. It had reached a boiling point and it was time for her to lash out; an impulse she didn't immediately understand had made her react totally out of character. She didn't know how else to call for help. There was nobody there so I footed the bill.

I was okay with that.

I felt her pain.

But now there was a problem.

Vera had exposed herself.

And she was extremely fragile.

I could see her discomfort as she struggled with herself, trying to find the words to smooth things over. Weakly, she propped an elbow on the table with her chin in her palm and peered around the restaurant. When she caught me gazing at her, almost lovingly, she gave a sigh of relief and sank back into her seat. She couldn't be mad anymore, and as usual she retreated.

"I'm sorry, baby," she whispered thickly. "I don't know what came over me." A hint of sorrow briefly marred the smoothness of her forehead.

In response, I gave her a smile which radiated sweet simplicity and warmth, but above all, understanding. She nodded, smiling warmly herself. Though inwardly, I believe, she was checking me out. I had on a black Giorgio Armani tweed jacket, and my blue silk shirt was opened at the collar. She hunched forward and I kissed her lips tenderly. She went to pull back.

But I wanted more.

"Give me your tongue, baby," I muttered against her lips. She hesitated, purposely; I repeated the demand. "Give me your tongue." Tentatively, she let it slide out, and the kiss turned red-hot. I loved kissing Vera. I could keep doing it all night and still want more. That's how hungry I felt for her, hungry and frustrated that I couldn't have her when I wanted. After about a minute's time we both eased back into our seats. I noted that her glass of wine was nearly empty. She caught it also.

"Would you like another glass, Vera?" I asked, flashing her a seductive smile. I was under no illusion that she was locked in a grip of yearning for me.

She didn't answer, instead she paused to let the immensity of her desire sink in. She snuggled cat-like in her seat, posing suggestively, running long, red-lacquered nails over the splendid curves of her bosom, down into the folds of her blouse. Then, with her perfectly shaped brow arched, she said in the most affectionate tone I had ever heard, "No. I don't want anything. No wine. No food. Nothing. I only want you...deep inside me." Her usual shy, virginal manner had fallen from her like a cloak.

I smiled, and was hard as a rock, and I guess I was even blushing. I kept my eyes on her face, not on her hands at the curve of her breasts. I like to think myself different from all others. Sure, I would look at my clients but not obviously. That's not my style. I choose to speak courteously. I never utter suggestive or reckless comments, not unless I feel this is what a client wished. I strive to remain professional, discreet. But as I rose from my seat to take Vera's hand for departure, I made no attempt to hide the quite noticeable bulge in my trousers, a technique that always manages to unnerve her, probably because there was so much more than being advertised.

A whole lot more.

We took her vehicle, a black Lincoln Navigator, and headed to the hotel room I had previously arranged. While I drove slowly through the dark and semi-damp streets, we talked about cars, people, and music. Vera loved Marvin Gaye, adored him, actually, and she also liked Sade. Her jam was *Sweetest Taboo*, which we listened to. She was almost amazed considering our age differences, on how often we agreed on things. Actually, so was I.

She cranked up the music a bit and was really feeling the moment, popping her fingers and doing the neck-swiveling thing. She began telling me about the time she got drunk and got laid in the back seat of her father's old Pontiac. She kept going on how wild it was, how fucking spontaneous and hot it was. She found herself confessing private, freaky thoughts she had shared with no one before.

I took it all in, again reading between the lines. I found a little spot off the road, out of the way. She was almost unaware when I stopped the vehicle and turned to face her, giving her my undivided attention. My arm slid across her shoulders, and we moved closer together, as close as the center console would allow. We hugged each other tightly, for quite a while, in fact. When at last I kissed her, sweet and tender, our tongues dancing a slow, sensuous waltz. Judging by her sweet moans and the nails digging into my jacket, she had no desire for me to stop. She was flattered that a man so young and attractive, intelligent, and sensitive found her interesting. Even for the situation being as it was.

A dozen times and more, my demanding mouth sought hers. She willingly accepted my heated, forceful kisses that I never gave her a chance to return. It was good, wet and delicious.

It was not long before she felt my hand under her skirt, slowly stroking its way up her thigh. Her first time in a car, I was pretty certain, was with a young, inexperienced, hot-blooded teenager, and most likely he went straight for her breasts. Back then, I suppose, it was appropriate.

But not now.

For me to act this way would be purely amateuristic.

Vera was ripe, abundantly moisturized, and ready to go. I bypassed her upper torso and went directly to my primary target. Vera was aroused to the point where she welcomed my touch, and when she parted her legs for my hand, I knew I had her. She needed no foreplay, nor did she desire any. So there would be no exploration, only exploitation. Removing her damp panties with a skilled right hand, I stroked her inner thighs gently with the other while kissing her neck and ears. Once I removed her panties her seat was reclined, all the way, humming lightly, as her body folded back. When the seat came to a stop I knelt over her, like a bronze statue; a position that implied full dominance and control. Then I smiled. She stared up at me, with the look of a wild cheerleader, as well as the eagerness. I slowly undid the buttons of my jacket and shirt, then I unzipped my trousers. The boxers were next.

Seeing me this way, hard and lean, my jimmie jutting at attention with a slight bounce like rigid rubber—knowing what was coming next—her legs shot outward and clamped around my back. I could feel the heels of her shoes digging in the cheeks of my buttocks, drawing me in. With a hard thrust—so hard that she was already in the throes of a violent orgasm—I sank deep within her. My body smothered hers as she bucked her oh-so-eager hips beneath me. Though she had reached her peak, I was not through with her.

There was a point I needed to make: if I were a whore I was going to be the only whore she would ever want. I pressed harder and continued my thrusts. I brought her to climax once more before reaching my own. It was a nice one. I guess, a needed one.

Lying there with Sade playing softly in our ears, pleasingly exhausted, our bodies slick and slippery, we moaned and caressed each other. My mouth brushed her lips in a mere whisper of a kiss, lightly, rubbing and retreating, again and again. She sighed deeply then hissed in my ear, "This is what I call being made to feel like a woman." Smiling, I lifted a strand of hair and tucked it behind her ear, then traced the angle of her jaw with my fingertips. I ended up with her cheek in my palm. She smiled breathlessly, but it soon faded and the light in her eyes changed in intensity. "You're a wonderful lover, baby," she murmured.

With those words, coming from that beautiful mouth, I felt a sudden tightness in my chest at the discovery of how desperately I wanted to believe her. "Am I really now?" I chuckled, masking my emotions.

"Yes." She grinned and stretched closer, rubbing her mouth over mine. She tipped her chin. "Exciting, magnificent, greedy, insatiable, and *damn* good. Incredibly good." Without warning she assaulted me with a kiss; it wasn't rough, it wasn't demanding. It was just *hot*. Searing hot. Blatantly sexual. The heat flowed over me, followed by her hands. I went with it, and because of the hungry, open-mouthed kisses and heated gropings, we made love again. Once more, afterwards, we laid tangled together. Thoroughly pleased. But not merely by the act of making love, but by a solid and profound sensation. However, as good as it was it was time to leave.

Despite my profession a sworn agreement, a solemn trust, if you will, had been reached between me and Vera. When I was with her no condom was necessary. I wouldn't do anything to harm Vera, nor would she to me. So we had this understanding, and it was to be respected as long as we were together. However, because of this understanding, there was a slight problem creeping up, or should I say, seeping out. We quickly cleaned ourselves up.

The night ended with Vera and I finishing our date at the hotel. It was nice. I was in rare form. And because of this, I was tipped...*very* well.

Chapter 3

I was late for my weekly basketball game with the fellahs at the recreation center, despite me doing everything short of running red lights to get there on time. I was tired. Vera had worn me out. It showed up in my game. It was off, to say the least. One of my shoes came off, my grip was slippery, and to add insult to injury, there were several honeys in the stands witnessing my humiliation. After sending up back-to-back air balls, I decided to pass the ball instead. The next three assists went into the stands. Everything went wrong. My jumper was pathetic, lay-ups unmentionable. The harder I tried, the worse I got. Grateful for a timeout, I took a seat on the sideline.

"You're not planting your feet before releasing the ball," my cousin Will, the basketball star, noted, getting ready to get back into the game. "And you're not getting close enough for lay-ups, not enough follow-through, my brother."

"I'm considering golf," I replied, my frustration surfacing.

"Look, cuz, your game is good. You just ain't concentrating. Take your time, focus, and follow the ball." He popped me in the chest with the back of his hand. "And keep your shoelaces tied." With that said inside of a sneer, he scooped up an insulated water mug which sat on his side. He shook it to see how much was left then tipped it up and guzzled down half before dousing the rest over his face and shoulders. He used a towel to wipe the water from his face and neck, then ran it over his chest and stomach, making a couple of quick swipes under his arms before tossing it back in the chair next to him. The moves and mannerism of a true jock I grinned.

Will was soon called into the game, and he demonstrated his skills, handling the ball like it was an extension of his hand as I watched jealously. He had chiseled muscle definition, liquid coordination, and he could, without effort, take you to the hole without you ever knowing that you'd been taken. I wondered if magnificent athletes had any concept of how they made the rest of us feel.

The game ended and because Will's car was in the shop, I drove him back to his house. He settled in the seat and smoothed back his wavy hair with the palm of his hand. Will was a handsome dude, about six-one, with a solid, streamlined physique. His skin was the color of creamed coffee. Believe when I say, women were the least of his problems. He glanced over at me. There was a sly expression on his face and one of his thick eyebrows rose upward. I could tell by the look it was interrogation time. Will knew everything, even about the men. However, he never judged me; he knew it was all about the money. But he just couldn't understand *why the men?*

As if the words were being forced out of him by a deep but involuntary nudge, he started in on me. "You still fudge-packin' them faggots, cuz? You know that makes you one, don't you? Even if they ain't doin' you."

"Man, don't start that shit up again." I couldn't restrain myself; I faced him directly, showing my irritation plainly. "Do you ever have anything else to talk about, *besides* my life?" Thinking I knew what was coming, I winced inwardly and gripped the steering wheel harder.

"Nah, cuz, not really," he admitted with a smile. "I mean, my cousin, Mister Pretty Boy, a man who could have his choice in bitches, is bangin' bitches *and* niggas? Now you tell me, what else *is* there to talk about? I'm just sayin', what can top that shit?"

"Your life," I snapped back. "What's been going on in your life...*playa?*"

He sighed happily. "Bangin' bitches and workin', what else is there?"

"Plenty."

"Like what?"

"Going to church, maybe?"

At that he whistled his astonishment. "Well, ain't that the pot callin' the kettle black! You got a lot of nerve! Dippin' your jimmie in a different hole almost every night!"

I didn't respond, not yet; my mind was on a comeback, a good, stinging one. I couldn't find one, however, so I just said, "Why don't you and I go to church this Sunday...together?"

He hesitated and gave me a strange look.

I nodded slowly, studying him; the strangeness of my expression cooled his ebullience. Unable to face me, he turned his head. He stuck his hand from the car, palm up, and let the rush of the wind push it back. Without turning his head he said bitterly, "Preachers ain't nothin' but ex-pimps. The whoring business has been squashed now them dudes done found somethin' else to do."

"You don't believe that nonsense, not for a minute," I replied.

"The hell I don't."

"So you're saying that your mother is wasting her time by listening to Pastor Jones?"

Sharply, he turned to me. "Nah, man, I'm not sayin' nothin' like that. I'm just sayin' if they close shop on you, you've got to open another." He frowned. "Hey, let's just drop the subject, all right? Besides, we were talkin' about your ass." He shifted his weight in the seat and stared at me, fully absorbed. "For the life of me, I can't figure out how you can go from sweet, delicious, delectable, wet, and oh-so-good punany, to a sweaty, nasty, hairy *man*. How do you do it?"

I chuckled and shook my head. I knew what Will was trying to do. He was grateful for anything that kept me from questioning him about church. Plus, I think he liked hearing about my life. My background was as a complete contrast to his everyday comings and goings; but it was also attractive—as strange and wondrous as a fairy tale. And it always kept him in awe. He wanted me to tell him *every*thing. And most of the time I usually did, however, with limited honesty, without names or explicit details.

"Money, cuz," I replied simply. "I do it for the money."

He slumped in his seat. "Man, can't no money in the world make me go that route."

"Bullshit," I retorted. "Every person has a limit."

"Not me."

"You mean to tell me, if a man offered you a million dollars to stroke him a few times you'd turn it down?"

"You damn straight."

"Bullshit. You're just saying that cause ain't nobody going offer you anything like that."

In response he threw up his hands. "Listen, cuz, all the money in the *world* couldn't make me bump another man in the butt."

"Well, that's what I used to say. But all that has changed."

With that, he gave me a drilling glare. "Do you enjoy yourself when you do that? Do you get off?"

Involuntarily, I scowled to keep myself from flinching; my face darkened. "What do you think?" I asked stiffly.

He couldn't answer that. He was too ashamed of himself. Softly, as if he were apologizing, he said, "I just wanted to know where you stand. I'm not here to beat you down, cuz..."

"Then what is it?" I cut in.

Surprised and a bit taken back, he answered, "I mean, when we shoot ball, are you...well, are checkin' out the fellas on the court?"

A pang went through me. My own cousin thought me to be straight-up gay. Well, I wasn't! I was far from it! Not quite able to meet his gaze, I announced, with bold authority in my voice, "That's it...I ain't playin' no more ball with you guys, all right? If you think I'm stretching a hard-on for the fellas, then how can we possibly win?"

Will put a hand to my shoulder and gripped me hard. "Listen, cuz, I really don't care what you do or who you do it with. What you do is your business, all right? If your thang is pushin' up on men, then..."

"It ain't my *thang*," I murmured in a clenched voice.

He nodded. "Well, *whatever* it is you're still my blood, man, all right?"

Abruptly, I took hold of myself with an almost visible grip of will and forced down my anger. I looked at him, and suddenly without warning, he did something that amazed me down to the soul. Nothing in the world could have prepared me for the way he swallowed his pride and said, "I love you, cuz. You're my favorite people, man. I mean it, you mean a lot to me. We go a long way back, almost as babies. I may fuck with you every now and then about what you do, but you can always count on my back. I mean this, cuz." Afterward, he gave me a smile like a gift.

His words, his smile, had moved me deeply, though he couldn't tell. I swallowed a lump in my throat. I tried to remain unaffected but then I became so overwhelmed that I leaned over, without thinking, and kissed him on his cheek. At once, he pulled away and rubbed his cheek roughly. His eyes went from side to side, hunting for comprehension, then his pleasure became so bright that he started laughing. It was infectious.

In fact, we were still chuckling when I dropped him at home.

Chapter 4

When Regina came out onto the tiny stage, warm tones picked her up, bathing her in brilliant light that reflected from the sequins in her hair and on her leopard outfit, and especially from her eyes. Even from where I was sitting, at a table off to the side and four rows back, I could see how bright her eyes were.

The crowd in the club, the high rollers, were putting out a steady stream of oohs and aahs, high-fiving each other. They knew it was showtime. Waitresses in slave-girl costumes moved among the tables, and in the beams of light, a haze of smoke drifted. But then Regina began to stir, and the noise subsided until the only sound you heard was the hard-hitting, raucous tune of Prince. I believe the tune was *Head*. Every eye in the place was fixed on Regina.

Her body gleamed under a thin coating of oil. The girl was looking righteous, and her tits were amazing, even if they weren't real. She also had good musculature, not that hard, in-your-face look, but firm and inviting. She went into her routine, standing before the crowd and seemingly making every muscle in her body vibrate. Then slowly, she turned, presenting the perfect ass. She threw the crowd a sly expression over her left shoulder then made her butt cheeks dance.

It was awesome, a sight to behold.

The muscles in her cheeks jumped and rippled, seeming to flow in one direction and then another, like turbulent waves in the ocean. She kept it up for a minute or so, building tension in the room, hypnotizing the men with her glistening, twitching flesh.

Then she turned, and leaned against the wall. She began gyrating her hips. She clasped her hands over her head and starting moaning with an agonized expression. In the seconds to follow, she began to work her hips like grease lightning, almost in a frenzy. It seemed as if she was being electrocuted; her body convulsed violently. Startled, the crowd gasped, and there was scattered applause. Nobody knew what to do. At that point, she stopped her movements and slid to the floor.

Lying on her back, she arched and began a slow grind, rotating her hips. She did this with an exaggerated swivel and a hard emphasis at the peak of her thrusts.

The lighting changed, filters altering the beams from one color to another, soft orange, to yellow and then blue deepening to gold, each one more dazzling than the one preceding it, until Regina was drenched in fiery red, as hot as the writhing, twisting gyrations her body was going through. She threw her head back, her eyes closed, then, with sweat glistening on her body, her fingers touched the hidden clasps on her costume, and the entire front melted away. The entire audience was bug-eyed, the men wild with desire and the waitresses with what I supposed was jealousy, although there could have been some admiration in there, as well.

Head back like a swan, chest thrust out, back arched, mouth open, sweaty muscles writhing in perfect synch with the music, Regina bucked her hips faster and faster, the bass seemingly pounding in her head with a rhythmic frenzy—you didn't need much imagination to understand what this was supposed to represent. When the climatic moment hit, the music and the lighting in the room hit also—one long blast to coincide with the scream from Regina's throat.

The music suddenly died, all at once, and Regina shuddered, her muscles taunt and trembling. She held the perfect stance, on her back, her hips in midair, and she held it, and held it, until the stage faded to black.

For a long moment, the room was dead silent. Then it exploded with thunderous applause. When the lights came up seconds later, the stage was bare.

The applause and dog barking went on for a full minute, calling for an encore, but I knew Regina was done. She'd told me once, when I'd asked why she didn't return, that she never forgot the words I had said to her: always leave your clients wanting more. So who was I to argue?

"Hit you again, Terry?"

I looked up to see a waitress standing over me, her breasts jutting out from a skimpy bodice. "Yeah, and bring me a bottle of Cristal, too, please."

She picked up my empty and sauntered off. The noise level had resumed to what it had been before Regina's performance, and people were starting to file out. For the majority of the patrons the best was over. There was nothing left to see. I mean, who wanted to see the clean-up acts? They were nothing compared to Regina; it was about as exciting as watching a presidential debate.

The waitress was back with my order. She placed the champagne and two glasses on the table and I requested my tab.

"Just give me a twenty, Terry," she smiled. "You buy a bottle damn near every week so the owner said this one's on the house."

I hadn't expected this, but this was cool with me. I fished a fifty out of my wallet and dropped it on her tray. "That okay, Beth?"

She smiled. "Yeah, it'll do." She tucked the fifty inside her deep cleavage and it disappeared, which appeared as magic, considering the skimpiness of her outfit. When she walked away, I took note of her rear. It was nice and full, with a slight jiggle. Just the way I like it. I began opening the champagne when I felt a tap at my shoulder.

"Hey, you." Regina gave me a quick peck on the cheek and sat down. "For me?"

"You know it is." I poured her a glass then myself.

"Thanks, you're a lifesaver. I'm thirsty as hell." She clinked my glass and tossed most of hers down. "Damn, this shit is good." She set the glass down. There was subtle tension in her face as her eyes scanned the room. She was obviously looking for her boyfriend. But she quickly changed her expression, smiling brightly. I guess she was feeling great at having put on such a good show. She did three a night, four times a week, and now she was finished and was feeling good about closing on a high note.

As she took another sip, her gaze moved around the room and then back to me. "Did you like the show?"

I grinned. She was wearing a large dress shirt and jeans, no makeup, and her dark hair was tied up in a knot on top of her head. Not a speckle of sequin or glitter marked her skin. None of the patrons would have guessed she was the same girl who'd been firing up their crotches only a short time ago. "You were magnificent. Like always."

Her eyes searched my face, and a smirk quipped her lips. "Did you get hard? Tell me the truth, Terry."

I chuckled. The girl probably left every man in the room with a wedge of steel in their pants, and here she was asking me, her best friend, was he as hard, as well. Was she trying to see if I had a thing for her? Or was she slyly testing my sexuality? Probably the latter. I thought about it more. Yes, definitely the latter.

"Yeah, I got a little wood watching you," I smiled.

Her face lit up in a little-girl grin and she sipped her champagne. She drained her glass then refilled it. As she poured she looked up. "You haven't seen Derrick tonight, have you?"

"No, I haven't. Were you expecting him tonight?"

She rolled her eyes. "No, not really." There was something on her mind, something she wanted to talk about. She let it go. Instead she nodded her head toward the stage. "I tore that motherfucker up, didn't I, Terry?"

I shrugged looking at the stage, as if the question was obvious. "You always do. You're one of a kind, and nobody can come near to what you do."

"Thank you, baby." She went on smiling. "It's an art form, you know? Dancing."

This proved to be a safe topic; she seemed very relaxed. "I agree. It takes a lot of work to perfect an act like yours. I tip my hat to you." With that, I gave her a mock salute. She nodded her appreciation.

After an hour or so, there were only about eight people left in the place, including Regina and I. I asked her if she needed a ride and she said yes. While Regina gathered her things I shook a few hands. I hollered at the DJ and spent a couple of minutes with the owner, thanking him for the bottle of Cristal. I waited back at the bar and sucked on a few fruit slices, where I overheard a few of the waitresses bitching about the cheap-ass niggas not tipping worth a damn.

Five minutes had passed. With a duffel bag straddling her shoulder, Regina rounded the corner. She was wearing a slouch hat and had on a light overcoat that couldn't completely conceal the curves underneath it. Something I suppose I had noticed a few too many times. I got up from the stool and we headed for the exit. I held the door as she passed through. The night air was cool and crisp as we made our way to the well-lit parking lot. We turned to see Tyrone Kellum, the security guard, a tall and lean brother, with a face that was as black as the night. A man who had passed his prime several years ago. With his slick black hair pulled into a ponytail, his fingers lit up with jewelry, he was about as flamboyant as a guard could possibly be, given his position and pay, always hitting on the women as they left the club. He was smooth, I'll give him that, and because the brother took special care of my ride, keeping an attentive eye on it, I took care of him.

Smiling brightly, he strolled toward me with an upturned palm. I reached into my wallet and slipped him a prearranged, tightly-folded twenty. He nodded graciously, while sliding the twenty deep into his trousers. As I walked away I had to smile. It seems as if everybody wants something extra for doing what they were supposed to be doing anyway.

Regina and I approached my Benz, which beamed like glass. I opened the door and she slid inside, smiling charmingly at me. I peeped a glimpse at her firm legs, even though they were covered in jeans. They *were* nice. I waited until she was seated properly then I proceeded to close the door. I walked around to my side and slid inside. I hoped Regina hadn't caught it, the fierce erection in my pants, because it was there. I hadn't a clue why I was like that, and at the moment I could have chipped concrete with it. There had to be a reason.

Apparently Regina's dance was still fresh in my mind.

Chapter 5

It was Sunday morning. I was in church. I distanced myself from
the usual hoopers and hollerers, and sat near the back. Somehow,
today, I didn't wish to be near them. It wasn't because of their
behavior, I just had a lot of things on my mind. A whole lot. I tried
not to think about them. I tried not to think about the three clients in
the last couple of days, one being a male. I tried not to think of the
four I had lined up for the early part of the week, all women, ages
ranging from twenty-nine to forty-six, three of them married.

Which bothered me.

More than ninety percent of my clientele were married women.
Where's the goddamn husbands in this picture? I shook my head; I
didn't want to bog my mind with this stuff.

I stole a peek at my Rolex: eleven-fifteen. How long was church
going to last today? I wondered. While waiting to get the pastor's
wisdom I glanced around the sanctuary. The choir was on and had
the congregation rocking. It was a pretty packed house, I had to
admit. I like it like that. I took note of the people around me, and
from what I could see, they were dressed nice, a few designers' names
came to mind. I couldn't help but think that most of the members
came to church just to show off their threads.

Never mind the pastor's message, I could hear them saying, *but
did you see what Sister Ruth had on? Girl, can you believe she had
the nerve to wear something like that up in here?* I chuckled;
sometimes I made my own self laugh.

The service pressed on, and after tithing, dropping a check for five
hundred dollars into the offering plate, I returned to my seat. The
money was shuffled off in a hurry behind closed doors. The deacons
then took their rather comfortable seats in the pulpit. Then, with the
strike from the organist: It was showtime! Members of True Meaning
Baptist Church, it was time to be entertained!

I know I shouldn't think like this, but at one time or another one
cannot help but draw a comparison between a pastor about to deliver
a sermon and a soulful entertainer. The connection suggested a

mental picture as it brought to mind a pastor from my former church, the Reverend Clayton Michaels. Now he put on a show! To see him work out was a treat! It was like watching James Brown in his hey-dey, doing *Please, please, please.* I mean, this brother had the capes, the scream, the hair—everything! At one point during one of his rousing, electrifying sermons, I half-expected to see him shimmy on one leg down the aisle. He was a real character, really fun to watch.

I never knew what happened to him, though. He kind of dropped from sight. Last I heard he was preaching out of some run-down motel over on Cass and Third, the heart of lowlifes and corruption. This brought to mind what my cousin Will had said, about preachers being ex-pimps. Maybe he had something there?

I shuddered. I didn't even want to think about this, either.

In the moments to follow, after the choir finished up on a stirring hymn, the Reverend Levi Clarksdale made his appearance, grinning like a chimpanzee, flamboyant robe and all. He went into action; but despite his theatrics the message he conveyed was concise and inspiring, very powerful: 'No matter how atrocious our behavior or actions may be, God will still forgive you if you come to HIM with a willing heart and repent, and that HE will never abandon you in your time of need'. I found the message deep.

When service ended, I placed the bible I was using back into the rear rack of the bench seat ahead of me. I headed for the door when suddenly I was greeted, also mobbed, effusively, by a few women belonging to the congregation. One squeezed my hands heartily, the other two hugged me ecstatically, nearly feeling me up. I wondered what in the world was going on? Did I miss something in the today's sermon? I was overwhelmed, and a little confused.

That's when Sister Charles, a huge but shapely woman outfitted in a stiff-necked dress of drab beige, approached me. She had a stern expression on her dark, almost black face. Without saying a word, giving no warning of her actions, she took hold of my forearm and hurriedly whisked me from the herd of women, who threw a very menacing, unchurch-like look at her backside. With her firm grip still in place, she escorted me out to the parking lot, then to her car, a dark blue GS300 Lexus. I didn't want this. I wanted to see the pastor. The pastor personally bestowed farewells to each and every member passing through the exit with his wife by his side. I wanted to thank him on such an inspiring sermon. But thanks to Sister Charles' bumrush I'd missed the opportunity.

And judging by the smug expression on her face, she didn't give a damn.

She turned my arm loose, then with short, angry movements she reached into her purse and pulled out a cigarette. She gave me a sour smile as she lit up. She took a deep drag and shot a stream of smoke upward.

"Sister Charles," I asked with a puzzled look, "why did you bring me out here?"

She watched me mildly, seemingly pulling her thoughts together.

With an effort, I repeated slowly, "Sister Charles, I would like an explanation, please."

"So would I," she said to the confused look on my face. "Got anything you want to tell me? Got anything you want to get off your chest? Feel the need to repent?"

I shook my head and tried again. "You literally dragged me out of the church like I was a child and now you're playing twenty questions." I cocked an eyebrow. "Well, now that you've succeeded, want to tell me what's up, Sister Charles?"

She sighed irritably and took a drag from her cigarette. She exhaled at one side of her mouth. Then she leaned against her car and rested her elbow in her palm, narrowing her wide-set eyes. "My dear Terry, there's a rumor going around about you." The strong deliverance in her voice told me she had rehearsed a confrontation with me, and had no plans on losing.

I saw it otherwise. "Don't believe rumors, Sister Charles, it's not church-like."

She didn't care for my sarcastic reply, and grimaced humorously, "Boy, don't run that crap on me, I'm twice your age."

In response I shrugged. "Your point being...?"

"You think you're smart, don't you, Terry?" she remarked unexpectedly, without taking her eyes from me, giving me a mirthless smile. In lugubrious concentration, she took a pull from her cigarette. This time she exhaled through her nose. It wasn't a pretty sight.

I was getting pissed. "Look, Sister, if you've got something to say, why don't you say it. I've got better things to do with my time."

She saw her chance and went straight for the jugular. "I'm sure you do. Like fucking and getting paid for it?"

I answered her simply, stepping closer and coming to a halt before her, "Yes, and time is money. So speak your mind." I thrust my head forward and adjusted the tie knotted at my throat, a simple enough motion, yet, the way I did it, it emerged as terribly intimidating. I could tell she was unaccustomed to such intimidation. It probably did something crazy to her stomach, most likely between her legs. But she amazed me, and kept her cool, waiting until I was finished; she already knew what she was going to say next.

She wedged her cigarette between her lips and with a single nail, pushed me back. Then she forced her aggression aside. She thought for a moment, smoothing her hair with a curved palm. Clearing her throat first, removing the cigarette from her mouth, she whispered in a sultry tone, "As a Christian, I cannot, in good conscience, let you continue to go on with such unacceptable behavior..." She reached out and adjusted my tie. Her voice dropped lower still, until it was little more than a breathless whisper, "...not without checking things out firsthand."

I looked at her questioningly, watching her face, trying to *see* if what my *ears* had just heard was true. Sister Charles—a pillar of the church, of the entire community, it seemed—was coming on to me! This couldn't be! I shivered. Not her! Not Sister Charles—the woman was like a mother to me! I thought about her proposition. I couldn't do it. Uh, uh, no way, no how. Not for all the money in the world.

Baffled as I was by this revelation, my professionalism kicked in. My training had taught me to say the appropriate things for any given situation, though I knew this was going to be a stretch. I reached out and clasped her hands in mine, mindful of her cigarette. I shot a gleam at her and began to explain. "Sister Charles, while you're a very attractive woman, with a voluptuous body, don't you...well, don't you think we'd be compromising a treasured relationship by taking it to that level?"

In response to my words, she dropped her head. Apparently these were not the words she wanted to hear; she appeared wilted; her hands became weak in my hands. I chose to remain silent, to let the meaning behind my words sink in. I remained silent for so long that she glanced up. She was considering me with her head tilted to one side. She moistened her dry lips.

"I don't know what I'm saying here," she murmured, with a low, crouched voice, her hand concealing the slight movement of her lips. "It's just that…after Manny left me for another woman five years ago I get so lonely. I can't get a man to even look at me, you know?" She puffed on her cigarette a few times then held it near her lips as she stared at the church. "They say you're supposed to find your soulmate in there. Well, where's mine, huh?" Tears were starting to well in her eyes.

Before they could fall, I said in a tone—a voice strong and formal, and yet unwittingly charming— "You *will* find your soulmate, Sister Charles. You've just got to believe you will. And you know as well as I do, he's out there, searching for you as we speak." I gave her hand a quick squeeze. "Don't you let this man wander out there while you hide. It isn't fair for either one of you. You understand what I'm trying to say here, Sister Charles? You've got to believe."

Slowly, gradually, she turned to face me. I guess my words restored the logical reality of the situation, took away the illusion that I was a male prostitute, and that she had propositioned me. She looked at me. She wanted to say something. In all actuality, none of this had anything to do with me. But she couldn't tell me what it was. Often I felt a quiver of hurt and personal fading when I saw people in this state.

Slowly, tears streaking her cheeks, she decided then to relieve her mind. With quivering lips she uttered, "Manny was selfish. It was always his wants, his needs, his ambitions. He expected me to do all the compromising, all the adjusting, have all the understanding. As long as my wants and needs coincided with his, everything was just fine. And when they didn't, he made my life a living hell…then he up and leaves me for another woman…"

Looking for an escape from her dilemma—or at least from my presence, so that she could try to pull herself together—away from the embarrassment she felt—she turned her head away and said dutifully, "I've got to go." As soon as she spoke, she realized there was something she had to ask, for her peace of mind, if nothing else. Slowly, she brought her gaze on me. For the first time since she had startled me with her proposition, she seemed herself. She smiled. At once, her expression and relief made her look ten years younger. Trying to keep a level voice, she batted her fake lashes and said, "Tell me, Terry, the truth, please...if we didn't have a treasured relationship, as you put it, would you have..."

"In a heartbeat, Mrs. Charles," I added swiftly. I reached out and ran the tips of my fingers down her cheek, along the curve of her jaw. "After all, you are one well-stacked little honey." Then, as a cherry on top, though it was a strain, I let my glance drift down to the vee neck-line and the succession of buttons and loops that ran down the front of her dress—an outfit which appeared to have been designed for a woman of eighty who had lost her figure. I brought my eyes to her eyes and licked my lips, aware that every muscle in her body was rippling under my gaze as surely as they would under my touch.

She smiled and blushed; her expression held the shape of my compliment. I could tell it was enough for her. She took one last hit from her cigarette and flicked it away, as if it was a former problem. She opened her car door and slid inside. She started the engine and then powered down her window.

"See you in church next Sunday, Terry?" she asked, leaning her head out the window.

"Wild horses couldn't keep me away, Sister Charles," I replied with a strong, confident voice, accompanied by a warm, understanding smile. "And when I see you next Sunday I want to see you in something a little more risqué, you know what I mean? Show your figure, girl. It's in there." I winked a slow eye.

She nodded, and I smiled, warmer—and she was smiling so hard herself—that she began laughing. But I could see she remained close to tears; but laughing over the situation was an improvement over crying. The fact that she wasn't crying enabled her to turn her gaze in front of her as she slowly drove away.

I watched as her Lexus left the parking lot. I wanted to leave also. But for a moment I remained where I was. I thought about the recent escapade, and then I decided it was dead and over with. I headed for my car however, as I did, I found myself going in another direction, back to the church, back to the sanctuary. I felt the need to pray. However, I had no desire to kneel at the altar to confess my problems—or in front of the pastor or any of the deacons. No, I wanted to pray alone.

I made my way toward the church. Then abruptly, I was stopped in my tracks, as if there had been a hand on my shoulder. A thought came over me, more like a chill, as if the sun had sailed behind a dark cloud and taken its warmth away. *An omen?* I wondered. On impulse, I clenched my teeth, then I peered hard into the sky. *How could someone like Sister Charles get wind of what I was doing? How could she possibly know my business? Who could have possibly told her?*

These unexpected questions made me feel strange, as though I was being violated—conspired against. Without warning, my curiosity was replaced by rage. The sense of impending disaster was strong in my gut which caused a faint chill to fiddle through my nerves. It was the way a sense of trouble always came to me. Something was definitely not right. I turned and headed for my Benz.

The need for prayer was gone.

The building seemed typical of the ones that you saw depicted in the movies set in New York and Chicago, during the late fifties and sixties, faded brick with a canopy out front and a uniformed doorman. It was clean and well-preserved but had none of the flair and limelight you found in the newer high-rises in the bigger cities today.

Attired in a black doubled-breasted suit and a smart, catchy yellow tie, I strolled past the doorman and entered inside. I walked up to the apartment clerk and told him who I was and what room I needed, and then waited while he spoke into a house phone just out of sight behind the counter. I glanced around. Even though I had been here at least three dozen times, the place still held me in awe. The lobby was huge, done up in gray, with thick carpetry and several pairs of upholstered benches.

The clerk hung up and looked at me. "Eleven C. Turn right off the elevator."

I knew the way, and I suspected he knew I did too. I nodded then walked toward the elevator. As I was about to push the button, the doors to the elevator opened and a beautiful white woman with a thick mane of golden hair cascading abundantly over her shoulders emerged. She was wearing a white cashmere sweater and jeans which she filled out nicely. Her age was hard to gauge—anywhere from twenty to thirty. We exchanged glances, seemingly doling each other compliments as I stepped inside. I rode the elevator to the eleventh floor. When I came to the apartment I pressed the buzzer and a man opened the door.

I knew at once the guy was gay. He had on a loud, florescent green tee shirt and super tight white jeans. His features were big in a small, narrow face, and even though he was dark skinned, lifeless blond hair fell across his forehead, and his arms were embroidered with tattoos. Around his eyes was the heavy art work of mascara.

"Hi, you must be Terry," he announced, with a heavy lisp, swishing his hips from side to side.

I couldn't help but notice the guy had a third leg poking from his crotch. I held a casual expression. "Yes, that would be me. I'm here to see Mrs. Brooks."

The man in green and white stepped back and aimed his chin inside the apartment, and when I entered, he closed the door. I looked around the place, which was filled with the aroma of perfume, or perhaps, I reasoned, some kind of potpourri.

"Eve will be right out," he said with a girlish glee in his voice.

I nodded, still looking around. To my left, a splendid buffet had been set up off to the side on a large silver platter, filled with crab, lobster, some kind of soufflé, and a salad of marinade asparagus tips. There were also grapes, brown bread, a thick wedge of deep yellow cheese, and a steaming bowl of something God only knew. The man sampled some of the crab declaring it superb, and offered me a taste, which I declined.

I watched him stuff his face then asked, "Who might you be?"

He smiled, and spoke around a mouthful of crab. "My name is Patrick Woods. I'm a dear friend of Eve's." He went about the crab, saying it was wonderful, seasoned exactly the way he liked it, with all the right spices.

I sucked in my cheeks. "Why don't you fix yourself a big plate? Instead of pecking at it?"

He tore off another piece of crab and popped it in his mouth, looking at the platter appreciatively. "This stuff is really outstanding." He looked at me with a bright smile. "You sure you don't want some?"

"No, thank you. I just ate." My disinterest was nearly flawless.

He then looked at me eagerly, slyly. "Wanna do a line of coke? It's some grade-A shit?" He punctuated his recommendation by kissing his closed fingertips sensuously, then tossing the short-lived kiss to the heavens.

"I'll pass." My tone was patient, as always, but he could sense my irritation.

He took my cue and rubbed his hands clean. "If you'll follow me, please."

I followed the guy, taking in my surroundings. From what I could tell the living room hadn't changed much since my last appearance, it was still laid to the bone—waxed pine floors under Chinese rugs, high plaster walls, a carved teak ceiling, and lots of stylish, comfortable-looking furniture. A few pieces had been added, but basically nothing major. Mrs. Brooks was a woman who loved to spend money on home furnishings.

From there, we went into the dining room. This room had been changed dramatically. A new table stood where the old used to be, surrounded by ten mahogany high-backed chairs. New pictures hung on the walls, and the wallpaper was now a bluish green. A far contrast from its former color. To my left, an open door revealed the kitchen; white and pink curtains had now taken the place of light blue and beige. We headed on. I knew where we were going.

At the far end of the hallway I saw the door to Mrs. Brooks' bedroom. It was closed. The swishing gay smiled at me then knocked on it, and a woman's voice, Mrs. Brooks, I presumed, said to come in. He opened the door and stepped inside. I went past him into the room. Inwardly, I gasped. There were dozens of four-inch cinnamon-scented candles scattered about, which provided the only light in the room.

What the hell...? Then I turned.

My jaws nearly dropped.

Mrs. Brooks was quite a sight!

I wasn't sure what I'd been expecting, but it wasn't a forty-six year old widow perched on her bed seductively with her tits billowing out of a little something she had picked up since our last encounter. Actually, to tell you the truth, though I would have given my little finger sooner than admit it, I got a little wood. With her body garbed in leather and lace, and a striking black garter belt, she looked quite inviting, as if she could be a working girl. Her face was also quite spectacular, nearly flawless. At least it was until you got close enough to see the hairline wrinkles at the edges of her eyes and mouth.

Sprawled out on the bed, a huge, turn-of-the-century mahogany four poster, made up with crisp, white linens and a green wilted-silk spread, she studied me as I approached.

"Thank you for coming, Terry." She glanced at her friend standing in the doorway, then back at me. "I thought I'd add a little spice to our get-together this evening." She drew a deep breath and announced formally, "Terry, darling, I would like very much for Mister Patrick Woods to join us. There's enough of me to share with everyone." With that said, she dipped a hand down within that ample valley of hers and, after a struggle, pried a giant breast out of her outfit. It hung there in front of me like a big, beige punching bag.

"Oops," she smiled, her eyes fixed on mine. "Look at that. It seems as if something has fallen out." She moved her hand over and tugged out the first breast's mate. "Uh, oh," she giggled, "there goes the other one." She then gave me a dazzling smile.

There were two chairs in the room and I sat down in one of them. I gestured to her friend, who took the other.

I undid the two buttons on my suit jacket. "Listen, and listen good…whatever you two had planned tonight consider it a bust. I don't do threesomes. When I commit to an agenda I rarely stray from it. I'm sorry but that's just the way it is with me. I don't like surprises."

As I sat back in the chair, calm, aloof and bored, Mrs. Brooks made no reply, but continued to look at me with dreamy, lazy eyes, rubbing the tips of her breasts, thrusting them provocatively, casting long shadows against the walls with her arms. She hit an irritating nerve when she threw a clawed hand in my direction while emitting a tigress-like snarl.

The gesture, as erotic as it was intended to be, did absolutely nothing except set my teeth on edge. I felt myself losing it. I closed my eyes and silently counted to ten. I opened them at Mrs. Brooks. "Mrs. Brooks," I said, feeling I wasn't getting through to her, "I can see you went through a lot of time and planning for this, but I meant what I said: I *don't* do threesomes."

Hearing those words, she appeared deflated, and her lips compressed into a thin line.

I sat back in my chair. "Look, let's understand something. In spite of my title, I'm very discreet in who I sleep with. I'm also very careful. I only deal with referred customers from established clients."

With no trace of my simmering words evident, her gay friend rose from his chair and placed a hand to my shoulder. I didn't want it there. His hand was like the rest of him—long, slim and scaly. He gave me a hazy glare and went on about how gorgeous I was, how deep my dimples were, how I almost seemed tropical, that I had a disarmingly perfect mouth, that I was truly blessed.

When he was done I frowned. I couldn't help but note the rehearsed quality in his words. I suspected they were words he'd repeated endless times. "Thank you for that embellished compliment," I said sharply. "I'm deeply flattered, really I am. But nothing has changed. First of all, I don't know you from Adam. Secondly, *I* choose with whom I sleep with. Thirdly and finally, I *don't* do threesomes. What part of this do you have difficulty in understanding?"

He went silent for a few seconds, then said, "Let me ask you something, Terry, do you trust Eve?" He gave Mrs. Brooks a warm glance.

With that, *I* glanced over to Mrs. Brooks. There was nothing warm in my expression. She was still sitting seductively, still stroking her tits. Yet she knew I was doing everything to remain calm—everything short of screaming, *Call off your boy, lady! I mean it! Tell this flamer to back the hell up!* Yet she said nothing, did nothing.

I turned my head. "Yeah, I trust Mrs. Brooks. What's that supposed to prove?"

He lowered his body so that his green eyes, obviously contacts, met mine. I could smell seafood coming off his clothing. I wanted to take my fist and drive it right through his face. But I didn't, of course; my professionalism means everything to me and I wasn't about to blow it on some flamer.

He hesitated then said, "Oh, on the contrary, I beg to differ, it proves a lot. Do you honestly think, given your relationship with

Mrs. Brooks, that she would do you any harm? Do you think she'd risk that for a lousy roll in the sack?"

I took his words personal, me being a lousy lay, I was far from it.

Smiling from ear to ear Mrs. Brooks cleared her throat, as if sending me a signal to ensure me of her trust, her good intention. But I paid her no mind. I looked up at the vaulted ceiling for a moment, and then my gaze came back to fasten on the flamer. *Getting fed, getting high and getting off,* I thought disgustedly, *the three things this jerk probably wanted most in life.* I peered over to Mrs. Brooks, something akin to a ravenous hunger also showing in her expression. I closed my eyes, silenced by the thought that suddenly flashed in my mind. I felt like a slab of meat, to be tugged and pushed, to be served up in a crockery for their bathing tongues, chewed and digested for their enjoyment. I shook my head and then stole another glance at the flamer; the gleam of interest in his eyes was undeniable. It only took a white-hot second to make up my mind—*the two of them can find themselves another boy! Screw this shit, I'm outta here!* I rose from my chair and headed for the door.

The flamer started after me. Mrs. Brooks stopped him with a snap of her voice, as if chastising a child, "Back off, Patrick! Take a seat in the chair," she added in what sounded like an order. "I want to speak with Terry...outside."

We met in the living room where she told me she would pay me two thousand dollars above my standard fee. That suggested a rather interesting picture of my portfolio; I could actually hear a "cha-ching" in my head. I thought about it, the money, the flamer, the money. I told her to make it three and she quickly agreed, saying this was the fantasy she'd always wanted to fulfill. I didn't give a shit what the reasons were, I just wanted to get paid.

She was deliriously giddy, and her expression was so lunatic that she nearly shouted aloud. She brought balled fists to her mouth and spun around with whetted anticipation.

I settled her down and laid out my ground rules: I do the penetrating. Absolutely *nothing* enters me—*nothing!* And that this was the absolute last time she would have me to do something like this, and that she was not to pull any sneaky shit like this again. I fixed her with a glare that threatened to make her face catch fire. My words had hit home, I could tell. She gaped at me as if I had threatened to strike her.

"I understand, Terry," she murmured under her breath.

That established, I showed my enthusiasm.

We turned and entered the bedroom, together.

The night went off without a hitch.

And even though my stomach turned a few times all went well.

And I got paid…well.

I left Mrs. Brooks' apartment four hours later. I was feeling kind of good. I had every reason to. Along with getting off twice with Mrs. Brooks, I'd just turned a nice piece of change. I summoned the elevator. As I waited a familiar feeling crept up my spine causing the hairs on my neck to prickle. I tried to shake it off but the feeling wouldn't go away, like an irritating mosquito buzzing around your ears, knowing it had you at a disadvantage.

When the elevator doors opened there was an overweight lady inside. She was no doubt one of the tenants in the building, taking her poodle for a piss. It was a horrendous-looking thing. She was no pretty sight, either. Her silk robe was tattered at bit at the hem. The sandals on her feet were worn, and the hair protruding from underneath her floppy hat made her look like a derelict, a real piece of work retrieved from some gutter I thought. I stepped inside and the doors closed. The woman tried to engage in some light, friendly conversation. However, I didn't respond. I just stared at her—or avoided staring at her—in misery, disgust, or rage. All of a sudden I reveled in my reactions toward the woman. Why was I pissed at her? She hadn't done a damn thing to me? Actually, to look at her, she wasn't all that bad looking.

The doors opened and I allowed the woman and her dog to pass through first. It was a gesture which held little merit. Apparently she thought me mean and rude. She turned and gave me a drilling glare. Her beak-like nose jutting with fierceness, and her wrinkled, tight mouth and narrowed eyes adding to the glare, struck me with such a chill that several moments had passed before I realized that the doors of the elevator were closing. I caught them and they retracted. The woman gave a loud snort of disapproval then with bowed and spindly legs, sauntered off with her dog trotting behind her.

I left the building and walked to my Benz. I cranked the engine but didn't drive off, not right away. Instead I slumped in my seat, propping my elbow on the armrest, supporting my head with my hand. Like an old friend the gnawing feeling returned. I turned on the radio, trying to break the silence, the feeling in my head. It wasn't working. I pulled down the visor and peered into the vanity mirror and noticed that a scowl had twisted my face, and my eyes seemed to flash anger. But most of all I looked like I wanted to weep.

In the moments to follow, beyond the music and the dim illumination of the vanity mirror, beyond the knowledge of knowing I had a knot of bills secured in a gold money clip, that I would most likely use as blow cash, beyond the fact I had a look that wouldn't hesitate to demand an audience of *anyone*, beyond the fact I was sitting in a brand new—bought and paid for SL500 convertible Mercedes Benz—beyond the fact that I was living so-ever-nicely, I felt myself searching for something else, an explanation for why I was feeling like I was.

What was it? I fumed.

I made a noise between my teeth that echoed through the interior. That's when it hit me.

Hard.

Abruptly, I sat up in my seat and turned off the radio. I knew at the moment I looked like a lunatic, but I didn't care. I think I had something going here. I came to the conclusion that Mrs. Brooks had no idea that I had men clients. So how in the hell did she find this out? As far as she knew I was strictly heterosexual. I gave no indication to contradict this. So how in the hell did she know?

I was a man who crept in the shadows, stayed strictly low-key. I never tried to attract attention the way a lot of people in my profession do, and I never wanted to build a rep. All I wanted was to handle my business. So what happens? Some jealous prick sees me making a few ends, and decides to make my body a punching bag—a dartboard, for a better choice of words.

The thought of this left a trail of petulance across my mind.

I could feel a dull flush overtaking my face.

All at once something dark and sinister seemed to conspire around me, and brought drops of perspiration to my forehead. And it was because of this eerie sensation that I decided then I would finish out the week with my last client. After that I wouldn't book anyone else. It was time to get less physical and more mental.

Chapter 6

It was Wednesday, late in the afternoon. I was kicking it with my cousin Will. We were standing in the driveway of his two bedroom home in Royal Oak, listening to the sounds of the Isley Brother's *For the Love of You.* Will was in the process of removing in what had to be the hundredth coat of wax from his ride, his pride and joy, a Cadillac STS Seville. It wasn't a new one but it sure looked like one. He kept it in tip-top shape, serviced dealer only. The bright September sun picked up the car's brilliant black finish, and the 22-inch 10-spokewire chrome wheels were nearly blinding.

Will had called me earlier that day and told me to stop by. I hadn't seen him since our basketball outing so I told him I'd be right over. Will had the day off, a rare event, so I knew I had to move before some honey pulled his nose in another direction. There were a few things I wanted to run by him, about the rumors. When I did he listened very carefully, giving me his full attention, at least as much as he could spare between swipes over the hood of his car. But I knew he was taking it all in, sorting the different things I'd said with a heedful consideration.

I really appreciated my cousin.

He was a cool brother, relaxed, his own man, speaking his mind without sugar coating anything. He was a factory rat, a hard worker, and loved to get paid. However he now did this legally. For nearly four years, since he was nineteen, Will slung grams of coke for a living. He dodged a few skirmishes with the law, and made some mad ends. But after his three year old daughter Kelly was born, he had lost all his illusions about running the streets and making underhanded drug deals, having decided it was much better to earn your ends without peering over your shoulder. It was a wise decision; he never once looked back.

"You can't be serious," Will said, looking up at me with a beige chamois cloth in his right hand, still working the wax into the car's exterior.

"I am," I said.

Will toyed with the chamois cloth, flipping and folding it expertly, jockeying for a clean spot. When he found it he put the finishing touches on the quarter panel. He stood up and peered at me with a half-amused, half-curious expression. "You really think somebody's spreadin' venom on you? Whassup with that? You ain't pissed nobody off, have you?"

I thought about it. If there was one thing I couldn't stand was being in the dark, especially on something like this. I forced myself to take a breath and let it out before answering. "No, at least I don't think so. You know me, I'm pretty smooth with everybody."

"Yeah," he nodded, "that's you, all right. So, you don't have a clue, huh?"

I shook my head. "Zilch."

He chuckled. "Maybe it was a disgruntled customer. Maybe you didn't lay the pipe right and they felt cheated." He elbowed me in the side. "You ain't slippin', are you, cuz?"

I smiled, inwardly finding the notion hilarious. I was *good*. My thoughts surfaced, and I said, "Not hardly. I still wear the crown—undisputedly." With that, I cupped my crotch and gave a hard tug. I knew this was totally out of character, but at the moment, I couldn't help myself.

Will reciprocated with a good-natured grin. "So, Mandingo, what are you goin' to do about your rumor problem, if it really is a problem?"

"What do you mean?"

He hesitated, then said, "Maybe all of this is just in your head. Maybe you're just imagining things are being said about you. Or maybe somebody spotted you with some dude and assumed the worst. Whatever the reason, I wouldn't lose any sleep over it."

I looked at Will, feeling myself powerfully drawn to the probability of his words. "Maybe you're right," I conceded. "Maybe I am being a little paranoid over this. I think I'll just chill on the whole matter."

"That's what I would do. You can't sweat every little thing that's bein' said about you. Man, people are always goin' to find somethin' bad to say, some negative shit to keep things goin'."

I took a deep breath and sighed heavily. "Yeah, I guess you're right."

"I am, cuz, take my word for it." Will gave my shoulder a light squeeze. "Don't sweat this shit too tough, cuz, it ain't worth it." He curled a lecherous eyebrow. "Besides, if you sweat it too hard you might not be able to get it up for your date tonight." There was a definite mockery in his expression.

"Never left a client unsatisfied," I countered smoothly, unruffled.

With that, Will paused, and gave me that look, that probing, inquiring look. I knew what was coming. No longer able to contain himself, he asked, "Ever have a problem with that, you know, gettin' your jimmie up?"

I shrugged, looking the perfect picture of a polite nobleman, leaning against the car, my arms crossed over my chest. I began studying my nails; there was no expression on my face, at least none that Will could read. Finally, I said as cool as ice, "Never."

"Bullshit," he retorted, elbowing me once more in the side. "All the bangin' you doin', I know your shit dies in the water every once in awhile." He cocked a brow. "Cuz, you ain't no goddamn machine. *Every* man has an off day."

My eyes narrowed with a cool, triumphant expression. "Speak for yourself, cousin. Ain't no nuts and bolts loose here."

There was a note of legitimacy in my voice, on my face, and Will looked at me as though I were a real, honest-to-goodness, bona-fide stud. "No shit, cuz? Even if the bitch is dog-ass ugly, you can still get it up and hit it?"

"Like a sledgehammer," I replied in a silvery tone. "When a client drops the loot, I knock the boots." To myself, I laughed. Sometimes I could really be a character.

Shaking his head, licking his lips, and then clearing his throat, Will grilled me on every possible scenario his mind could come up with, and no matter how disgusting, vile, uncouth and unsettling the things were that he threw at me, I emerged victorious, telling him I could get it up no matter what. Finally, after ten minutes of this, he relented, saying he'd met his match. There was little left to be said, only that I was the *man!*

Will and I talked for about an hour or so, and touched on a variety of things, his daughter's mother, on how she was impossible to deal with, his job at the plant, how they were going to send him to an early grave making him work such long hours, on how much the world had changed in just ten short years, our friends and family, it seemed we'd covered everything. Except cars. That was our topic. We both loved cars. But there was a prerequisite we had to follow; we had to get all the preliminaries out of the way to clear the way for our cars. We loved everything about cars. The sound systems, the tires and rims, the colors, engines—everything. Absolutely nothing was overlooked.

We were about to debate SUV's over cars when a light blue Geo Tracker cruised slowly down the street. Inside were two nice-looking women. The Tracker came to a halt in front of us and the women flashed their bright red lipsticked smiles in our direction. Will immediately became receptive, flashing his pearly whites back at them. Though the brother appeared cool and in control he had the inner look of a drooling dog.

I nodded kindly at the women, showing no noticeable effect.

Having decided who was going to be paired up with who, the two women looked at us conspiratorially. Their demeanor—despite the fact that their combined age couldn't have been more than thirty-five—resembled two women on the prowl for a serious, sexual beat down.

Like a starving man about to eat steak, Will hiked up his jeans and went for it, the makings of a cool stride materializing as he approached closer. As for me, I just yelled, "Catch you later, cousin!" I wished him all the luck in the world. For me, the two women—the two *girls*—were a waste of time. My time meant money.

Like the song said, 'No romance without finance'.

And I *knew* I had the romance. I could turn those girls inside out, upside down, right-side up, forward and backward—a full three-sixty, if I wanted to, and not worry a single minute about giving out. I wouldn't, however. Nah, not me. It seemed as if over the years tits and asses were no longer a driving factor for me. I mean, they were nice to look at, but as a whole, I was no longer impressed.

In my world, money spoke the last and the loudest.

I turned and headed for my Benz.

I had a date tonight.

Good God, Terry Allens was handsome thought Vera Armstrong as she stretched out on her bed. He had it all! He was tall and athletic-looking, with pretty skin, beautiful brown eyes, and a drop-dead dimpled smile. She pictured his raw, masculine body in the nude...his broad, muscled chest, the flat, ridged stomach...down the arrow of dark hair from his navel to the widening curls between his golden brown, leanly muscled legs, focusing on the full, rigid flesh that filled her so completely. She closed her eyes and felt a sharp, hot stab of pleasure, feeling his arms around her, feeling his mouth, his lips nipping and tugging at her breasts...She shuddered. She wanted to see him, *feel* him. Even though it had been just a week ago when she was in his arms she couldn't wait any longer. She needed to have him by her side.

With a determined look in her eyes, she rose from the bed and strode over to the ivory and gilt telephone sitting on the nightstand. She dialed Terry's home but he wasn't there to pick up. Instead of calling him on his cell phone, not wanting to appear desperate, she left a rather nice message on his voice mail, requesting her need to see him. She hung up the phone and walked over to her closet. For some odd reason she felt the need to look sexy, to feel and look like a desirable woman.

When she opened the closet door a perfectly-arranged world was presented to her. Dozens of blouses, jeans, pants suits, blazers, of every texture and style, hung on silk-lined hangers, and scarves in every color in the rainbow had been threaded through brass hooks, looking like streamers. She grinned, then like a knife, her hands sliced through the middle of the clothing and she pulled them apart. In the bottom of her closet, hidden in the back under a dozen or so shoe boxes, stacked like bricks, was a little something she had bought for her next date with Terry. It was a peach and white-laced negligee, made of silk, with painstakingly detail given to its unique design.

She smiled as she pulled the glossy black box free. She crossed over to her bed and removed the lid, which was bordered with fancy red scroll-like lettering. Next came the fluffy tissue paper. Giddy as a schoolgirl she lifted the silk negligee from the box, and her breath caught in her throat. It was so beautiful! she marveled, feeling a certain exuberance overtaking her. She had to try it on, just for a second. Her every move and gesture was thrilling as she slid the garment on, which molded perfectly to her frame. To complete the look she was after, she stepped into a pair of white calf Andrea Pfister pumps, walked to the three-way mirror, and surveyed herself.

She was pleased by the reflection.

The outfit was both dazzling and alluring, and because she shared the family trait of clear gray eyes, it gave the outfit a new depth and luster, which only made her more phenomenal. Sensing she was missing the last needed touch, she added a sprinkle of perfume to her outfit and then into the air. Afterwards she stared into the mirror.

She was definitely pleased, more than pleased, and could hardly wait until Terry gazed upon her. She knew he would really like it. No, she smiled, he would *love* it.

She closed her eyes for a second, imaging what the outfit would do to him, what reaction it would evoke, and how he would show her how much he'd been affected. Then a door slammed and Mel Armstrong was home.

He was mad. That went without saying. "Shit," he snarled, "that asshole union rep thinks he has me over a barrel! Well, he doesn't, the cocksure motherfucker!" He threw his keys on the kitchen counter. "Damn," he frowned, "this kitchen is like an oven, and it stinks in here! Ver...what's that stink?"

Vera quietly emerged from the bedroom as if she were walking on eggshells and hurried into the kitchen. "There's a roast in the oven. It's been warming for nearly an hour. I didn't know you'd be coming home this early." She looked at him lovingly, nervously. "Why don't you sit down and I'll fix you a plate."

Mel Armstrong's eyes lit up when he saw the outfit his wife had on. He strode over to her and, with deliberate, purposeful expression of a man trying to stifle his emotions, lifted the outfit up and began to examine it. As he did so, he snarled.

"Where did you get this thing?" he asked, still snarling.

"Victoria Secrets," she replied, hoping that her husband would like it, even though she didn't have him in mind when she'd bought it.

"How much?" He looked up and peered with drilling eyes.

She swallowed. "Two hundred and fifty dollars."

Two hundred and fifty dollars!" he exclaimed with as much shock as if the outfit had been purchased from Paris France costing a thousand. "Two hundred and fifty dollars! Just what do you think I'm made of, anyway?" He snatched the bottom of the outfit and stared hard, trying to decipher its worth. "One stinking nightgown. Peach colored. Two hundred and fifty bucks plus tax! They gotta be joking! Why in the hell would you buy something that cost this much?"

"It's very pretty, Mel," Vera explained timidly, "and I thought you'd like to see me in something pretty."

In response his eyes flew over her body. Her breasts encased in shiny peach fabric into a mound of titillating flesh, her golden thighs long and supple, he thought she looked very alluring. But he couldn't stand to give her the compliment.

"You bought this for me, huh?" he leered, a little skeptical. "You sure you bought this for me, Ver?"

"Yes," she frowned, shrugging evasively, "who else would I buy it for, silly?"

"I don't know..." he said, narrowing his eyes. "...at least not yet. But I will, my dear Vera...believe me...I will. You can bet your ass on that." The look he now shot at her gave his threat full credibility.

For an instant, ferocity came over her face. She clinched one eye closed so that she could scowl murderously at her husband with the other. But he didn't flinch, in fact, he met her expression with a fiercer one. She had to turn away. "Goodnight, Mel," retreating from the kitchen, "fix your own goddamn plate, I'm going to bed."

"Bitch!" he shouted. "You don't walk away from me when I'm talkin' to you!" He reached out and took her by the arm.

"Mel, you're hurting me!" she protested, trying to wrench her arm free.

He gritted his teeth. "You better not be fuckin' around on me, bitch! I'm Mel Armstrong—I made your ass! I can make you go away, too!" With that, he reached out and grabbed her by her long, jet-black hair and jerked back hard. "You understand me—I'm Mel Armstrong, goddammit! You don't fuck around on me!" He twisted the silken black strands tighter and tighter until his large fist rested at the base of her skull. "You understand?"

I'm not fucking around!" she started to scream, turning her head away. "What the hell is wrong with you, Mel! Have you lost your goddamn mind?" Her voice dropped lower, softly, "I bought this outfit for you...so we could have a romantic evening...I wanted to please you." She was grateful for the hint of perfume which lingered on her body. Slowly, deeply, after her hair was released, she brought her gaze back to his face. That's when she saw him get that look in his eye...that special, fiery look that he always got before he started in on her, and she knew what was coming.

"You wanted to please your old man, huh, Ver? Then show me," he said, looking thin about the mouth. His voice was not rough anymore. It was low and caressing, though there was a faint, accusing overture in his tone. "Come on, baby, show me." He pulled her to him and put his tongue in her mouth. His spit tasted of brandy. The kitchen was hot, and she gasped for breath when he dug his hand between her legs and started rubbing back and forth on the silk fabric. For a split second, her head spun with the moment, and a fire shot up from her crotch; for a moment she actually wanted him to take her, right there in the kitchen.

He sensed his wife's submission, and gave her a lusting, lopsided grin. With a smooth gesture his suit jacket disappeared and landed on the black and white marble floor. His eyes were wild as he clutched at the peach material like a wild beast tearing at its prey. She gave a shriek of surprise as the pretty outfit was ripped mercilessly from her body. She flailed out wildly, trying to pull away as his rough hands began mauling her breasts. He pushed her against the refrigerator and humped her violently, grabbing her buttocks roughly. He swore and pulled at her hair, forcing her head up and bruising her lips with another punishing kiss, not letting up for a moment. Tiny hands came up against broad shoulders. She squirmed and pleaded, but she was a kitten battling a tiger, and soon she yielded, giving up her body to him willingly. There was no use in fighting.

In the moments to come Mel Armstrong pounded his wife relentlessly, and all Vera could do was pray...pray that he would hurry and finish his business. Five minutes later he did, and went to shower. She laid there, on the kitchen floor, motionless, her gray eyes blank, nearly colorless, as she stared up at the ceiling. She'd gotten her wish, she thought...they'd made it in the kitchen.

Tears cascaded down the side of her face, streaking her cheeks. She began to weep, though silently. Then slowly, she rose to her feet. Tears still streaking her cheeks, she picked up the shreds of peach fabric from the floor, then she went into the bathroom just down the hall. She eased the door shut, and gradually began removing what was left of the negligee, which hung from her body in tattered strips.

She turned and stepped into the shower, where she rinsed her body for nearly an hour, in the hottest water she could stand.

Chapter 7

My tongue probed and prodded, coaxing the small bud from its protective sheath. In response she moaned, stroking my head like I was a sick child, pivoting her hips and whispering my name over and over. *It shouldn't be too much longer* I told myself. She purred with pleasure as I used the tip of my finger and dipped it into her moistness, and she cooed in answer as she did some dipping of her own, her long, red fingernails raking through the waves in my hair.

Though I knew I could bring this session to an end, with a flick of my tongue, so to say, I purposely delayed it from happening. Instead, I toyed with her, while my mind drifted off to other things, other places. I thought about my life, my profession. I worried sometimes that it would one day take its toll on me, and whenever I felt a little under the weather, it bothered me. But I always get myself checked out, and as usual, I'm good to go. And as long as I stayed in this profession, I'd make damned sure it would stay that way.

I pondered a few things here and there concerning my life, and after going through my own self-evaluation, I thought about Regina.

I worried about the girl.

The things she'd told me about Derrick made my skin crawl. He was one cocky, sick bastard, and he sure knew how to control Regina. Maybe it was something in his cold black eyes that scared her. Regina said they were old eyes, with all the youth drained out of them, eyes that never seemed to look straight at you, yet at the same time pierced you through. She said he had a depraved sense of humor, and would tell her stories he'd heard while in prison. She would try to laugh or smile, despite the fact his stories weren't really funny at all. In fact, she confided in me, some were just plain gruesome and frightened her tremendously, like the one about some lifer who said if he ever escaped he would 'make himself the perfect woman' out of bits and pieces of dissected corpses, or about the hard-looking, militant inmate who had a plan to infect every white person he could with the HIV virus to 'even up the odds'.

For a man to sit there and tell his girl this kind of shit as a joke made me wonder. I was soon convinced: Derrick Collins was a truly sick individual, and if that wasn't enough, Regina told me that Derrick had deep scars on his back he'd gotten while in prison, his badge of fierceness and defiance, he'd boast, that proclaimed, 'I've lived through things you motherfuckas couldn't even begin to imagine. I live by my own rules from here on out'. But I knew guys like Derrick, all too well. They came off as loud, boisterous individuals, and preferred large, noisy gatherings, where public conversation was impossible. Yet, at smaller, formal gatherings, they'd sweat bullets, afraid somebody with a little intellect would engage them in some light conversation, something to do with politics, or computers, or technology as a whole. And when that happened they'd react hastily to divert the rather uncomfortable, incomprehensible topic or better yet, they'd sacrifice themselves for a moment or two to talk—very evasively—about something they really didn't want to talk about at all. Then slowly, when an opening was made, they'd jump on it and ease themselves away.

By now, Regina should have had her fill—sick and ready to heave—of Derrick. Time and time again I told Regina she should leave him, but she said he wasn't unbearable all the time, and they did have some good moments together. I didn't like her situation, but what could I do, the girl was blinded with what she figured to be love.

My thoughts of Regina were broken by the low moans coming from my date. Her name was Julie, a dark, petite and very pretty woman I'd met on an incoming flight from Atlanta. She was quite a number. Though she lived in Detroit for many years, everything about her appearance bespoke California. There was a polished, big-city, pulled-together look that most Detroit women just never managed to achieve, no matter how long the time spent at the beauty shop. At that time I was stirred by Julie's dramatic ensemble, it was striking, and as the conversation progressed, I was impressed by the entire woman, with everything she had to say. I listened intently, thoroughly, and was pleased with what I had learned, especially relating to her father's financial portfolio.

Julie's old man had plenty of money, and footed the bill while she tried her hand at becoming an aspiring actress. And it seemed as if she had everything working in her favor, down to her hair, which was tousled in the deliberate disarray favored by so many models in magazine ads. She told me she had done a lot of commercial work, and was heading for the big time. She'd thought about going to New York or L.A., but she wanted to ease into stardom, which I thought was smart on her part. We had a great conversation, and she had a terrific sense of humor, and for a minute we seemed like old friends hooking up, and she sensed this.

She didn't want this, and at the time, I guess, neither did I. She grilled me a bit, about mid-flight at this point, and I told her what I did, and by the time we'd landed we had exchanged numbers.

It wasn't long before I had her sprung.

Julie's breathing became louder and more ragged, and once again I was taken from my thoughts. Her breath snagged a few times, and then she began emitting small, infantile gasps of elation as my tongue lashed out blindly. She was very close, indeed. I held back however, and bathed her inner thighs with my tongue, moaning deeply with her, expelling an air of atonement and understanding. Inwardly I guess I was trying to extend the moment, expand upon it, and utilize the time to think and sort things out. I did, and Julie reacted warmly, almost expectedly, writhing in sweet delirium, in her own world. I took this opportunity and thought of Vera.

I had to admit to myself, I had a thing for her. A big thing. There was even a part of me that genuinely hungered to win her heart. To me, it would be a means of proving my own worth, to go after something I *really* wanted. To tell it, she represented the perfect woman, breathtaking, charming, well-preserved, smart, witty; she was the closest thing to perfection I had yet experienced.

As always, the thought of Vera sent an involuntary chill down my spine, and I began to feel the need to see her, to hold her in my arms. But I knew I just couldn't "call her". She was married, and had her own obligations and responsibilities. Still, that couldn't stop me from wanting her. Nothing could stop that.

I took a deep breath, inhaling the arousing scent coming from my date.

It was time I felt. *Time to finish up here.*

Employing my experience, my tongue went up her thigh, around the opening, and found a spot just above her pubic area, where I flicked modestly at her navel. The silky hairs along the top of her mound brushed lightly against my chin, enticing my mouth downwards.

"Please," she whispered urgently, "don't make me wait any longer, please..." Gingerly, she raised her hips until her urgent spot found my mouth. I brought my lips to hers, then slowly, gently, expertly, I ran my tongue where she wanted it most...twiddling it again and again with a skill which grew more mischievous by the milli-second. She began to moan, and her hands gripped the sheets like talons, then, like a car stuck in the snow trying to gain purchase, she moved back and forth.

"Terry..." she cried out, sweet and low, but got no further, for suddenly, with a final thrust of her hips, she hit her peak. She held the moment and kept her spinning hips in the air as my quickly administering tongue unmercifully performed gymnastics. A minute or so had passed and gradually, as the burning subsided, her hips settled into place on the bed. In a pleased, more than satisfied voice, distorted by lingering pleasure and the need for air, she raised up and uttered through slitted eyes, face drenched in sweat, "...thank you." She groaned, and then fell back in a wasted heap. There was a quiet, contented smile on her lips as she reached out and drew the sheets to her body. She covered herself almost protectively, as if her body could no longer stand to have pleasure placed upon it, even if she wanted to.

Soon her steady breathing told me that she was fast asleep. The sun had set by this time, leaving the room bathed in soft shadows. I rose from the bed and showered. I dressed and headed for the door. I turned and stared at Julie. She was really out. For some reason I experienced glorification. I hadn't even made love to her, and here she was, dead to the world, totally oblivious to my departure.

Damn, I thought, incredulously, I didn't use my jimmie, not once; all things considered, I felt I *was* pretty good at what I did.

Smiling, I threw a kiss at Julie, then slowly, silently, I closed the door behind me.

The weather was unkind that afternoon as Vera and I talked at an out of the way restaurant. The rain was coming down in buckets and the winds were strong and cruel. Because of the weather, the crowd was light, which was fine with Vera and I, we had premium seats near the back, and we liked it like that. In addition to its excellent food and fine settings, the restaurant served alcohol, the strong kind, and Vera had ordered a double shot of vodka over ice. When her drink arrived, she took a hard pull. Her brain seemed clouded, and she said her temples throbbed with pain. With a deep sigh, she finally told me her mind had been wandering over the past few days.

It was obvious that Vera wanted to do the talking, so I relaxed somewhat, listening, thinking. Vera had told me about her husband, and what he had done, and why she believed he'd done it. Though she dismissed his behavior as job related, I couldn't...too many things were beginning to add up.

Over the last week and a half, three people had given me reason to take heed: Sister Charles, Mrs. Brooks and the flamer, and now Vera. Something was definitely up. This was more than pure coincidence.

I watched Vera and thought she looked worn-out and depressed, with every tiny line around her eyes magnified tenfold after the ordeal with her husband. But between the vodka warming her system and the coziness of the atmosphere, and I'd like to think being with me, her face became relaxed and she looked so much better, like her former self, vibrant and lovely, yet a hint of anxiety lingered just beneath the surface.

Thinking about her husband I fumed in my seat. I could barely sit still.

Mel Armstrong...he could be such a prick when he wanted to. Here he was a rich and powerful man—so what if his wife chose to get a little on the side? I'm sure he wasn't masturbating when Vera wasn't around. And I had to think Vera knew this too, and as I glanced at her expression, her face seemed to confirm and reinforce my view on things. She did know. Her eyes narrowed and her fingers had turned nearly white from the force with which she clenched her drink, as though it were her husband's neck and she was trying to squeeze the very life out of him.

I thought it an expedient moment to defuse her rage. But there was no denying I felt her rage; I wanted to strangle the bastard myself. Though Vera was married I still felt as though she were mine. I reached my hands to hers, and to my surprise, she pulled hers back.

"No," she said painfully.

I stared at Vera, too stunned to think in logical sequences. *She had withdrawn from me!* For a second I experienced a deep pang in my heart, but then I understood what was happening, and why she did what she did.

She was scared.

"I understand," I whispered.

Her face wilted as she peered into my eyes. "It's not that I don't want to...you know I do. It's just I..."

"You're a bit nervous that maybe he's watching us," I continued for her, earnest and concerned. "Or maybe having us watched. In either event, I understand our dilemma."

"It's not your dilemma, Terry," she murmured vaguely. "You're not married to Mel...I am." She turned her head, and I could see she was sinking deeper into gloom.

I countered, "But that's just it, Vera...I feel as though I am married to you."

At that she looked at me strangely, with mingled astonishment and incomprehension. The words were intended to mean something, and they did. Hadn't she been thinking the same thing herself? About some kind of attachment being made, something other than our meetings? A bond welding us together? But as she stared at me she seemed unsure of it. I could tell this was too much for her; she looked as if instinct told her to get up from the restaurant and leave. But she didn't. Instead, she looked at me with soft, piercing eyes. It was a look of delicate tenderness, one that made me think she really did belong to me. Nevertheless she said nothing to justify her look. As if I knew she wasn't strong enough to be pushed, I urged nothing, erecting a tactful emotional distance.

She shook her head. I could see she was experiencing memories, some good, some bad, but mostly bad, I figured, for she appeared so lost, so forlorn. Her head bowed as she confessed, "You know something, Terry...back then, Marvin Gaye was the only man I ever loved...other my husband. *Marvin Gaye*, he was the *shit*—that nigga sure knew a thing about singing." She smiled with glazed eyes, imagining his voice in her ear. "When I'm alone I never play any other kind of music. I loved me some Marvin." At that she raised her eyes and held them on me. "I even have a scrapbook with pictures of him that I cut from magazines and newspapers when I was younger. I used to tell my friends how one day I was finally going to get up enough nerve—I call it my "personal pilgrimage" —and place flowers at his headstone. And when I do," she smiled, with now narrowed eyes, "I'll be going by myself, without a solicitous husband peeking over my shoulder."

I watched Vera closely; she was breathing harder that she should have been, and her face appeared flushed.

A moment later, she shrugged the expression away and looked at me directly. A softness came back into her eyes as she continued, "Like I said, except for my husband, Marvin Gaye was the only man I ever loved, so it just seemed natural when things went horribly wrong for Marvin Gaye, that I'd give my heart more and more to Mel. I tried. He wouldn't have me. You know, I cried for three days when Marvin died, till Mel slapped me around and told me to stop that bawling shit or he'd smash those 'goddamn Marvin Gaye records' over my head. I wasn't crazy, Mel had a violent temper even back then, so I stopped my crying, but he knew deep inside that I was the only woman in the world who loved and understood Marvin, and that I would continue to hold a place in my heart for him, and that made him jealous as hell."

She looked around, moistening her lips with a quick tongue. When she turned back to me there was a distant, peculiar expression on her face—an expression that might have been one of defiance. "Well, fuck you Mel," she murmured, "Marvin is mine, goddammit." She sounded like she was speaking to herself; but the look she gave me showed that she was aware my presence. "That tight bastard can have all the money he wants, but Marvin is *mine*."

Vera's sudden dedication interested me, although it didn't appear to interest her quite as much as it did a second ago. Her look was now one of thoughtful consideration. "I'm sorry, Terry," she said. With that, a lazy half-smile curved her beautiful mouth. And when it hit me it came as a sudden, hot quiver that struck like a dart, deep in my stomach. Then, as if involuntarily, she leaned across the table and kissed me. Her tongue stroked my lips, giving me a taste of her mouth I had never experienced. Her gestures were new. And yet...familiar. My mouth dipped to hers, and I kissed her lips lightly: once; again. We hungered for more, aching for each other, but reason prevailed, and we settled in our seats.

So while it rained hard and forceful, and as fierce and brutal winds slapped against the restaurant windows around us, we shared each other's company. I noticed Vera seeming to fall into a kind of static calm, abated not by the weather outside but by a certain inner peace. I watched her. Her eyes were less burdened, voice lighter, at times almost giddy, savoring the atmosphere of the restaurant after every third sip or so of her drink. In the moments we had, she did essentially nothing but this, sitting, drinking, and smiling...talking whenever the need arose. And that was fine with me.

As rain careened off the windshield creating a clear, mudslide design, she stared at her cellular phone with mounting disgust as the touchy device refused to accept the number. Every time she started to dial, the phone would cut off after the fifth digit and taunt her with a blank display.

"Goddammit," she blurted out, rolling her eyes. Her cheeks were flushed with frustration, and she was breathing hard.

She didn't let an inoperative phone dismay her, however. A little thrill ran through her as she reached into her purse. With a look of a startled owl, she smiled and grabbed what she'd been looking for. She settled back into the leather seat, and waited. She watched as water ran thickly from the roof and sides, as it streamed off the eaves in a downpour. Already the parking lot resembled a black haze as people bustled in and out of the restaurant, wearing cloaks and holding newspapers over their heads.

For a moment she was baffled because she couldn't make out anything. She frowned in an effort to concentrate. Then the silvery curtain of rain eased up a bit, and the sight drew a smile from her. She could see clearly now...the rain was gone.

Chapter 8

Sometime later in the evening, I heard my doorbell ring. I was in the shower so I dried off the best I could and hurried to the door. It was Regina, dressed in light gray-flannel slacks and a faded rose turtleneck sweater.

"Sorry for not calling first, Terry," she said as she entered carrying a large container of Chinese food. "I hoped you'd be home and not on a date." She winked. "I'm not interrupting anything, am I?"

For no very admirable reason, I thought it might be fun to scream at her for barging in on me. Or maybe not *fun*, exactly. Maybe *satisfying*? But I didn't, yet, feeling a little violated and at the moment impervious to her smile, I said, "No, but you might have been."

She glanced down at the wet towel covering my body. "I see you're dressed for the occasion, if the need came up." She walked over to me and stopped; there was less than a yard between us. When she looked up, her face wore a veil of slyness, and the corner of her mouth quirked. "You hungry, big boy?"

I watched her with a quizzical expression; however, I made no comment. The tempting aroma coming from the Chinese food and the way Regina looked temporarily held me at bay. Finally, unable to suppress a grin, I shrugged my shoulders and told her to set up the food while I finished up in the bathroom. I stepped back into the shower. Although the water was nice and warm like it had been before answering the door, it wasn't balmy. There's nothing worse than leaving the shower and restarting again. I grabbed the soap and went to work. The hot water was beginning to feel good. Soon I rinsed, however, as the water cascaded over my face and body, I felt a presence. Then I turned.

I thought I heard something.

Seconds later I felt a cool draft.

I pulled back the shower curtains. The first thing I noticed was steam clinging to the outer edges of the bathroom mirror and condensing into little beads of water that slipped and slid their way down the slick surface.

I brought my attention to the door.

That's when I saw Regina.

Completely nude.

I struggled to understand. "Girl...what the hell are you doing...?" I found myself frowning a bit. Nevertheless I thought Regina looked fascinating. In fact, I found her more fascinating than I could explain. Something about the way her mouth curled, in the suggestion of a pout, and the way she leered at me made me suspect that she knew exactly what she was doing—there *was* cunning in her actions.

She shut the door behind her, then stepped closer. Swallowing whatever reluctance she'd been holding, she whispered, "Make love to me, Terry."

My mouth gaped, so I closed it, and stared at Regina with question and utter surprise in my eyes. She had apparently been thinking about this moment when she came over here, her body lightly oiled, smelling of sweet perfume. She looked at me and raised a delicate eyebrow in intrigue. Her expression was no more intriguing than mine.

"Please, Terry," she pleaded, her features composing into a look of need, "let's make love."

At this point in my life I should be accustomed to such come-ons, but now, it was an all-out effort to collect my scattered wits. This was *Regina! My girl!* My shoulders seemed to droop and I sighed inwardly. Lately, this was becoming the story of my life. Nothing made sense anymore. And as I thought about it, I felt as if I were in need of a frontal lobotomy. But as soon as Regina worked her way closer to me, I felt the edge of sexual awareness kick through me like the explosive heat of excellent whiskey. I really found myself excited, and couldn't find the words to protest.

Fortunately, Regina was sensitive to my ignorance. "It'll be just between you and me, Terry," she whispered, supplying more reassurance than the situation superficially required. "It'll just be two friends sharing an unmentioned moment...never to be revealed...to anyone."

I felt helpless, struck as much by the moment as by the strangeness of hearing those words coming from Regina's mouth...directed toward me. At first I was taken aback; I seemed almost suspicious, as if I thought she had some ulterior motive. I swallowed my concern, however. Brightly, I found myself smiling, "No one?" Just for a second, her face showed a relief she couldn't conceal. Apparently, one of her fears had been proven groundless: I did find her desirable.

She inhaled deeply and smiled back. "No one."

"Okay," I murmured warmly, extending my arms to take her. Although Regina was my girl—and I loved her dearly—and we were the best of friends, mind you, her offer seemed too reasonable to ignore, and as I gazed at her warm, inviting, succulent body, I was more than ready.

Regina smiled, it was a naughty one, although the assessing quality of her smile suggested that her lusting expression was more complex, that there was more to it than what was on the surface. Yes, I figured, there had to be something else. And I soon found out that I'd been right in what I was thinking. As I held her in my arms, showering kisses over her throat, her ears, her closed eyelids, everywhere, as our hands glided over the other one's body, her eagerness began to change. What had started as a simple case of heated sex was turning down yet another path in her quest to procure her needs. I detected this immediately as her manner became less aggressive; she even went so far as to say she loved me, and for me to hold her tightly and never let go.

I knew what it was, it didn't take a brain surgeon. She was lacking all the things a woman required; intimacy, to be held, to be wanted...and most of all...to be loved.

As the warm water danced and played over our bodies, I held her, tightly, tight as I possibly could, trying to fulfill her wistful needs...every last one of them...inwardly thinking of Vera.

I sat in the living room of my apartment working on my fifth glass of Crist and staring at the telephone. It had been a week since I last heard from Vera. I was worried, and it showed. I still wore the same clothes I'd worn for the last two days. I hadn't really eaten and my face was in serious need of a blading. By now, Vera should have called or at least paged me. She did this every so often, just to let me know she was thinking about me, leaving me her special "155" code on the digital display. But I hadn't heard anything from her. Something was wrong. What, though? I wondered if her husband had gone ballistic on her and the thought of this made me cringe.

After leaving the restaurant a week ago I recalled putting my arms around Vera, as if for the last time. There were tears in her eyes and her embrace was strong, but she knew it had to end, and so did I. But where was Vera now? I wondered, closing my eyes.

Somewhere in all the mind-twisting clatter going on in my head, I heard a series of fluttering chimes, but my mind and body were heavy with thoughts, and the fact that I was working on my fifth glass of champagne didn't exactly help matters. The sound filtered through my conscious again, and I forced my eyes open. Although the room was dark, I could see daylight seeping through the edges of the blinds. I heard the sound once more and realized it was my cell-phone sitting on the coffee table. Suddenly alert, my adrenaline pumping, hoping it was Vera, I pushed myself from the sofa and answered it.

It wasn't.

It was a client, Mrs. Johnson, an executive for a major advertising firm, a well-to-do woman in her mid-thirties. Though this was the last thing I wanted to do, I still booked the date for eight-thirty this evening, at her place. It wouldn't be a hard one I thought. Mrs. Johnson had told me all she wanted was a good, straight-up fuck. Which was cool with me. That meant I wouldn't have to go downtown! I hated doing that with Mrs. Johnson. I mean the woman didn't smell offensive or anything like that, it's just that she's...well, she's very excitable, and when she hits her peak her hips buck and heave like a wild bull with its nuts bound in a sling, and she grunts like a bull, too, braying loud and forceful to the point I expect to see steam blast from her nostrils one of these days. On top of this, she has the annoying habit of digging her nails in the back of my head— grinding my face in her muff. Now, combine all of these unforgettable sights and sounds and you can see why I'm so grateful to bypass the event. I could only hope and pray she wasn't going to change her mind once I got there.

Still, as I thought about it, I didn't mind doing Mrs. Johnson, even if I had to go downtown. To tell it, she was a nice-looking woman and she tipped very well, and that made things a lot easier. She also had a decent-looking body, a little on the heavy side, but all the extra weight was in proportion. If there was anything on the fat side it was probably her chest—which was big, even for her—with areolaes the size of pancakes! I guess if I had to describe Mrs. Johnson in a word, it might be *stacked!* There was an additional feature to Mrs. Johnson that I liked, loved, actually. The woman had a wicked mouth, a demented sword swallower, and loved to use it, especially on me she said, and I was always more than obliged to have it on me. The woman was indeed exceptional, the best I'd ever had.

I nodded, sure of the evening ahead, and suddenly I felt a bit elated, it seemed as if I had a purpose, something to do, and I was really up to doing something—anything. Besides, the fresh air might do me some good...and keep my mind off Vera.

I went to the bedroom and selected my standard attire: denim blue jeans and a white silk shirt. However, tonight, I would wear a dark blue blazer to complete the look, along with my dark blue gators. I shaved and showered, really sprucing myself up and after sliding into my apparel, I was feeling even better and looking *damn* good. I checked my Rolex. It was six-fifteen. I had some time to kill. I decided to check out the latest fashions at Spotlights, a clothing store over on Telegraph Avenue.

When I got there the place had a moderate gathering of customers, a few brothers here and there, mostly browsing. However, there were a few brothers at the register who were purchasing some big-ticket items, but nobody seemed to be in a buying frenzy.

"Yo, Terry," a voice hollered out, "what's up, my brother!"

I turned to see the owner, Elgin Kirtz, a slim, dark brother with an alligator smile, who dressed impeccably. The man was a living legend around the area, and everybody wanted to see him for the latest fashions scheduled to arrive in Detroit. When it came to clothing Elgin knew his shit, and greeted this fact with equanimity, never coming off cocky, or like he knew it all, though he did.

"Hey, Elgin, my man," I smiled, shaking his hand with a firm grip, which he met. I always did respect a man with a firm handshake. "Okay, Mister Magic, you know why I'm here. Show me the happs."

Elgin went to work. Turning to a rack of blazers, he sailed toward it as if he were leading a fleet. Like many salesmen in the business, Elgin had charisma, and demonstrated all the savvy needed to secure a sale, but he was also street-smart, and knew how to hit you the right way, nickel smooth and as sharp as splintered glass.

I followed him and he turned with a gold blazer in his hand, in my size. The blazer was tight I nodded, and the color was really slammin', something I would definitely sport. He handed me the blazer and the sumptuously smooth material seemed to conform to my hands. "This is some fine shit, Elgin," I had to admit. "And you can take this as testimony to the quality of your entire store."

He bowed in humble pride. "Just here to keep the brothers from lookin' crazy when they step out with their ladies."

"And you do." I tried on the blazer then stepped to a three-way mirror. I couldn't suppress a grin. It was me—no doubt about it. I shrugged my shoulders and the blazer fell into place, molding to my physique like it had been tailored. I brushed the length of the sleeves. Soon Elgin had three blazers of the same caliber for me to sample.

While extending my neck and rotating my shoulders, I asked, "How much?"

Elgin was bold enough to say, "Three hundred, but I'll cut you a deal for two-fifty if you buy two."

With that, I turned my attention to the question of quantity. "How many you got in my size?"

Trying to be casual, knowing what I was about to say, Elgin feathered through the rack. He looked up and said, "Seven, in every color in the rainbow, baby."

"Nothing loud in there, is it?"

"Not a one, baby."

"Can you have them ready to be picked up tomorrow afternoon?" I inquired, still shrugging my shoulders in the mirror.

"Which one?" he asked, with a gleam in his eyes, rubbing his palms together.

I grinned to myself, I was so much better at nonchalance than Elgin was. I threw him a sideways glance and the makings of a smile pinched my mouth. "All of them. That won't be a problem, will it?"

At first he seemed too happy to reply, then he said, "No problem, baby, I'll gift-wrap 'em myself. Hell, I'll even deliver them to your door!"

"No, Elgin, that won't be necessary," I chuckled. I began to remove the blazer and he assisted me. He draped the blazer across his arm. While Elgin selected all the remaining blazers in my size, I went on checking out more things in the store and in an hour or so, I had purchased over five thousand dollars worth of clothing. Elgin proved to have a good eye. The outfits he selected for consideration were excellent—some light and durable things for everyday wear, some fine and handsome outfits for formal occasions—and the colors he advised were right for my hair and eyes and skin. I settled my bill, telling Elgin I'd be back tomorrow.

I checked my Rolex. I still had some time to kill so I decided to get a jump on my date. Maybe I could get in there and get out.

The trip to Mrs. Johnson's place took forty-five minutes, not bad considering I was on the other side of town. My Benz can really fly. When I arrived there was an automobile with out-of-state plates parked in her driveway. I wondered whose it was, the car was a piece of shit, and by it sitting in such an upscale neighborhood it really stuck out like a sore thumb. I parked my Benz in front of Mrs. Johnson's house and walked to the front door. I rung the bell. Seconds later, I was greeted by a light-skinned, heavy set woman with an extremely bad weave. She was at least fifty and looked as country as hot-water corn bread. Black polyester pants were stretched over extra wide hips, a blue blouse was buttoned loosely at her neck, and she wore black flat loafers. The woman gave me the once-over with spirited eyes, then her face lit up in a grin, flashing two gold teeth in her mouth.

"Well, hello *there*, sugah," she oozed in a low, sassy tone. She craned her head and announced my arrival over her shoulder, "Hey, Rose, yo' man is here!" She turned her attention back to me, shaking her head. "And he is mighty, mighty fine. Lord have mercy." She raised a devilish eyebrow, a sly glance drifting over the front of my jeans. "What's yo' name, sugah?"

I could tell at once that tactfulness was the least developed aspect of her character. "Terry Allens, ma'am." I'd said this as politely as I could. Between the strong aroma of alcohol coming from the woman and the faint music I heard in the background, I felt a seething headache coming on. It was enough to make me want to turn and leave. I didn't need this shit, especially now. I would stay, however.

"You Rose man, or somethin'?" the woman asked, again tracing me from head to toe. Then she had the audacity to push that birdnest of a hairdo into some semblance of order—as if somehow—by some absurd notion, I'd be interested.

I blew air out between my lips in an expression of contempt. "No, ma'am, I am not Rose's man. I'm just a friend."

The woman paused, and then her face went blank, then a little leery. "A friend, huh? Yeah, right, I bet you are. You work with her, or somethin'?"

"No, ma'am, now may I see Mrs. Johnson, please?" I kindly urged.

With all the morals of a mink in heat, she looked at me with a thoroughness that told me her eyes had touched on every inch of my body. When she finally finished she brought her lazy gaze to my face. "Why sure, baby...you can see her. Hell, you can see more than just her if you want to." She held her gaze, daring me to deny her open invitation. Then she reached out and brushed an imaginary strand of hair off my temple, needing an excuse to touch me.

Hearing that and feeling her hands on me, I was really tempted to leave, thinking this was headed into the direction of another threesome, and I'd had my fill of that. Instead of leaving, I slithered through the doorway, ignoring the woman's yapping. Once inside, I detected the sound of Marvin Gaye's *Got to give it up*. I immediately thought of Vera, and a pang shot through me. The music was coming from the den. The wide-hipped woman led the way. As unprofessional as I knew it was to do it, I found myself staring at the woman's rear end. It was enormous, four feet across if it was an inch and looked like a couple of down-filled pillows jammed together. And man-oh-man did it wobble something fierce; the movement was flaccid, like bladders without enough water in them. I wondered how she could wipe herself with such wide, full blown cheeks.

I entered the den and could see that there was a little five-person party going on, and from what I could tell the party was just getting started. But apparently one man had been drinking heavily before things even got a chance to get going. He was a short, thin man with a large bulbous nose, and boy was he hammered, as rumpled as ever, his tie askew, the blue suit looking as if he'd slept in it. There were two other men, apparently a bit more in control, who were holding him up by the arms, and whenever they let him go, he would sag and they'd have to grab him to keep him from falling to the floor. I looked over to Mrs. Johnson sitting in a chair off to the side. She shrugged her shoulders and had a weak smile on her face. I nodded, understanding fully that she had no knowledge of this sudden affair.

As time pressed on the music got louder, the drinks flowed heavier, and the dancing turned vulgar. No longer a spectator, I found myself in the mix, dancing with the big woman, who yelled out loudly, "When I get home to Alabama, I'm goin' to get myself a young-ass man!" The party ended two hours later and everybody began filing out. The old drunk, Uncle Smitty, I'd learned, staggered toward me and slurred, "This has been a stone gas, baby. Make sure you call me on the next one." With that, he hitched up his trousers with his wrists and swaggered out the door. I smiled and shook my head, praying he wouldn't have anything else to drink, at least not tonight.

With everything back to normal, Mrs. Johnson and I took a seat on the sofa. She looked at me with wilted eyes, seemingly very apologetic, saying she was sorry for her relatives barging in on her so unannounced. I told her there was no need for explanations and that family was family, no matter what, and that I was a little early anyway, so I essentially barged in on them. Actually, I had to confess, I'd had a pretty good time, and that her aunt was something else, a real outgoing, spirited, touchy-feely kind of woman. Mrs. Johnson grinned and then snickered like an adolescent, telling me how her aunt was always pushing up on somebody else's man, never getting one of her own. We laughed and went on about our relatives, saying in spite of their behavior, we wouldn't trade them for the world.

But then, after the last chuckle, I placed my hand on Mrs. Johnson's lap and sensuously slid it up her leg. I looked into her eyes. Then in a deep, rumbling voice, I asked her if she were ready for me. As startled as if she'd been caught doing something forbidden she nodded, then practically ran to her bedroom. Her sudden reaction sort of took me by surprise; an involuntary twitch made my heart skip a beat. Nevertheless, I rose from the sofa with ease and confidence, and there was even a hint of swagger to my stride as I approached the bedroom. *The woman was prime*, I smiled, fully assured that it would be an easy night.

As the night progressed I couldn't have been more wrong. The woman was impossible! I tried everything—every position—missionary, doggy-style, sideways, her on top, against the wall—everything! The woman was impossible to turn! At one point, I asked her if she were on some kind of medication, to which she denied. Strangely, she threw a look at me and asked me why I would even ask such a question. Instead of answering I shook my head, giving her a grin which was probably intended to say, *never mind, it was nothing*. To tell you the honest truth, I didn't know what it meant.

Gasping and grimacing, determined to complete my task, I positioned Mrs. Johnson with her backside to me. She took her cue and leaned forward with her face on the pillow. I clutched her by the shins with both hands. Then, with my body arced, I went for broke—giving her everything I had—thrusting relentlessly—moving like a well-oiled machine—determined to get this woman off—no matter what! Sweat streaked my face, my body glistened with it as I thrust harder. *Keep pounding, goddammit!* I urged myself, picturing Mrs. Johnson rolling her eyes in affectionate ridicule, as if telling me it would be okay if I didn't bring her to a climax. *To hell with that—I would!*

For nearly twenty minutes I kept up my grueling pace, my body now drenched in sweat. It was turning to physical obsession. I had to do it! I grabbed at the brass headboard with both hands. My feet dug frantically into the bed sheets. Hell, I needed all the traction I could get! Ten more minutes had passed, at least I presumed it had, and soon I felt myself giving out. I mean, even *I* have my limitations! Just as I was about to wave the white flag and throw the towel in, like an athlete realizing that the game was over and it was just a matter of waiting until the buzzer rang, going through the motions, I heard Mrs. Johnson let loose with an explosive, agonizing wail, which reverberated off the bedroom walls, "Oooh, you mother*fucka!*" She threw her backside into me and grunted like a bull, grinding and smashing, sinking me deeper.

Afterwards she collapsed on the bed with her head buried in the pillow. Her massive breasts were forced out on either side of her billowing body like a pair of bottom-heavy sandbags. I came down over her, balancing myself on my elbows. I guess she was still in the throes of post-orgasmic sensation, for her body started shaking as if she were chilled to the bone, and then I heard throaty, sobbing sounds.

What the hell...? I wondered, at the moment not sure what it was, thinking I had hurt her. I raised up from the bed. "Mrs. Johnson," I asked, in a worried, concerned voice, "you okay?"

Moaning delightfully, she pushed up on her elbows enough to glare around at me. She was a mess, in a haggard, sexy kind of way. Sweat had plastered her black hair to her face and what wasn't layered down shot in every direction. Despite her appearance, I detected a look of astonishment and intense satisfaction written in her face.

Realizing that she must look like a dripping mess, she made a futile attempt to smooth her disheveled hair, running her fingers through it haphazardly as I watched with a small, amused smile on my face. She moaned long and deep, and her dark eyes were vague and dazed as she whispered, "I'm fine, Terry...believe me, just fine. Listen, baby, can you let yourself out? I'm just too exhausted to get out of bed."

Looking as if I had just been hosed down myself, I smiled and nodded my head. I went into the bathroom and showered. Afterward I dressed, gathered up my pay, and let myself out. I got into my car and headed home. I'd like to say the night went off without a hitch but it hadn't. No, there was some serious work done on my part, I really had to earn my ends. But nevertheless, none the less for wear, I was pleased with the outcome. *I still wore the crown* I smiled, and I guess every now and then you had to prove yourself worthy of wearing it. The thought of this brought to mind an old saying, 'You gotta pay the cost to be the boss'.

And tonight, I'm proud to say, I did.

It wasn't too late so I decided to drop in on my mother, the Black Pearl, I like to call her. She was a night owl and I hoped she was still up. She stayed in a senior citizens complex, a nice one, I made sure of that. I arrived there in twenty minutes and after punching in my security code, I let myself in. I walked to my mother's apartment and fished out my keys. Slowly, silently, mindful of the time, I entered. Although it was September, and there wasn't a trace of winter in the air, the apartment was steamy when I walked in. My mother, like most senior citizens, evidently felt that the hotter it was, the better.

But this was a little too hot, even for her. So I went around opening a few windows and blinds in the small living room. The breeze felt nice as the cool moonlight poured in, tinting everything with a blue-white glow.

I knocked lightly on my mother's bedroom door. There was no answer. I nudged the door open and peeked inside. She was out like a light. I loved my mother dearly, and really liked talking with her. She was my best friend, *the* best friend: kind, loving, caring, helpful, and almost flirtatious when we'd talk, as though she were trying to see what kind of line I ran on the ladies. She knew I was a ladies' man. However, Moms knew nothing of my business, not a thing, and if I had my way, she never would. The shock would send her to an early grave. I told her I was a sales consultant at a major firm in the area, and in a way, I guess I was.

I smiled and said goodnight to my mother. I went back into the living room, to the thick brown sofa sitting against the wall and in a matter of seconds, there was a soft bed with crisp sheets staring invitingly at me. I crawled inside and pulled the sheets to my chin. I heard my mother in her bedroom moving around for a while, and then all was quiet. It was comforting to know she was there, much nicer than being at my place by myself. I turned over and settled in and as I laid there, my glance strayed to the oval-framed picture on the wall, to my right. Its antique bubble glass protected an old black and white photograph of my mother when she was but a mere girl of sixteen. She was dressed in a long pleated skirt, a wool sweater, and flat shoes. A pair of white gloves were molded around her hands.

She was beautiful...the most beautiful woman to ever walk this earth. There was a fineness about her features that suggested royalty. She could have been a queen I smiled. Yet, to me, she was. A queen with more than just beauty. Yes, there was something else to this queen; she carried that extra edge, that certain aura...strength and determination. I couldn't admire another person more. As I stared at the photograph, seemingly with every muscle in me shutting down, I smiled. At the same time I was filled with a kind of exhilaration that made any physical depletion seem distant.

I soon drifted off, and for the first time in weeks, I slept soundly.

There were no dreams.

Just a welcomed, brain-relieved slumber.

Chapter 9

The Mirage was on Second Avenue, near the corner of Lafayette Street, an upscale strip club where Regina danced. It was definitely a cut above the rest, with Tiffany lamps and polished mahogany tables, sedate wood paneling and brass fixtures everywhere, and believe it or not, clean bathrooms. It definitely stood out on its own accord; not like other strip clubs where one looked like the other until they all blurred together.

The place was frequented by the high rollers, people who had money and had no remorse about spending it. The taxi dropped me at the front entrance, and when I'd paid the driver and turned to go inside, I saw that there was standing room only—which was to be expected on a Saturday night—which is why I chose not to drive. I knew the parking lot would be on jam, and I wasn't about to park my Benz on some side street and have it broken down or stolen. Actually, if I had to choose between the two, I would prefer to have my Benz stolen and never recovered. There was nothing worse than seeing your ride violated. It would be like witnessing a national tragedy.

It was around eight-thirty, and The Mirage was really brewing. It was a popular meeting place, as well as one where you could get the most premium drugs, if that was what you were after. However, not many people came to the place for that. The Mirage wasn't about drugs and making underhanded deals. Instead, it was a place where only the finest tits and asses were showcased, almost exclusively.

Regina had invited me to come down to see her new and revised act, around nine-fifteen, and to be on the lookout for her circulating around the place. I had some time on my side so I decided to browse. I looked around, hoping to spot Regina. I noticed that there were quite a few women in the place, dressed fierce and looking very nice. *Very* nice. There's nothing like a black woman when she's hitting on all cylinders. I was dying for a beer, but with the crush at the bar, I wasn't sure it was worth it. Still, I pushed my way through the mob, conscious that a number of women as well as jealous men, were looking me over. And then above the noise, I heard someone calling my name. I turned.

Low and behold, it was Regina's boyfriend: Derrick Collins. He was dressed *ROCA WEAR* down with Timberlands on his feet, sitting at one of the small tables grinning foolishly and gesturing me over. I nodded, inwardly cursing. He was the *last* person I wanted to see. Still I went, threading and slipping through the crowd, inadvertently bumping into a waitress, who smiled, almost lovingly. I think she'd planned the mild collision, to draw attention to herself. I get that a lot. I gave her a warm grin then made my way to the table. His bald head gleaming like a cue-ball, Derrick stuck out a ringed hand and smiled.

"What's up, pretty nigga?" he boasted slickly, two gold teeth beaming brightly despite the dimness of the place. "Welcome to the madness. Take a load off, partner."

I shook his hand and took a seat, and although it was a relief to get out of the mainstream of bar traffic, I really wished it hadn't been with Derrick. Not only did the dude make my skin crawl, he was fake, as fake as they come, and then some—stealing someone else's line, ripping off a style here, mimicking someone there, sampling something from somebody way over there—nothing he did was original. And it showed in his speech, an ever-changing slanguage dictated by the young hip-hop artists.

I looked over at him. Just the sight of his cocky, loud, blunt-smoking ass made me want to push up from the table. But I didn't, instead I said tiredly, "What's been up, Derrick?"

Almost immediately he grinned, even harder, and said, while rubbing his palms together, "Just big pimpin', baby, spendin' cheese, know what I mean?" He pointed to a glass in front of him on the table. "I'm sippin' on some yac. What you want, dog?"

I knew Derrick to be a heavy drinker, but I had to admire his cleverness. Even after knocking down a dozen shots of the strongest liquor, he could still count money with machinelike accuracy. "Cognac also sounds like a winner," I said. I never drank the stuff. In fact, outside of my usual bottle of Cristal champagne, I almost never have anything stronger than beer or an occasional glass of wine, but I wanted to be sociable, though it turned my stomach to do so.

Derrick nodded, then summoned, more like grabbed, a passing waitress and placed my order, hitting his drink again in the process. He looked at me with a sly expression scrunched at one side of his mouth. "Our shit will be right up, dog." He hunched forward. "So, pretty nigga, you still workin' that nine to five?" With that said inside of a sneer, he sat back in his chair and picked his teeth with a fingernail.

In response, I smiled vaguely—not as if I weren't listening but rather as if what I'd heard from Derrick had triggered a wide range of thoughts. I wondered if he knew more about my pretense world than he was letting on, like everyone else it seemed.

"Yeah," I said, "I'm still at the firm wearing a suit and tie and punching the clock." I looked at him directly—eye to eye. "You still doing your thing?"

This tidbit pleased him to no end. He slapped the table and threw his shiny head back, grinning fiercely. Then, casting an enigmatic look, he waggled his eyebrows. "Oh, no doubt, baby, it's 'bout that, makin' mad ends. And as long as these crackheads is hungry, I'm goin' feed 'em. Know what I'm sayin', dog?"

I shrugged, then hesitated. "Yeah, I guess you gotta do what you gotta do."

"And you *know* this," he agreed, as if we actually shared a common bond. "And I'm here to make all the mad ends I can, baby. I'm here" —suddenly, he raised his voice until it rang around the room— "to get paid! I'm a hustler, baby! Ain't no shadowboxin' here! I'm the real deal!"

A ripple of low laughter traveled through the crowd as they exchanged glances and nods at Derrick's response; it was precisely the kind they had expected him to make. As for me, when his voice had died down, I gaped at him. *The man was a straight-up idiot. Definitely stuck on stupid.* What in the hell does Regina see in this man? I took note of his attire, the loud-ass "bling-bling" jewelry, the thick rope around his neck, the roll of bills he carried, the Range Rover he drove, and felt that might have something to do with it. But still...

Derrick leaned back in his seat and folded one leg across the other. He brought his hand to his mouth and stroked his crooked, razor-thin mustache contemplatively, then trailed his goatee. "So, what brings you down here, pretty nigga, you come to get your freak on?"

"Actually, Regina invited me down, to see her new act," I replied.

Derrick's grin was like his gaze—at once proud, possessive, and vastly amused. "Yeah, my Regina's a bad bitch, ain't she?"

I didn't respond. I faced Derrick, instead. Inside of an exasperating sigh, I said, "Regina is an exceptional woman, who is very talented. I think her dancing is one of a kind."

"You ain't never lie," he chuckled, his crooked mustache in harmony with his mouth, "that bitch works that body like she's makin' a baby, and not only that," chuckling harder, "she gives good brains, too."

The muscles at the corners of my mouth flinched. At that moment I wanted to slam his face into the table. I felt myself trembling with rage. Many times in my life I'd tried to imagine what it would feel like to kill a person—to dole out final punishment to a worthy soul, and now, as I sat there, Derrick Collins seemed a fitting candidate. I took a deep breath to settle my nerves, then said, "Derrick, Regina is your woman. Instead of degrading her you should be treating her like a queen. The girl loves you, man."

"Loves me?" returned Derrick instantly, in a tone of disbelief and humor. He coughed without covering his mouth. "Man, that bitch don't love me, never has. She's just ridin' my jock for some free blow, baby." He chuckled out loud. "Regina, loving me, yeah, *right!*" More laughter greeted this assertion as he hunched forward. "That bitch can go through an eight-ball in no time flat. Hell, she snorts more shit than I can sell."

A sudden thick silence swallowed every sound in the place, which caused a jolt to go through me as I stared at Derrick, who sat perfectly still with a horrendous grin on his face; the expression was suspended still as a stone in the silence. I shook my head and blinked my eyes. Not quite able to meet Derrick's expression, I said, "She can really put it away, huh?"

"Like a fuckin' Hoover," he snapped brashly. "Hell, she gets a nose bleed almost every other day." With that stated, he fished a wood-tipped cigarillo from out of his jacket, and lit it with a chrome lighter. Sucking in deeply, he examined his surroundings with a flinty stare and blew smoke through his nose.

Shocked and a bit curious, I stared at him then inquired, "Is that right? How long has she been doing this?"

Derrick stared at the ceiling, then settled back in his seat, unbuttoning his jacket and stretching his neck. "'Bout...a year or so, I'd say, give or take a few months."

I made no effort to hide my feelings. "Did you hook her, Derrick?"

For a moment he said nothing, and the two of us glowered at each other like two rival stags about to lock antlers, our bodies rigid, our gazes unblinking, the charged atmosphere between us like that which presaged a storm. My attention stayed on him, sizing him up with eyes that were narrow with suspicion and cold with warning. As for Derrick, the glitter of hatred in his eyes was almost tangible, and all of it was being directed at me with a vengeance. Finally, Derrick was the first to react. His face crumpled, then he raised an eyebrow. "What the fuck you sayin' here, pretty nigga? That I strung my own bitch out? Well, fuck you, I didn't. She wanted somethin' and so did I. It was a trade off."

I looked at him with a snarl of revulsion, fearless and defiant. "What could you possibly want from her? You can have your choice of any woman in this place. Why her?"

Derrick winked at me, as if the answer was obvious, and as if I were too dumb to figure it out. He sniffed lightly and thumbed his nose, then his eyes looked as piercing as a hawk's. "You never struck me as a fool. Maybe you'd better take a look around you. It's status. That does it for me." He held his arms out. "Can't you *see it?* Can't you *feel it?* Status is king here, baby. When these niggas come down here and see Regina on stage shakin' that ass and snappin' them fuckin' hips, they all want to know who that bad-ass bitch belong to...and that'll be me...Derrick Collins...with the baddest bitch in the joint. See my point, pretty nigga? It's status, and nothing else. And besides, if you must know, I keep a grip on her rent, keep her ass laced in eel and snake, and I throw her a bone every now and then. So you see, I ain't no slouch. I handle my business."

Hearing those words did something to me, and I could only look dumbly at Derrick. The explanation he gave for what he did wasn't entirely satisfying, but it seemed to be true. Maybe the yearning look in Regina's eyes wasn't love. Maybe I was wrong in thinking that she was looking for a man to hold her. Maybe there was an understanding between her and Derrick, like I have with a client...I scratch your back you scratch mine. I thought it about more. That would explain the weathered look in Regina's eyes at times.

I stared back at Derrick. If I hadn't been struggling so hard with this—and if he wasn't so damn bullish in his demeanor—I might have catered to his juvenile mentality and shook his hand. But I couldn't, and had to rise from the table. I was done here. Besides, the loud music made any further attempt at conversation impossible. I would have had to shout to make myself heard. And Derrick wasn't worth the effort. I reached into my wallet and laid a twenty on the table. "That should cover my drink when it arrives." My voice was harsh and forceful.

When I turned to walk away, Derrick took the twenty and balled it up in his fist. I felt something hit my back. I knew what it was. I kept my pace and headed toward the exit. I had to get out of there. I felt as though the walls were closing in on me. Everything was going wrong; Regina was yet another item on the list. And somehow, I felt as if the worst was yet to come.

I flagged a taxi and went straight home. For the life of me, I couldn't have stayed and watch Regina dance...no, not tonight. I just could not.

The taxi dropped me off in front of my apartment. I paid the driver and he drove off leaving a plume of blue smoke in the air. I stared at my apartment, as if for the first time. To me, my apartment was more than just a place to live; it was a refuge. And tonight, it seemed, I needed it just for that. I walked up to the front door and inserted my key. I was about to enter when suddenly I heard a feathered voice calling my name. I turned to see who it was.

My breath left me in a rush.

I couldn't believe my eyes.

It was Vera.

She was dressed in a long burgundy overcoat. Her hair was covered with a black scarf and large sunglasses partially obscured her face. She'd been apparently traveling incognito. I remained motionless, glaring at her. A feeling that I was acting out a dream washed over me. The feeling was real and fierce, as hard as a slap and as penetrating as razor-sharp nails. My first reaction was mild shock, and I held my breath while my heart shook. Desperately, I wanted to babble, *Where in the hell have you been? Why haven't you called?* The pressure to give up every possession I owned so that I could know was maddening. Somehow, I kept it under control.

In the next few moments we just stared at one another, at a loss for words. Then through the silence I heard a faint sound like muffled cries. I looked down at Vera's hand and saw that it was balled tightly into a fist around her purse strap. Something was wrong.

I swallowed the lump in my throat and said, "Hello, Vera, won't you come inside?"

She looked around, scanning the area. She turned her head back to me. "Yes, but only for a minute." She wet her lips and stared at me like a bird caught by a snake.

I exhaled heavily and stared back at her. Something was definitely wrong. I opened the door and then turned, holding the door for her. She took a deep breath and closed her eyes as if she were controlling herself with great difficulty. Then she walked up the three steps and stepped inside. As she passed me I felt my insides tremble. She stood by the sofa with her shoulders bunched. I turned on a few lamps to shed some light in the room. Vera looked around. This was her first time inside my apartment, and it showed on her face.

"Can I take your coat?" I asked lightly.

She unbuttoned it as she took a seat on the sofa, saying she'd keep it on. With shifting eyes, she scanned the living room. "Nice place," she uttered. "You have" —she looked like she would have been happier if she could have fainted— "great taste in furnishings."

I took a seat next to Vera with a couple of glasses of wine. I handed one to her. I set my glass on the coffee table. "Vera, where have you been?" I went to put an arm around her shoulder before she could answer. "Baby, why haven't you called me? You had me worried to death." My voice was raw with concern.

"I...I needed some time to myself." She turned her head away, gulping in air. "I needed some space."

With my free hand, I scrubbed a palm over my face, holding her tighter with the other. "Vera, what is it?"

She jerked away from my hold, fidgeting with the rim of her glass, unable to sit still. "We can't see each other, Terry. Not ever again. I'm sorry..."

"But why? Tell me why?" An instant silence gripped the room as my eyes glued to hers with a tense expectancy. I needed an answer—desperately.

She opened her mouth to do just that, then clamped it shut. She swallowed hard and stared at the ceiling. My hand snaked out and cupped her jaw delicately. That's when her skin cringed, and a sob escaped. My heart leaped as I heard the pathetic whimpering sound, only realizing after a moment that it had come from Vera. I cradled her face and turned her head from side to side. Tears stung my eyes when I saw that there was a bruise by her lip.

"What happened here, Vera?" I demanded mildly.

She pulled her face away and her chin lifted in a rigid composure. "Nothing happened." Her denial came in a rush. "Nothing at all. Okay? Absolutely nothing."

I didn't believe her. I folded my arms and looked at her through lowered lids, and she had to turn away from my doubting expression.

"I was reaching for a can of peas when the can tumbled out of the cupboard. It was a large can..." Vera slanted me a look but couldn't tell whether I accepted what she was saying. "...and the tip caught the side of my face." She managed a self-effacing laugh. "It was dumb of me, I know, but I needed to have dinner fixed..." She let the rest of it fade away as she lifted her hands and dropped them.

I cradled her face once more. "Your lip is bleeding."

In response, she licked it gingerly, wincing when her tongue encountered the wound. "It still hasn't quite healed yet."

Carefully, slowly, tenderly, I shifted in my seat and removed the sunglasses from Vera's face. Her right eye had been blackened, but at the moment it was barely noticeable. I said nothing, did nothing, nor did I react in any way. I just stared at her. She looked like a little girl. Her eyes were still puffy from crying, and the expression in them was so forlorn that I wanted to put my arms around her in a protective embrace. I tried to compose myself, but the effort only made me weaker. I slid the glasses back onto her face. Yet my eyes never left hers. Even when she tried to turn away, tried to be strong, she could feel the power of my disapproval boring into her.

Finally, I had to say, "That motherfucker did this to you, didn't he, Vera?"

In response, she jerked around to the sound of hatred in my voice. She shook her head slowly. "No, Terry, Mel didn't do this to me...I did."

With that she remained motionless, as motionless and as passive as I had ever seen her.

"You did nothing, Vera," I pleaded.

She turned and faced me for a long moment, then replied with a glare that would have split a wooden plank, "Oh, yes...I did. I'm the cause to all of this." Shuddering, she stood up. "I'm married, Terry. I shouldn't have come on to you. I see now that it was wrong...so, so wrong." She stared vacantly at nothing. I noticed she was trembling, but she didn't let that stop her. "I should have been there for my husband, to pray and support my marriage. Instead, what do I do...I sneak around fucking some young stud—trying to hide my hurt, my pain."

I couldn't respond; what she was saying was true, but, on the other hand, her situation, her marriage, was not real. It was a sham. I looked up at Vera. "How can you call what you have a marriage?"

For a second, her face radiated relief and understanding, as if what I had said held some merit. It did something to her, her outward appearance. Even with her glasses on I could see the vitality that made her so attractive slowly surfacing. She even managed a weak smile. But then the smile turned, to an expression of indignation.

"What the fuck do you know about being married!" she lashed out, ripping the scarf from her head. "You don't know jack-shit! You don't know the first thing about even *being* in a relationship! All you know is when the phone rings it's time to get paid! Now you tell me, how can someone like you understand the inner workings of a marriage!"

The words cut through me like a hot knife. My jaws knotted, and I clasped my chin in my hand. My deliberate blankness said it all. I was hurt. Deeply. I didn't know what to say. But I knew what I felt.

Abruptly, Vera's rage failed. She sat down next to me and bowed her head, trying to hide behind her hair.

"I do understand," I said quietly, rubbing her back. "More than you can ever realize."

Vera shook her head and sighed. She was smiling at nothing in particular. "What can you possibly know about being married?" she asked me silently with her palms extended.

"I suppose ignorance is an excuse of sorts cause I really don't know about the intricacies of marriage," I enunciated softly but distinctly, "but I do know about relationships...the one you and I share, Vera."

With that, she raised her head and peered at me strangely, like she was beginning to understand what I was saying, partly from the look I gave her, but mostly from what she felt, that there were more things going on within herself than she could identify. Removing her glasses, she watched me in expected suspense as I looked on. For a moment I thought I was getting through to her. There was a favorable expression on her face, and it did appear hopeful. Though there was—hidden deep within her eyes—a twinge of reluctance. And I guess she had every reason to have it there.

Suddenly, as if I were peering at her too deeply, with too much persistence being heaped on her—looking to see how she would react—she lowered her head to hide her frustration.

"We can never be." She sounded tired. "Maybe in another time and place, but not now, not in this day and age."

"But I need you, Vera," —my voice had an edge of desperateness which I never heard— "I need you in my life."

"You don't need me, Terry," she breathed. "You just think you do. You're just caught up in the moment, caught up in the mystique of having something you can't. What you feel for me is not need, it's just a strong, temporary longing, and it'll blow away, like a feather in a breeze."

"But I love you, Vera." I took her hands in mine.

Tentatively, as though she wished to avert any fractured feelings, she asked, "Do you really love me or is it just the thought of losing a good-paying customer?"

I sat stoically, unwilling to take offense. "You're being cruel now, Vera. I deserve better."

A flash of passion showed in her eyes. "That you do," she said with a nod, "and I hate I ever said those words. Please, forgive me. But you can't honestly say that you love me, not doing what you do."

"But I do." At once, I could see a wonderful and delighted aura coming over Vera. But it lasted for only a few seconds; but while it had endured she seemed so very happy. I half-expected her to leap into my arms. I wanted this more than anything. Of course she didn't. Instead she rose from the sofa and paced the floor.

From across the room she asked me, "Can you honestly say you love me, while you hold all these other people in your arms?"

"Yes," I sighed. "Those other people mean nothing to me."

At that, she gave me a hard, drilling glare—perhaps frustrated that I didn't provide a clearer, more truthful answer, perhaps hesitant to consider the drastic consequences for a question she appeared to have proposed in her mind. Finally, after a moment or two, her hesitance vanished and she said through her teeth, "What about the men, Terry? How about when you're holding them?"

I was stunned, feeling as though I'd been kicked in the stomach. The direct question, the sight of Vera's crushed, pained, scornful look made me momentarily dizzy; my head seethed with a building migraine. I felt I was going to fall face-forward into the coffee table. But I closed my eyes and pushed down my queasiness. When I looked up at Vera, she held herself steady by concentrating on my eyes, and as I looked back, we seemed to be groping blindly toward an answer, as if *both of us* were seeking a reason for my actions.

—of how and why I could do this to her.

So softly that I doubted Vera could even hear me, I murmured, "I'm sorry I didn't tell you, Vera. I...I don't know what to say. I..."

"You don't have to say anything...not a *goddamn* thing," she rasped, standing over me, growing steadily angrier. "In fact, I wouldn't want to hear the shit anyway—it'll probably turn my stomach!" Unable to contain herself she slapped me, and the crack of her hand across my face rang through the room like a verbal declaration of war. She was about to slap me once more but steeled against it; yet her tone was thickened with vibrations of anger. "Bastard!"

That one word "bastard" stung more than all her raging venting or expression.

I could only stare as her face went dark, hard and closed. And despite the passionate bond we'd shared, the intimacies we'd known over the years, at the moment, just then, she seemed a stranger to me all over again, transformed by the broth of powerful, disturbing emotions bubbling beneath her skin. I watched as she swallowed, deeply wounded...to the point it was almost frightening to see her in this state, as she fixed a quelling glare on me, in the depths of my eyes.

At that moment, something had happened. And I knew what it was.

There was something between us that had been taken away. It was something we feared our love, however deep and true, could never recover.

A combination of regret and fear stained my face. "Vera, listen to me..."

"No," she challenged hotly, the breath she released heavy with disgust, "you listen." She reached into the purse straddling her shoulder. Her hand emerged with a brown envelope. She reached inside the envelope and pulled out a sheaf of photographs. She threw them down on the coffee table. Afterward she clenched her hands together until the knuckles whitened. "We were being watched, Terry. And I guess I'm taking a risk by coming here to tell you this. But I felt the need to tell you, in person." She grasped me gently by the chin and peered deep into my eyes. "Watch your back, Terry," she warned, urging me carefully, trying to make her point felt, "somebody's out to do you a great injustice. The person who took these pictures told Mel about several other...clients, that you are partnered with. Terry, your background is being scrutinized."

With that, Vera turned and headed for the door. I rose from the sofa and pulled her in my arms. She drew back and gazed into my eyes. We blinked at each other with uncertainty. A grip of passion overtook us and we savored the moment but did nothing. Instead we relapsed into silence. After a minute or so, Vera shifted in my arms as if she wanted to say something, then thought better of it. Looking at her, she appeared to be shrinking in my arms; she might have been making an unconscious effort to leave my embrace. I wouldn't allow it to happen. I clenched my arms around her like a man who felt like holding on and never letting go. Furiously, she met my embrace, then slowly, with a great reluctance, she drew back and slid her glasses back on.

"Be careful, Terry," she sniffed, "I don't want anything to happen to you."

Still gripping her hard, I waited until my breathing was under control, and then whispered inside of a weak sigh, "Don't worry about me, Vera. Mel Armstrong doesn't scare me."

As if shocked by what I had just said, Vera shook her head violently. She took hold of my jaw and chin then she said stiffly, like a breaking board, "I guess I didn't make myself clear. So you listen to me carefully, Terry. Someone came to Mel…" her face wilting, "…Mel didn't go to them. Don't you see, Terry? Someone has been watching you…*they* came to Mel—in person—face to face!"

I couldn't help but digest Vera's words with great difficulty, and I know the look on my face had to resemble apoplexy. I was almost bursting at the seams in a daze, sort of in mild shock. *I'd been right. Somebody was out to get me. But who? Why?* After a short moment while sweat formed on my forehead and my heart hammered in my chest I brought my attention to Vera's face. She took her cue promptly. With a gentle gesture she swallowed her emotions and stroked my right cheek with a slow hand. Even through the glasses I could see her eyes watering, and she seemed so very weak, almost lost. She wished she were smaller, I could tell. Small enough to curl and hide in some corner until all this went away.

She stood there…totally crushed, totally innocent, and I felt totally responsible, totally helpless, battling to hold back the pain in my throat. All I could do was stare at her…and die on the inside. *Please, God, look after her* I prayed.

As if she had heard me she blinked her eyes. A lone tear escaped. I wiped at the wet tear-track on her face, accidentally rubbing the slightly bruised flesh where her husband had hit her. That's when my insides exploded. I couldn't take it! I reached to her and planted a light kiss on her lips and struggled to keep it light. She returned my kiss, matching my intensity.

Giving me one last sorrowful gaze, as if she had exhausted all of her emotional resources, she turned and left through the door. Before I could say goodbye she had already disappeared into the night. I stood in the archway for quite a while, hoping that she would come back to me, so she could tell me that this was all a dream. But it wasn't. I wrenched myself into motion and began closing the door until I heard the lock catch. I turned. The silence in the apartment was so sharp that it nearly made me cry out. I stared at the photographs lying on the coffee table. A bolt went through my heart; alarm closed around my stomach. I decided I would eventually look at the photographs, but not now.

I couldn't.

I was in too much pain, too furious; and at the moment nothing made sense. Nothing at all. I went into the bathroom and took a long, hot, scalding shower, trying to remove the feelings scaling my skin, my body. Unfortunately that wouldn't be as easy as it sounded. *How does one cleanse his insides?* I wondered. I dried off then went back into the living room where I thumbed through the photographs. The sight of them melted my bones and turned my innards into a seething broth.

Midway through my actions I stopped, as guilt flooded my face; my thoughts scrambled to make sense of what I already knew, with absolute, crystalline clarity…I was being watched.

I finished going over the photos. Feeling drained, as well as empty and hurt, I leaned back on the sofa.

I thought of Vera, and felt a twinge of longing and immediately rejected it. I had to stay focus, keep my mind clear. Besides, Vera couldn't help me; she had done enough by risking her well-being by coming to me and telling me of my dilemma. No. She couldn't help me anymore. More than that. I wouldn't let her. It was too dangerous.

I went over the photos again, almost blindly, but with a grief-born fury rumbling inside me.

After a while I set the photos aside. I was tired. I ignored the silent invitation of my bed and stretched out instead on the sofa. I took a sharp intake of breath and let it out slowly. I was so tired. *But could I sleep?* I wondered. *Or did I really want to?* I was afraid, afraid of what lay behind the floodgates of sleep. I rested an arm wearily across my forehead. I bit my lip, trying to keep my mind off the tainted, unreal night. I soon felt my eyes becoming heavy, however, when my eyes closed, I jerked upright abruptly. I had to beat back the wave of exhaustion that threatened to engulf me. *I did not want to sleep!* So instead I just laid there, and as I did I felt alone.

That's when it hit me.

In spite of everything I had, everything I had accomplished...I was alone...and on my own.

Chapter 10

The moonlight filtered gently through the trees and down to the car windows, bathing the interior in a misty glow.

Inside the car, she sat slumped in the driver seat, her head tilted back on the headrest, a contented grin on her face, as Vera Armstrong maneuvered her Lincoln Navigator from the inconspicuous location. There wouldn't be a need for anymore photographs, she smiled. The ones she had previously submitted were quite enough, quite valid, more than incriminating. She nestled back in her seat. Out of a cornered eye she watched the apartment. She figured Terry was in for the night. However, she decided to stay another hour or so, for good measure.

As she settled in she thought of Terry Allens. Some hidden force had drawn them together, of that she was sure of. When they'd first met she knew it was love at first sight. Her insides had instantly melted as he stood there before her. The warm look he had given her, the charming way he smiled—it was *there!* He wanted her as much as she wanted him! And because of this connection everything she'd resolved about herself and her past relationships with men had flown out of her head. It was at that moment, when he had stared into her eyes, that she found herself all emotion, all feeling. There was something so right in the look that had passed between them—so real and strong—and she could not deny the sensations that had stirred within her.

He *was* the one.

As she sat in her car watching Terry Allens' apartment, she toyed with the hem of her short skirt. "Terry..." She let the name roll off her tongue in a quiet whisper of awe. "Baby, I want you bad," she cooed, her lips parting in a sensuous invitation, her tongue dampening the glossy lipstick that donned her mouth, "so, so bad." Her eyebrows lifted. "Do you want me, too, baby? Huh? Do you? I know you do, baby..." She felt herself losing control. "Terry...baby..." Her voice vanished, and she could not finish her sentence. A rush of desire and yearning came together inside her. Her breathing became labored and ragged. Slowly, as she moaned lightly, her right hand trailed her thigh. She sighed deeply, reclining into the soft leather upholstery.

As if some force were manipulating her body her legs parted, and she ran a palm over the moisture building up between her legs. She wore no stockings. With deft fingers she tugged her panties aside. She soon found her spot. She began to massage herself lightly and as she thought of Terry Allens, her hips thrust and she started panting and moaning incoherently. She pictured him on top of her, their lips fused together while his hands roamed and gripped her body. She imagined his questing tongue moving to the generous curves of her breasts, their fullness overflowing the width of his palms.

She literally lost her breath as she lifted her hips to meet her stabbing fingers, imaging his thick penis plunging deeply into her. Then she screamed, cupping one of her breasts through her silk lilac blouse, massaging it roughly, and pinching the tip, "Oooh, Terry!" then slowly, she collapsed in her seat, breathing hard. The draining event left her body limp and satisfied. Nevertheless, her lacquered nails still spiraled around the tips of her breasts as her body remained content and lazily stretched out. *That was so good,* she smiled, *so fucking good.* She was in seventh heaven.

All of a sudden her mouth twisted in a look of distaste. In an explosive move like someone had poked her in the ribs, she sat up and gripped the steering wheel tightly. A hardness had come to distort her face as she stared at the apartment. Still gripping the wheel hard she waited until her calm was restored. In the seconds to come it had. She was herself. Back in control. If anything, her manner was more nonchalant than ever; but there was a certain look in her face—especially in her eyes—a new excitement, a taste for the game she was playing.

But to her, it wasn't a game.

She kept her riveting glare on the apartment. Then she said in an acidity tone, her words breaking like a dam, "You had better love me, Terry, after all the shit I'm about to sacrifice for you. You had better be the one. But there's no need for me to worry, I know you are. Oh, I saw the look you gave me. You can't fool me—you want me, too. Don't be tryin' to mack, you gorgeous son-of-a-bitch, you want me. I know this—*you know this.*" In a heartbeat her voice turned sweetly, "And we *will* be together, okay, baby? Just give me a little time, all right, darling? There's just so many things I have to do...for us." A grin of anticipation bared her teeth; but she said nothing else. Instead her eyes filled up with chagrin, and she began to blush like a little girl. It was then when she decided it was time to leave.

With evident difficulty, she started up her car. She gave the apartment a final glance. She smiled, but the way she bared her teeth gave her an air of lugubrious savagery, and her eyes glittered coldly. "Remember what I said, Terry," she declared, speaking more mildly, "you will be mine." Then her face tightened in a ferocious grin as her voice dripped venom, "This is not a request, baby." Her features were hard; there was no trace of gentleness or compassion, no warmth anywhere in her face.

She gave the apartment a long, measuring look.

Then quietly, she pulled off into the night.

It was Monday morning.

Will said nothing as I sat in his kitchen. He just stood there against the refrigerator with his arms folded as though he had been stricken mute, unable to interject an opinion on the matter. The situation had him by the tail also. A snarl twisted his mouth as his brow knotted. After a moment, he said to me, "What about this Armstrong woman, think she's tryin' to pull a fast one?"

"Vera?" I replied with surprising promptness. "No way, cousin, she's not that kind of person. Besides, what would she possibly gain from all this?"

He shrugged his shoulders. "Nothin', I guess." He then gave me a strange, wondrous look. My hasty reply concerning Vera must have interested him, although it didn't appear to interest him to the point of asking me anything about her. His look was now one of thoughtful consideration. "Somebody is most definitely droppin' dimes on you, cuz," he admitted. He walked over to the table and pulled out a chair next to me. "Have you noticed anything unusual happening to you? Like somebody suspicious following you or watching your apartment? Somebody creepin' in the shadows, maybe?"

I thought about it then shook my head. "No, not really. I mean, I never really paid any attention to my surroundings, or my comings and goings. I didn't feel the need to." However, for a moment, I was struck by the wild notion that Mrs. Brooks and the flamer had something to do with my situation. But I quickly pushed it from my mind. Those two were just looking for a good time, and nothing else.

In the next forty-five minutes, Will and I went through every "suspect" we could and came up dry. Nobody seemed to have a reason, a motive. Both of us stumped, the conversation, inevitably, had turned to cars. It was a great way to defuse a tense situation, for me at least. Once again Will and I hit on every point. Nothing was overlooked. After exhausting the topic I rose from the table. I told Will I'd catch up with him in a couple of days. He agreed and told me to bring the incriminating photographs with me next time. I nodded and left his home. I climbed into my Benz and decided to cruise by Regina's house—unannounced! It was time to pay her ass back. Plus I really wanted to see her, but only if Derrick wasn't there. If his Range Rover was parked in front of the house I wouldn't stop.

I hit the Lodge Freeway and in twenty minutes I arrived at Regina's place. I didn't see Derrick's ride. Actually, by it being Monday morning, I didn't think he'd be there. Regina wasn't in the limelight so his presence wasn't required. It was nearly noon so I knew Regina's kids to be in either daycare or school. I walked up to the front door and pounded away, trying my best to awaken her. After peering through the peephole she opened the door and let me in. She had on a robe and her hair was in curlers. Her eyes widened as she looked at me, and when I walked in, she shut the door behind me and led me straight into her bedroom.

"Get undressed," she said. "We can get in a quick fuck before I pick up Damion from the daycare center."

I took a seat on the bed. "I'd rather talk."

Her tone was firm. "Don't argue, Terry. Let's just do this, okay?"

I shifted my weight uncomfortably on the bed and refused to drop my gaze. "No, it's not okay, Regina. I didn't come by for this."

She didn't want to hear these words and looked away with her hands cupped about her elbows. She gripped them tightly. "Don't you want me?" she muttered.

"Yes," I explained, "but not in the bed...not as a lover. I want you as my friend, like we are."

"What's wrong with you, nigga?" she whispered harshly. "A girl throws you some ass and all you want to do is talk?" She shook her head questioningly. "Shit, sometimes I just can't figure you out. Don't you like to have a good time?"

At that, she stared at me as if I were less than a man. I met her eyes—forced them to meet mine—and held the moment for a while. And what Regina saw was a look that seemed to unsettle or alarm her; she was the one who looked away. The silence in the room became strained as she frowned into the distance, looking for self-possession. Stiffly, she sat down beside me on the bed.

"What's wrong with me, Terry?" she asked tiredly. "Why can't my life be normal? Like the ones on television? I—just once—want to be normal, with a man who loves me, where we could get married, and grow and prosper as a family, you know? I want to be the perfect housewife, having dinner for my husband, keeping a clean house, having a warm bath drawn for him when he steps through the door, give him nothing but good loving at night...waking up in the morning, gazing into each other's eyes. But how did it all turn out: a failed marriage, three kids, and I'm a stripper at a club shakin' my ass and fake titties for a living. I guess...I guess I really missed the mark, huh?" When she finished, she groaned, then fell silent.

Before she could groan again, I took her hand. "Regina, listen to me, you're a beautiful, talented woman, with three wonderful kids. You have nothing to be ashamed of. You're a terrific mom and you provide everything for your kids. Private schools, the best daycare, the finest of clothes, everything. So you see, you have nothing to be ashamed of."

Just for a moment she smiled at me, then sudden weeping closed her throat. It sounded like the rustle of dry pain, so deep and far away that I could hardly believe what I was hearing.

"Regina," I beckoned sternly, impossibly weak, hurt, crushed—and agonized myself, yet determined to reach her, "you have nothing to cry about. Come on now, don't do this to yourself. You're a strong woman."

"No, Terry, I'm not." Her plea came to me from some place entirely out of reach. "I'm just a woman who acts like she's strong."

"That's not true," I retorted.

"Yes, I am." She locked her teeth to keep from screaming.

"Bullshit." Somehow, I managed to speak more strongly. "You are a strong woman who has everything going for her—I envy you at times."

For a second, I startled her out of her downward dismay. Tears streaking her cheeks, she stared at me blankly. It appeared as if she had come back to consciousness without any notion of where she was or why—

"Terry?"

"Yes, Regina."

"You're really jealous of me?"

"Yes." I fought to control my emotions.

"Why? You have nothing to be jealous of?"

"Oh, yes...yes I do. You have something special. You have someone to come home to at night. You have someone you can love and cuddle...someone to call your own. I don't have that luxury. My life is empty. I have no one."

She looked at me. With a clench of will, she fought to push her pain aside in order to help me with mine. "You have me, Terry. You'll always have me. We need each other. The two of us are like two peas in a pod, two people who need and feed off of the other."

Until I heard the edge of need in her voice, I didn't realize how much she was depending on me. And if I lost her, I, too, would feel a void. We hugged each other and then slowly, she pulled back to face me. Her gaze held; her eyes looked dreamy and faraway. With a voice that sifted like sand blowing in the wind she said, "When I was a little girl I wanted to dance like a ballerina, with a pretty white flaring dress with white tights and ballet shoes, to be as graceful as a swan. The stage would be beautifully decorated, and I'd be the only one out there...the center of everyone's attention, and I would dance like an angel with newfound wings."

I cradled her softly and added, "And I would be there in the front row, cheering you on."

She kissed my cheek and smiled. She had such a pretty smile, and I guess with this smile she was reassuring herself that she was special, that she was still a viable human being with a lot to be thankful for. But as I studied her face I detected another look just below the surface. It was the same look I had seen in the past. I knew something heavy was on her heart, and I could tell she was ready to talk about it.

Slowly, tenderly, she reached out and took my hands in hers. "Terry." She wanted to explain everything clearly, make the importance of what she had to say plain; but she felt hindered, as if I would somehow lose respect for her, as a friend, if she spoke her mind. But deep down she knew me well enough to know this would never happen.

Not between us.

I was a dear, close friend.

And because of this I knew what she was trying to say.

It was about her addiction.

Squeezing her hand tightly, I looked into her eyes. My face betrayed no reaction; yet my sudden stillness suggested that I had touched on some inner part of her. Slowly, she lowered her head.

"You know, don't you, Terry?" she whispered weak and ashamed.

"Yeah, girl," I smiled inside of a sigh, nudging a shoulder into hers, "I know. But you're going to beat this thing, right?"

At once, my unobjectionable attitude was like magic; it made her firmer, stronger. Almost immediately her distress receded. "You damn straight I'm going to beat it!" she let loose. With that proclaimed, we embraced each other fiercely. *She would beat it* I grinned. *Of that, I was sure of.* I would like to think that our embrace had everything to do with it—the confirmation was building mightily between us, strong and sure. At the moment, I don't think anything could have been stronger between two people, and whatever I had to give Regina, she was more than welcomed to it.

Chapter 11

A couple of days had past. Too many things were playing in my head: Vera. The photographs. A gut feeling.

I parted the curtains. At three in the morning the street in front of my apartment complex was deserted. I could tell easily if I were being followed. Enough was enough. I had to find out what was going on. And I knew if I stayed at my apartment I would be at a disadvantage. Whoever this person was, be it man or woman, one or a hundred, there was an odds-on-end bet that they knew where I lived and how I moved about. My apartment was no longer a safe refuge. Instead it had now become a telltale location to where I was.

I had to leave.

I would come back only out of necessity, and hopefully, I could persuade Will to do that for me.

My destination had been previously arranged. I figured I would stay away for at least a week or two. However I couldn't take the chance of hauling suitcases out to my car. It would be a dead giveaway. So I stuffed a weeks worth of clothing into two large plastic bags and sealed them with plastic ties. Dressed in a pair of Levi's, a light blue sweater, and low-top Nike sneakers, I left my apartment. I secured the front door and walked casually to my Benz. Looking around first, scanning the area through narrowed lids, I opened the door, threw the two bags in the back seat, then slid inside. Cautious of every little thing around me I drove to the Marriott Hotel off Northwestern Highway.

It was three forty-five.

Fifteen minutes later I was in my suite and on the phone with Will, who said he'd be there whenever I needed him. I knew this to be true. I gave Will the name and location of the hotel as well as the room and telephone number. After talking with him for about ten more minutes I hung up. I knew the brother was tired, having just gotten off work. Actually, so was I. I glanced around the room, really taking it in. I was more than pleased by what I saw. The place was clean, nicely appointed, and spacious. There was a thick blue carpet on the floor and I really liked the tasteful combination of paint and wallpaper. I glanced out the long plate-glass window. It was a killer view. Still, I walked over and blocked out the extravagant neon glitter of the city by closing the heavy drapes. With long, restless strides, I crossed the sitting room and went into the master bedroom. I bobbed my head in approval. A king-size bed filled the room, its covers turned back in precise folds. A double row of plump pillows lined the headboard. I turned and went back into the sitting room, where I caught sight of the two garbage bags of clothing sitting by the door. The bags were less than ten paces from where I stood but they might as well have been on the other side of the world. I just stared at them...too tired to sort through my things. Tomorrow, I would, I told myself, for sure.

I took a hot shower and climbed into the king-size bed. The cool sheets felt good against my naked body. It wasn't long before my eyelids grew heavy, and I soon drifted off to sleep.

I dreamed.

It was autumn in Northern Michigan. I was with my father. We were laughing and skipping stones across a pond. The sky was blue, the leaves were bright and the air was crisp. The year was 1984, and I was six years old. I remember the year well.

It was the same year cancer had come to claim my father's life.

There was a deep scowl on her face.

In the last four days she had tried unsuccessfully to reach Terry Allens at his apartment. But the bastard wasn't there. Today alone, she'd called seventeen times, only to hear that silly-ass voice mail message. She hated that fucking message—cringing every time she'd heard it—making something wet and heavy slosh in her stomach. She dialed the number once again, and once again, she was met by Terry Allens' voice mail. She became so angry that she hurled her cellular phone into the passenger window, but neither her phone nor the window shattered.

But her nerves were.

And she knew why.

The bastard wasn't there.

He had taken flight—*like a little bitch!* she fumed.

It was then that a concern she had been subconsciously keeping in the back of her mind surfaced and became a distinct fear. Gripping the sides of her head violently, she had to force down the pain of ingrained rejection. She had to remain in control, continue to function, to hold on to her faith, which meant she would have to spend as much time as possible with Terry Allens—talking, trying to make him understand that they were meant to be. Nevertheless the frightening knowledge that she would not find him to tell him this wore on her heavily. She couldn't shake free of a dark gray depression that took the edge off everything she thought and felt; her behavior resembled her former existence, when she had to be passive and follow orders.

As a result, her face crumpled and her eyes melted into submissiveness. Her mind mingled with doubts and incomprehension. She was losing her fragile sense of purpose, of direction. In fact, at the moment, her reason for being where she was, sitting out in a dark, cold automobile, watching some man's apartment, seemed almost ludicrous. And try as she may she could not seem to be able to invent a valid reason for being there. At that moment her mind was paralyzed. Then slowly, after a minute or so, she came out of it, and her gaze was coaxed toward Terry Allens' apartment.

That's when she remembered.

She was unable to suppress a grin, which emerged suspiciously like a sneer.

She wanted this man—but she was inwardly afraid that he didn't want her. *But she wanted him!* But did he want *her?* Opposing viewpoints made her forehead ache. She was torn in two directions and had no idea what to do about the intense struggle. As if she knew she wasn't strong enough for this tug-of-war, she chose a side. With a delicate gentleness that made her face appear as peaceful as a quiet sea, she stared at the apartment. In just that second she became a completely separate person, one who was deeply in love. She fell into a kind of static calm, thinking of Terry Allens. She rolled her eyes and sighed.

Then, like a bolt of lightning, her eyes erupted in a blaze of furor!

She may never see her man again! Her dream man, her love— *their love—everything*—it may never come to blossom! All of a sudden she wore a baffled expression. *What was she going to do? How could she make him see that he was wrong in leaving her—abandoning her—especially in her time of need? When their love was so new and fragile?*

These questions closed around her brain like a clamp, squeezing out a solution to her dilemma. Her hands like talons, she gripped the steering wheel with compressed rage. But oddly, as her inner anger manifested, her face gradually softened. Her demeanor became less hostile; she even went so far as to attempt a smile, it was ghastly. At the same time, her mind hit on something.

She knew what she had to do.

She released her grip on the wheel.

She'd found clarification. The vision struck her as so simple that she laughed. It was as plain as the cute little nose on her face. All she had to do was flush the cowardly son-of-a-bitch out into the open, make him show his fucking self—like a *real* man!

Although she hadn't devised any plan of strategy to bring about her desires, she felt free to smile with assurance, and did this with distinct pleasure. In fact, she felt so strongly of herself and of what she had to do, that she proclaimed boisterously, "You can't hide from me Terry Allens! You pretty motherfucker! Your ass belongs to me, goddammit! And I *will not* have you play these childish-ass games with me!"

With that said in a raw, grinding voice, she fell silent. Her mind now worked intricately, methodically, on a way to tip the scales back in her favor. She needed to secure Terry Allens, *her man*, by her side, no matter what. But she needed more than that from him. She needed better—she didn't deserve to be hurt like this.

But he did.

He needed to be taught a lesson: You *do not* treat a beautiful and desirable woman like shit, depriving her of a wonderful and tantalizing life. No. Not her. It wasn't right. He would have to pay. Better yet, someone close to him. She smiled. *Yes, someone dear and close to his heart. Yes! Oh, HELL yes!* She grinned, harder. If she experienced any personal regrets over the fact that someone was going to feel her wrath, it was secondary. All she knew was someone was going to pay! There was no question about it; and she would have fun doing this. She wouldn't overdo it, however. Just enough to make Terry Allens recognize and take note that she wasn't a woman to be fucked with.

She started her car. She revved the powerful engine. She was ready to peel off in a show of readiness, of combat. However she didn't want to call attention to herself by pulling off harshly. At the same time, she couldn't contain herself. She was hyped, ready to devise a plan and put it into play. But she knew she had to remain in control, it would be the first step in her scheme, to act ladylike. Which she did, most of the time, at least. She cleared her throat and then prim and proper, ran a palm over her hair. After an instant of hesitation, she pulled off...leaving a trail of burnt rubber for nearly half a block.

Chapter 12

At eight-twenty in the evening, Will came out of the stylish department store carrying a handful of shopping bags. On his right arm a beautiful woman was also carrying her share of bags. It was nearly dark and the mall parking lot had thinned out significantly. With a lazy stroll the couple made their way to Will's car parked a little ways down.

That's when it happened.

The first gunshot brought Will and his lady friend to attention. The second and third had sent them running with crouched heads. Seconds later a screeching car pulled off from the shadows and disappeared. Looking up over the hood of a van, Will peered around, his eyes scanning the area, his heart pounding. It seemed clear. He turned and took his lady friend by the arm and with a quick pace, he led her to his car. Moments later with nervous hands he started up his car. As he was about to drive away he saw something tucked under his windshield wiper. It was an envelope. He stared out the window, unsure whether or not to retrieve it. Though he had thought better, he took a deep breath and opened the door. He craned an arm and pulled the envelope inside.

Slumped back in his seat, he began opening the envelope where there was a letter inside. He started to read the typed words. His expression didn't flicker, yet he looked more like a threat of violence with every passing moment. Slowly, after finishing, he stared blankly out the window. His face was tight, as if he were stifling a yawn.

His lady friend fixed him with a worried look. "Will, baby, what's going on here?"

He didn't respond, he just stared out the window. For a long moment he kept his gaze straight ahead, stroking his chin as though he were deep in thought. Then he turned to his lady friend. His throat nearly closed against a mounting sense of panic as he whispered, "Terry." He spoke firmly yet he had begun to sweat. "I've got to find Terry. Somebody needs to see him. They said they need to talk to him. They said..." alarm tightened his speech, "...they said for me to find him and then wait for a call at his apartment." With that, he sat up eagerly and drove off. There was more to the letter than what was mentioned, but he could never repeat those words to her. The words would have sent her into shock.

After spending two days in my hotel room I needed to get out. I hopped into my Benz and headed for Belle Isle Park. Dawn had broken clear and I had to flip down the visor to keep the sun out of my eyes as I drove along Jefferson Avenue for the park turnoff. The sun really agitated my eyes, probably from the lack of sleep. If I'd slept at all last night, I didn't remember. Five minutes later, I came to the Belle Isle Bridge and crossed over. I found a familiar stand of trees and parked. A grassy field was circumvented by a muddy road that ran around its periphery and was lined with trees, some with leaves that were just beginning to turn. I got out and stretched my legs. I looked up at the sky, which was a peacock blue, the kind I'd only seen on crayons as a kid.

As a white butterfly flitted across my face, I glanced around. About fifty yards to my left, was a small pond. Swans floated serenely on the surface, like miniature black and gray dragonships, while ducks, with iridescent, emerald throats, bobbed about, quacking noisily and dabbing, tails up, in the reeds.

Lost in the scene as well as the serenity, I smiled, taking in the sights around me. It was nice, this time of year in early fall. The rhythm of life had slowed and everything was changing. Cool breezes floated off the Detroit River, the tempo of living was less hectic, and people who had run now strolled. It was as if time no longer mattered, as if everything were suspended only to be awakened later, with the coming of spring, evoking another time, another place. It was moments like these I liked best—at day's end or day's beginning, when there was time to appreciate and savor the sometimes extravagant and sometimes subtle beauty of the place.

I couldn't help but think of Vera.

This was our place.

We used to meet here several times a week, just to talk. It was nice, just looking and listening to her. We'd spend hours and hours, laughing, kissing, hugging. They were beautiful, treasured moments. The woman was my equal, there was no doubt. She was on my level in nearly every way: intelligence, humor, courage, in passion, and fire. All my life I'd wished for a woman like her. A woman who would draw a sword and fight at my side in one breath, race neck and neck with me in another, then match my passion, measure for measure, between the sheets.

Yet...for all these affinities, I just wanted to protect Vera. To keep her safe from harm and to do hurt to those who would hurt her. She made me want to share all that she was and all that she could ever be, with me by her side. And then, when our youth was spent, and the fires no longer burned within us quite so brightly, I wanted to grow old with her. To look up at her from across the room and see her smile at me, just as I imagined her smiling now...

I shook my head, still trying to fathom what had happened, indeed what was happening, when I realized I was walking in a daze. I found myself touching things, the limbs of trees, the leaves, the weathered rock Vera and I used to sit on, feeling and connecting with these things as if my tactile sense would give me a clue of how to deal with what I was going through. I picked up a handful of pebbles at my feet. I juggled them in my hand until I closed my hand into a fist around them. I looked up at the sky, a sheen of moisture in my eyes. I clamped my mouth tight, grimness pulling at the corners. I shook my head and dismissed my emotions. With a sighing, half-irritated shrug I looked around, for several minutes. After that I'd decided I had enough. It wasn't working. The place wasn't the same without her.

I needed her with me.

I needed Vera.

Badly.

I had never seen the sky so bright and precise. I was sitting in my underwear, tank-top and silk boxers, looking out the hotel window. The view was breathtaking.

It was ten minutes after nine in the evening. At seven o'clock I'd come back from a rental car company, having decided as long as I was changing residences, I'd might as well change cars, too. It only made good sense. The first thing I'd done after returning to my room was check my voice-mail. It was jammed, at least two dozen messages, mostly clients requesting my services, one being Alvin

Harris, the wealthy entrepreneur who lived in the exclusive Palmer Estates. But I wasn't going to call any of them. I was done with the "servicing" business. I was through with it all—the weird-ass fetishes, the whips and chains, the fake smiles, the laying up with people who I didn't really give a rat's ass about nor did they me, the endless scalding showers to wash my body free of the shame and regret—all of that shit. I was through!

Besides, the drive was gone, and that meant everything to me. Well, the money, actually, but these days this was also a non-valued factor. At this point in my life, sitting on a six-digit bank account, money was the least of my problems.

I stared out the window into the night, tired and disgusted. I thought about Vera, and what she had said about me and my take on relationships. Sure, there were a lot of things I wasn't up on, but I knew what I felt in my heart, what I needed, and it was her.

I *needed* Vera.

I knew there was a lost expression on my face so I shook it off, trying not to berate myself with thoughts and images of Vera. I walked over to the television and turned it on. I flicked through the channels and soon caught the rebroadcast of a classic basketball game on *ESPN 2*: the 1990 NBA finals. Game 5. The Detroit Pistons and the Portland Trailblazers! It had been one hell of a match-up—the Bad Boys in their prime! *Aw, shit*, I heard myself saying, *it was on!* Even though the game was a repeat and I knew the outcome, I was still grateful for the distraction. My mind really needed a reprieve.

As I settled back on the bed to check out the game, the telephone to the right of me started to ring. Cursing under my breath, I picked it up. It was Will. He sounded out of breath. "Hey, what's up, cousin?" I asked. "You sound winded, you got some woman blowing you, or what?"

"Terry," he flung back, "somebody took a shot at me!"

"What the hell are you talking about?" I swung my legs from the bed and clutched the phone tighter.

Will sounded hysterical. "Somebody took several shots at me and Angela while we were at the mall."

It was my turn to be hysterical. "You guys weren't hit, were you? Everybody's fine, right?"

"Yeah, we're cool," he said. "But Angela was a little shaken up. I just dropped her off at her crib. I wanted to talk to you alone. Listen, cuz, you were right, somebody has definitely got a thing for you. I'm talkin' big time."

At once my heart hammered in my chest. "Why? What the hell are you talking about?"

"Whoever took a shot at me and Angela also left a letter on my windshield."

"What did the letter say?" I urged, swallowing a huge lump in my throat.

Will paused, then stated in a rush, "The letter said for me to tell you that you'd better own up to your responsibilities, and for you to get your ass back to your apartment, ASAP...or else."

"Or else, what?" My reaction was so strong I sprung to my feet. "What the hell does *or else* mean?" Again, Will paused. I knew then something was seriously wrong. Will didn't pull punches for nothing. No way. Not him. Not unless he absolutely had to. "Or else, what, Will?" I demanded louder. "Tell me, dammit!"

I heard him sigh, then as forward as he could he said, "Or else I wouldn't be so lucky next 'fucking' time. That a bullet would find its way through my rear window and into the back of my skull."

Almost immediately, my blood pressure rose until I thought my head would explode. "What the hell is going on here? I mean, who the hell is this? I haven't done nothing to nobody! What do they want from me!"

"I don't know, cuz," murmured Will. "You ain't knocked some bitch up, have you?"

"Hell no!" I blasted back. "I'm strapped every time—doubled strapped!" I shook my head. "Naw, this is something else, something a little deeper. It could be a jealous husband or boyfriend."

"I hope not, cuz." Will then raised his voice, "You got a piece?"

"No," I replied vaguely, thinking that maybe I would need one.

"Well, I do," returned Will strongly. "A nine-millimeter. It's clean, no numbers, and this baby will blow a fuckin' hole in a sewer cap. Say the word and it's yours."

My jaws knotted with tension, but I knew what time it was. "I want it, and I'll take any extra rounds you have, too."

"You got it, cuz. Where do you want to hook-up at?"

"Meet me at the Amoco station on Telegraph and Twelve mile, in about an hour, if that's cool for you?"

"It is." Will hesitated then said, "What's the game plan, cuz?"

At that my eyes flashed with readiness. I was tired of all this ducking and hiding bullshit. I wanted to know what the hell was going on. I clenched the phone tighter. "Since this *person* wants me at home so bad, that's where I'm going—home."

"I hear you, baby," Will agreed anxiously. "Meet this punk-ass bitch head on. We'll lay in the cut for his ass."

Hearing Will's words caught me totally off-guard. *No way*, I thought to myself, *I wasn't about to let him do it.* In an apologetic tone, I said, "Sorry, cousin, but this one's on me. I can't have you in the middle of my mess, man. This is my problem, not yours, and I'll handle it. I'll just meet you at the Amoco..."

Apparently Will had anticipated my reaction and countered as if the subject was a closed issue. "Fuck you, cuz. I'm in it all the way. Now, push your ass up and let's get movin'. We got some business to handle."

She smoothed her dress self-consciously. It was a shimmering iridescent blue with long sleeves and a high neck. It fit her body like a glove down to her shapely hips, and then it flared into soft folds. She wore a silver bracelet, earrings, and necklace. Her dress fabric glittered, so she felt there was no need for fancy jewels, too. *It would be an overkill* she smiled, *and Terry probably wouldn't like that.* She was inordinately proud of the dress. It could stand on its own. She had purchased it just for this moment. It was designed especially for her, from her own pattern, so, in her eyes, it was one of a kind.

Her long hair was pulled up and back, though some black silky strands escaped to frame her face. All in all, she looked simply breathtaking. *He was worthy of her* she nodded, *as she was of him. They were meant for each other.* And now, by her looking so exceptional he would eventually see this. He would come to realize his errors and treat her like a fine lady, kind and gentle and loving. She looked down at her dress. Suddenly she became overwhelmed, and began to cry, not because she was sad, but because she would finally find her happiness, in a much finer man. Terry Allens would be so much better than *her first.* In fact, at this point, there was no comparison.

She nodded and dried her eyes, then she pulled a veil of calm around her and hurried from the room, smiling joyously as she headed for the phone. Two things came immediately to mind. One was that she would win Terry Allens over with her sweetness and charms, like he had done her; the other was that she was going to get him to confess his love for her, and she would not let him depart from the phone until he did; the devastatingly handsome Terry Allens would confess to the world—loudly—to the heavens—*that she was his!*

Both of these things were going to happen.

There were no doubts in her mind.

With long, slender fingers, lacquered beautifully in red enamel, she dialed Terry Allens' apartment...a strong heart pounded violently within her chest as the phone began to ring.

Chapter 13

"Hello," I said, my naturally deep voice coming out a little strained.

"Hi, might this be Terry Allens?" a voice inquired, sweet and charming.

A chill instantly came over me as I asked, "Who is this?"

"Now, now, now, I asked first," the voice came back, polite and refined.

I swallowed. "This is Terry Allens, now who the hell is this?"

"Terry, baby," she announced almost lovingly. "How have you been?"

"Who the hell is this?" I demanded. "I don't have time to play these childish games."

"Oh no," the voice snapped, "we will not start off like this, Terry. I'm a woman who demands nothing but respect, you hear me?" At once the voice was harsh, but it slowly gave way to spice and humor. "Now, let's try this again, okay? And please, be nice to me."

At that, I glanced sharply at the receiver as if to gauge the intent of the request. Whoever this woman was, she wasn't stable. That I knew right off. I took a breath and relaxed. I decided to meet her at her terms. I laughed softly and then replied candidly, "Okay, I'll be nice, and I do apologize for my rudeness." There was a silence, as if the woman was confirming the sincerity of my words.

"Apology accepted," she finally chuckled.

"Good," I smiled, "now, who am I speaking with, please? It would surely aid in the conversation."

There was a pause. "Just call me Darling," the woman replied seriously but was almost chortling. "That sounds so fitting for a moment like this," she went on, speaking now more like a long, lost friend, "and if you'd like, I could call you Darling, too" —she giggled behind her words— "eventually, I'll be calling you that anyway."

My lungs felt tight, as though I hadn't taken a decent breath for hours. *Who the hell was this? Was she the one causing so much shit in my life?* I waited as patiently as I could until my emotions and wits were replenished. Then I said, very coolly, like a card player about to bluff his way through a hand, "Tell you what, why don't I call you Darling, and you call me Terry, and then, when I feel comfortable enough with you, I'll let you call me Darling, too, deal?"

"Okay," she happily agreed. "I'd like that...I'd like that a whole lot."

I couldn't help but notice her reply sounded like an offer of rescue. "Okay, Darling, what would you like to talk about?"

"Us."

"Okay, would you like to book a date?"

"*What!* What the fuck did you say?" returned the woman instantly in a tone of protest and outrage. "Do you think this is what I'm calling you for? To book a goddamn date? Well, it's not, you presumptuous asshole! I'm here to talk about *us*—not about anything else! You hear me!"

I couldn't respond. I turned to face Will, who was in the room watching me, his chin out-thrust. Slowly I turned my attention back to the phone. Then, with extreme effort, I made myself heard through a calm voice, "I hear you loud and clear. And I'm sorry if—"

"You'd better be!" she interrupted rudely. "Let's get this shit straight—*right now*—I am *not* a woman to be fucked with, do I make myself clear, Terry?"

I paused, and while my heart thumped like an out of control bongo, I heard through my hesitation a faint sound, like muffled laughter. It was her. Abruptly, my senses came back. "I hear you loud and clear."

The woman responded with surprising promptness, and said in a voice that sounded like dry husk, "Okay. That's better. Now that we've got that established I think we should get a few more things straight here. Number one: you are not to book anymore dates. Number two: the only person you're to see outside of me, is your cousin Will, a few family members here and there, and maybe that whore-bitch Regina. Other than that, no women at all." She stopped and chuckled. "But your mom is okay. I've met her already over tea and cookies. Mary is a very nice woman. And I think her little apartment is just adorable. She said you bought nearly every piece of furniture in her place, even the pictures. It really is nice, Terry, you've got excellent taste." In a split second her voice became deadly. "And last but not least: stay away from the faggots. No man of mine is doing that disgusting shit." She drew a sharp breath. "Now, you think you can follow these simple rules?"

Hearing the words, my eyes glittered dangerously, but I didn't dare retort. It was obvious that she had the upper hand. I struggled to regain my calm stature. I did. Nevertheless the veins in the back of my hand bulged crookedly as I gripped the phone. "I guess so, I mean, that shouldn't be too hard to do." My voice cracked. Fighting for dignity, I said, "What about you…you're making a lot of demands on me but when do I get to see you?"

"Oh, you will, baby." Her tone betrayed neither disapproval nor doubts. "You will. You can count on it. And I can guarantee you, you will *not* be disappointed."

A dull flush spread over my face. "What exactly do you want from me?"

"For us to be together."

Who the f—Fortunately, my anger was quick to subside. "Listen, if we're going to be an item then I need to know who you are, what you look like, your hobbies, your likes and dislikes, things of that nature, know what I'm saying here? I don't know anything about you."

"Oh, but you will, Terry," she squealed delightfully. "Believe me, baby, you most certainly will. We just need a little time to get better acquainted over the phone. You know, twice, three times a day for about a week or so. You know, until the ice is broken."

"And what do I do with myself in the meantime?" I asked as if I were speaking into the air.

"You do nothing," she whispered quickly. "Not a damn thing, you hear me? You can come and go as you please, but I want your ass at home every night. I mean this, Terry. And don't go to the cops or snoop around trying to find out who I am. Nobody knows. And if I find out that you have, I'll make your life and those around you *very* uncomfortable. Do I make myself understood, Terry?"

"Very." Sweat trickled from my temple.

"Good." With that, her voice turned into that of an angel. "I'll be talking to you tomorrow night, okay, baby? And remember, don't break the rules. Goodnight, Terry."

I didn't response. I couldn't. Instead I conveyed an impression of desperation. Seconds later I heard a dial tone. But instead of hanging up, I just stood there, with the phone to my ear, heart pounding in my throat, as I felt danger suddenly thickening around me, but there was nothing I could do. I felt helpless. Then, in an unexpected move, I slammed the phone down, smashing it into pieces. Will rushed to my side, asking about the call. But at the moment I couldn't say anything. I was in too much rage. I recovered rapidly, however, and instead of telling Will about the call I turned to him and said dully, "I need to buy a new phone."

Chapter 14

I had tried unsuccessfully to reach my mother since near six o'clock the next morning. I'd called four times without response. The fifth time, I called the front office and asked if by some chance they had seen her. They had. It seemed that one of the maintenance men had seen her with Mister Carter, an elderly man who'd suffered a stroke nearly a year ago which had left him partially paralyzed and unable to speak. But I'd noticed, in the last few months or so, he could walk with the aid of a cane and speak, if slowly, without slurring. And now that he had paired up with my mother he could easily walk a half mile and without his cane, at times alone and unaided. Deep in my heart I knew my mother had a lot to do with this. She had this kind of effect on people, with her miraculous love and caring, sort of a black Mother Teresa.

The rain came down harder than before and the wipers drummed out a steady rhythm across the windshield. The combination was enough to bring me out of my reverie. To my left, I caught sight of the familiar spot visible through the dark of the trees that lined the road. Little more than a quarter mile ahead was the turnoff to the spot. I approached the area and I found my usual location. It was raining too hard to walk around so I shut down the engine and stared at the car's ceiling. It was a dreary day at Belle Isle Park. But I thought I'd utilize this time to ponder my next move. I figured I would go by mother's place a little later and ask her about this mysterious woman. I needed some type of description, something to work on. After that, using what I had gotten from my mother, I'd go to Will's place and try to hammer out some possibilities.

As I stared up vacantly, listening to the heavy truncheon of rain, I went over a few things in my head, concerning the mysterious woman who had entered my life so shockingly. Her intrusion had not been sheer coincidence. I was certain she'd been watching me for a while. She knew too many things about me, my lifestyle, the people I hung out with, my family. She *had* to be watching me for some time. From what I could decipher from last night's conversation, she appeared to be unstable, spiteful, embittered, and very vindictive. But most of all, she wanted to be in control. So there was only one thing I could do, at least for the time being: let her be in control.

Or at least let her *think* she was in control.

But I had to be extremely careful. I couldn't afford to lose my grip, not for a second. I had to become just as deceitful and cunning as the woman I was dealing with, yet I had to remain one step ahead of her, and oh-so-cautious. I'd like to think myself very good with the techniques of deception, although I am not always able anymore to deceive myself. I chuckled. "If I were, I wouldn't know that, now would I? Ha, ha." I shook my head. The woman had me talking aloud to myself.

I reclined further into my seat, analyzing this woman. Most likely she's beautiful; she said I wouldn't be disappointed. She has a strong, practical mind, she's tough and outspoken, definitely quick on the trigger, and she loves to bulldoze. She comes across as clever, articulate, intelligent. But I detected something else in our conversation: she seemed fragile and weak, almost timid.

And this unnerved me.

People harboring all of these attributes can be very unpredictable. In a nutshell: dangerous, as well as extremely resourceful.

And because of this I wouldn't go to the police, not just yet, not unless I had to. I feared for my family, especially my mother. I gritted my teeth. *If that bitch came near her...* I had to keep my wits, remain professional. I also knew I had my work cut out for me. But somehow, I was up for it, and if it wasn't for the disheartening threats thrown in the mix, I'd actually enjoy the challenge. I like a challenge, and I hate being bored. Even with my profession I have a tendency to get bored. Anything routine that comes along I'll most likely pass on, and that makes my boredom worse. It's a real problem to decide whether it's more boring to do somebody boring than to pass it up and then have nothing to do at all.

To tell the truth, I really relish my work when the assignments are risqué and daring and somewhat different and will stimulate my mind. I get nervous, but I usually perform at my best under this stimulating kind of pressure and enjoy my job the most. I rejoice with tremendous pride and vanity in the compliments I receive when I do my clients well, as I always do. But between such peaks of challenge and elation there is monotony and despair. And I find, too, that once I've succeeded in impressing a client, I'm not much excited about impressing that same client again; there is a tremendous letdown after the moment, a kind of empty, tragic disappointment, an almost inescapable depression. I frequently feel I'm being taken advantage of merely because I'm asked to do the shit I'm paid to do.

Except with Vera.

I could lay with her for hours—days, and not do anything but cradle her in my arms and kiss the whorls of her ears. Not like the others, when all I want to do is push up from the room and get the hell out of there.

But I guess I don't have to concern myself with such dreadful thoughts.

All of that is over with.

I'm done. I only had one final hurdle to jump, this sick-ass woman. And when I finally jump this mysterious, deranged, unhinged, bitch-of-a-hurdle, there will be no more.

Well, maybe one more, and perhaps, my toughest one.

It was eight o'clock in the evening when my telephone began to ring. Slowly, with an immense act of will and strength, I pushed myself into action. The caller ID read: unlisted. I reached over and picked up the phone before it could reach the fifth ring.

"Hello," I answered lightly.

"Good evening, Terry," a soft voice announced. "How's my baby tonight?"

It was her! I fumed. Almost at once, the veins in my forehead surfaced and stretched to the point of bursting. However, I took a deep breath and protested the strain. "Well, hello," I whispered back. "I'm doing just fine, how about you?"

"I'm fine, now that I'm talking with my man-to-be."

Heart pounding, muscles crying out with strain, I held on. "Is that right? So when do I get to see the woman behind this charming voice?"

"Soon."

"When?"

"Soon, okay? Let's not rush things."

"Okay. So, how was your day?" My stomach twisted.

"Just fine."

"Did you do anything worth mentioning?"

"No, not really, just drove around, takin' in a few new sights."

"Any place special?" My voice had an edginess which I tried to hide.

"A matter of fact, I did," she happily announced. "A quiet little spot, sort of tucked out of the way. There's trees, bushes, nature all around you as far as you can see."

"Sounds nice."

"Oh, it is. We have to go there sometime…together."

"What about tonight? This place sounds just right for a night drive. Care to indulge me?"

"No, not tonight, I'm a little tired."

"That's being a bit contradictory, don't you think? I thought all you did today was drive around?" I continued to speak carefully. "Now how tiring can that be? You're not an old lady, are you?"

"Hardly, baby."

Tentatively, as though I wished to avert a confrontation, I asked, "May I ask your age?"

She seemed unwilling to take offense. "Twenty-four." Then she added in a nasty tone, "You know that's not very gentlemanly of you to ask a woman such an embarrassing, upfront question? Don't you think you're being a little crass by asking that?"

I paused. I needed time to digest her question and marshal a reply. "I guess you're right," I finally acknowledged, "that was a bit intrusive on my part."

She hummed her agreement, then inquired, "What are you wearing?"

I glanced down at my attire. "Just some jeans and a tee shirt, no socks."

"Are the jeans tight?"

I smiled, and the smile on my lips didn't soften the glint of battle in my eyes. The woman was stepping into my realm. "Yeah, but not too tight, I need room to swing and sway, if you know what I mean."

At that she went silent, then recovered and countered as if she were immune to my words, as a drawling voice said clearly, "Yes, it's not too wise to wear your jeans too tight, it bunches things up and that's not good."

In the space between heartbeats, I smiled, "I agree, especially if you're packin' like I am."

"You shouldn't say such degrading things about yourself," she spat. "It's not very becoming of you...it cheapens you."

"I apologize, I just wanted to entice you."

"Your reason being?"

"I want to see you."

"Oh, really now. Cut the shit, Mister Terry Allens."

"But I do want to see you," I pleaded tenderly. "You sound so beautiful...so intriguing." There was silence. I took advantage of it. "I would really like to see you. You appear to be very secretive...a...how should I say...lurk-in-the-shadows type of woman, and that turns me on. I bet you're the kind of woman who loves to take a long, hot, soothing bath after a hectic day, the kind who lotions her body down afterwards from head to toe, with slow, skillful hands. The kind who takes the time to prepare for bed...like you're about to make passionate love to a long, lost lover. Yes, I know what kind of woman you are, all too well. You're a perfectionist...even though you're just shutting your body down for the evening, everything has to be just right for you...to the letter. Your hair, your face, your skin, even your nails, everything about you must meet an exact standard before you decide to call it a night."

On that note I paused...to let my words sink in, feeling a bit anxious but nevertheless going with the flow. Yet, I didn't want to push anything; I had to apply caution here. But as I held the phone to my ear I felt bolder and thought, *The hell with it. I'll go for it.* I wet my lips and continued, "And because of this perfection, I feel a burning need to see you. I would really love to hold your warm, exceptional body against mine. To be able to cradle you, to rub you slowly, stroke and caress the curves of your breasts. And in the process of doing this I'd become weak, to the point I would fall to my knees...only to see your moistness staring back at me, taunting me, calling me, inviting me to explore. And obediently, I would...flicking and licking between your legs, just the way you'd like it, just the way you'd tell me to...up and down...all around...stabbing...inside and out. My mouth would be everywhere—nuzzling you, biting you, surrounding you, rubbing you, eating you..."

"Stop..." she demanded inside a breathless whisper.

"*Non, ma chere*, I can't help myself," I countered, knowing she was weakening. "The burning is too strong. I'm so hungry for you...getting so hard. I need you, baby. I want to look into your eyes, the eyes that I long to see, and see the fire and passion and lust in them. I want to devour you, with every flick of my tongue, with every caress of my hands..."

"Stop it. You, you mustn't..." Her voice trailed.

"But why? Why torture ourselves? I want you so bad. All this secrecy shit is turning me on. I need to see and hold you."

She whimpered and repeated her rejection. "You can't...you just can't."

"Why? The moment is so right," I soothed, in a warm masculine voice. "Don't you want me? Don't you want me wedged deep inside you?"

The pleasure in her voice was so brilliant that she nearly started to sob. "*Yes!* Oh my, *yes!*—more than *anything!* More than anything in the world! Believe me, I do—really and honestly I do!"

Mustering a smile, I said, "Then what's the problem here? We're two consenting adults?" I moaned, deep and low, "Let's do this, baby...tonight."

She paused, then explained in a gasp, "Oh, I would just love to. But I don't want to rush you into anything. I'd like for us to take our time. It's nothing personal. I just want you to be sure, okay, Terry? This is a big move we're making...and I want you to be certain about me and about your feelings. I'm a very fragile person...I break very easily, know what I'm saying here?"

"I understand," I said, withdrawing. I tried to appear compassionate, though it was hard, sickening, actually. "And in the future I will respect your feelings, as well as your vulnerability."

"*Merci, monsieur,*" she uttered. "You're so very kind."

For some strange reason I found a brow raising. "Oh, I see you speak some French, huh? Where did you learn it?"

"From *par-ee*," rolled off of her tongue in a rich French accent. "I went there some time ago for an internship."

"I see." I rubbed my chin, very much intrigued. "So tell me, just how fluent are you?"

"Alas, *Je parle un petit peu de francais, mais ma francais n'est pas parfait.*"

125

"I'm sorry, you'll have to translate."

She giggled. "It means 'I speak a little bit of French, but my French is not perfect'."

"Well, I'm here to tell you, it sounds pretty damn good to me. It really does. I'm very impressed."

She paused, then said, *"Merci.* You know, I'm so glad we're going to be together soon. I'm really looking forward to seeing you again."

A jolt went through me. I relaxed on my bed and decided to probe a little deeper. "Do you remember what I was wearing?" As light sweat gleamed dimly across my forehead I closed my eyes. I blocked everything from my head, anticipating an answer that could give me some insight on who I was dealing with.

"Let's just say you looked very nice, Terry," she whispered as though she, too, knew what I was up to.

I wasn't going to push it. The woman was no dummy. Instead, I said, "Why don't you describe yourself. So I can get a mental picture of you. It doesn't have to be anything exact, just the basics."

The idea made her giggle. "Describe myself, huh? Okay, let's see here...I'm about five-feet two, very pretty—so people tell me—and I have a nice curvaceous body."

"Uh-huh. Why don't you tell me a little more about that body."

"What do you want to know?"

"Dimensions, baby."

"Oooh, you naughty boy. You got me blushing here."

"Well?"

"34-24-36."

"Nice. Care to elaborate?"

She cleared her throat. "So, I see you want the details, huh?" She cleared her throat once more. "I have very nice breasts, perky and pear-shaped, and I got a firm round bottom. Or should I be saying *ass*?"

"Oh, it doesn't matter. Either way sounds nice. *Very* nice. What about your eyes?" I went on.

"They're brown, almost hazel, at times."

"So I take it with eyes like that you don't wear contacts?"

"No way. I ain't covering up these babies with no contacts."

126

She appeared relaxed. This was what I wanted; it distracted her from my questions. "So, how would you describe your hair?"

Again, she giggled. "It's long and black and silky. I have it conditioned every week at Shear Ritz Hair Salon."

I smiled. I was making some headway. But instead of pushing my luck I retreated in another direction. "So, Darling, describe what you look for in a man?"

"He has to have all your qualities."

I chuckled and shook my head. "Well, let's forget about me and my qualities for the time being, okay?"

"That's not easy to do, baby."

"Well, let's give it the old college try, all right? For me?"

She paused then said, "Well, okay, since you put it that way how can I refuse. First of all, the man should know the basics, like how to brush and floss, and have clean hands and fingernails. And secondly, he should never break a promise to me. I hate that, with a passion." She drew a harsh breath. "But as far as dating goes, I like a man who can romance, you know what I'm saying? Romance…romance and more romance. I like to be primed for lovemaking. Give me some erotic thoughts before we make love. Call me during the day and say something sexy like, 'I've been thinking about making love you all morning long, and I can't wait to get my hands on you. Or tell me that you needed to hear the sound of my voice in your ear. Things of that nature. And when the moment happens *please*, be good in bed, or at least decent."

"You know, I can relate to that, almost to the letter."

"Oh, really?"

"Of course."

"Uh-huh. I forgot, you're the expert around here."

"Whoa, I never said that."

"You didn't need to. I know you're good, most likely exceptional. So tell me, what would *you* do, besides the obvious, to ease me into the mood?"

Though my stomach was flipping, I was ready. "Well, for starters, I'd leave a post-it note on your front door or maybe on your car window, saying how much I need to see you. I'd take you for a long walk, and then hold you tightly, while a slow tune played lightly in the background, all the while nuzzling your neck, looking dreamily into your eyes. Then, when we finally got together for dinner, I'd sneak a card in front of you saying I wish you were my dessert, but not in a sexual way, only as the last thing to savor."

She moaned. "Mmm, talk to me, baby. Tell me more."

"Well, before the actual act of making love, I'd give you my special, erotic, no-strings attached back rub, using all my skills to keep your mind stimulated, keeping your libido constantly humming by telling you how much you're turning me on. Then, when it's all said and done, I'd put your body in the meltdown mode."

I heard a gasp. "What would you do, baby? What? *What?*"

I hesitated, purposely. "I would be the most considerate and sincere lover you had ever known. No part of your flesh would be overlooked as I gave you the most healthiest, well-needed, deeply satisfying, lethal dose of lovemaking your body could stand." Afterwards I remained silent, hopefully holding that moment of intimacy in her head.

She joined in the silence, not saying a word, then concern soon edged her voice. "Terry? Are you still there? Terry?"

Leaving her on edge I broke the silence with a deep chuckle, changing the subject entirely. "So tell me, Darling, what's your favorite color?"

There was a pause; I guess she needed time to come out of it, to adjust. A few moments passed then she proclaimed decidedly, "Purple. I love everything in purple."

I nodded. "Purple is a beautiful color. It has a certain mystique to it...like you." I settled back. "I would love to see you in something purple, something sexy...when we finally get together." At that, I heard another gasp, followed by a squeal of pleasure. For one more moment while she expressed her joy, I held the mood as though I were about to squeal along with her. Then I whispered in a tone of sultriness, "Yes, a purple negligee, with your face and lips gleaming seductively. And to consummate the union I'd be wearing a silk purple robe, with matching boxers."

"No, Terry," she cut in smoothly, "a purple G-string, so I can see the bulge, baby."

"You've never seen it?"

"No," she breathed. "Is it big?"

"Oh, yes," I seeped out, "nice and thick."

"Is it long and smooth, too?"

"Very. I take it you like it like that...long and smooth?"

"Yes, and hot—I like 'em *hot!* Does yours get hot?"

"Yes it does, baby." My voice then dripped like slow honey, "I have it just way you want it...nice and thick and long and smooth and hot. Would you like to have a go at it? Wouldn't you just love to feel it sliding slow and deep inside you? Sawing wonderfully against your clit?"

"Yes, I...I would. I really would like that. You gonna give it to me good, baby?" she beckoned urgently. "Like you said you would?"

"Nothing but," I promised, in the deepest voice I could bring forth.

Almost instantly, she blurted out, "Can we do it outdoors, in the rain?"

"Sure," I chuckled. "Any special place in mind?"

In response she gave an answer that made my heart stop. "Let's do it in that place you were at today, you know, at Belle Isle Park, where the trees and stuff are?"

I lost it! I rose to my feet and came back in a fury. "You were following me! Isn't it enough you have me on goddamn lockdown! Now you're following me, too! What kind of sick bitch are you!"

"A bitch who has you by the fuckin' balls," she quickly rasped. "And you had better recognize this shit! I hold the fuckin' cards! Every last one of them! From the fuckin' Jokers to the goddamn Ace of Spade! Got it! Now you think about this shit while you jack-off thinking about me, you cunt-suckin' bastard! I'm through with your ass tonight!"

With that, she gave a sharp howl like a cry of battle and slammed the phone down. With my face clenched and bleak, my lower lip bitten between my teeth, I shuddered. *What the hell had I done? I was making such serious headway!* I toppled backward with the slow, unreactive violence of felled timber. When I hit the bed I stared up at the ceiling. *Boy, did I ever screw that up!* Then suddenly my heart was on fire, and I shot up from the bed. Every expansion and contraction of my lungs was a supreme effort as I reached for the keys to my rental car. I wondered, with each breath, if I had enough strength for the next as I bolted from my apartment.

Lockdown or not, I had to check in on my mother.

Ray Burton

At five-forty a.m., I sat on my sofa watching the morning sun coming up over a thick gathering of trees in the distance. A soft, liquid line of light oozed through a part in the curtains like a golden veil. Faint stubble had appeared on my face and I stroked it absently. The emotional arc I experienced went from shock, to fear, to indignation and ended in anger. But I was grateful. Nothing had happened last night at my mother's place. In fact, we had a good time just laughing and talking, and while I chatted amiably, praising her on her cooking as well as her timeless beauty, secretly drawing any suspicions away, I had inquired about unexpected visitors popping their heads in her apartment. In response, she'd mentioned a list of people who often dropped by unannounced, at all hours: Mister Carter, other friends, prescription deliveries, the fumigation man, maintenance men, office personnel, and recently, a census taker, who she had tea and cookies with.

When she'd rambled off "census taker", I could feel the hair beginning to crawl up the back of my neck. I had asked my mother to describe this census taker, and she did, stating "the woman" was very pretty and polite, showing nothing but good manners, a real down-to-earth girl who complimented her to no end on how beautifully decorated the place was, saying it was such an "adorable little apartment". When I'd heard this my insides screamed *You sneaky little bitch!* in a hundred languages. It was at that point when I'd excused myself from my mother's apartment and headed back to my place. For the life of me I couldn't sit there calm and casual, while some loony bitch held me by the nuts.

I just could not!

I knew I had to make a move in finding out this woman's identity!

The woman was breaking bread with my mother for Godsakes!

As I gazed out the window still rubbing the stubble on my face, a silent stir moved me, nothing overwhelming, just a light nudge of anxiety and apprehension. I wondered if this woman was really capable of carrying out a threat? Or was she doing all of this for some kind of attention? Hell, I didn't know, and I knew I couldn't take the chance. There was too much at stake. So what could I do? Apparently, nothing...just sit and stare vacantly out of my window and watch as another dawn came to the city. I felt helpless, alone.

At times like this, I think of Vera. Sometimes it would come to me as a quiet thought, or like a drifting mist; other times, as emotion engulfing me, coming as loud and startling as a crack of thunder wherever I stood, making my heart erupt on the spot. However, much as I like to think of Vera, I had to block her from my mind. Now was not the time. I shifted on the sofa and brought out the gun Will had given me and nestled it in my hand. I tipped it towards me and saw the hole where death came out. I wondered if I could actually kill somebody. I suppose I could if I had to, though I hoped and prayed it would never come to that. I wasn't a killer.

But I knew I could pull a trigger if I had to.

I placed the gun on the coffee table then picked up the envelope containing the surveillance pictures of me and Vera. I pulled them out and sifted through each one. Glancing over the photos a feeling came over me that I was juggling an extremely hot potato, that there was something in the photos I was missing. I stared hard, but found nothing which could aid me. There was nothing, nothing but images of Vera and I hugging outside a restaurant; some were close-ups, some were full-body shots. Yet there was something there. I was about to go on to something else when it occurred to me that I might have simply overlooked the most obvious thing, or failed to decipher it. But there it was, staring at me as plain as day. I wondered why I hadn't thought of it before.

The photos.

The woman had taken them.

She had given them to Mel Armstrong.

Mel Armstrong had seen her.

He could identify her.

I knew what my next move was. I had to get a hold of Vera, and convince her to talk to Mel, to get him to bring this woman to light. But would she do it? For that matter, would *he* do it? This wasn't exactly something he would want to rehash, nor Vera. But I had to take a chance. But I was facing two dilemmas: finding Vera and convincing her; the other being the presence of the psychopathic bitch monitoring me. The latter being undoubtedly the biggest obstacle to overcome. So I knew I had to bide my time, and win this psycho woman over. It was the only way. In the meantime I had to reach Vera, in some manner. But how? I was on lockdown.

Then it hit me.

I was, but Will wasn't, and this woman couldn't possibly be in two places at one time. I reached over and snatched up the phone. I called Will and gave him the gist of my plan, and though I talked fast and the brother was groggy, he knew where I was going. I told him I'd meet with him in a day or two where I would go into further detail, and in the meantime how I would try to contact Vera, so she would know what was up. He agreed. Somehow I knew he would. I laid the phone down. I was starting to feel pretty good, in spite of the situation around me, and was anxious to get out of the apartment.

That's when I smiled. Since the woman liked keeping tabs on me, I was going to give her a run for her money. I was going to take her ass on a wild ride! Hopefully flush her out!

At a quarter to nine I left my apartment. I was dressed in jeans and a light sweater. I had on a blue denim jacket with white Reeboks on my feet. My face was clean as a whistle and I must say, I was feeling as good as I looked. My implacable confidence transmitted itself into my stride as I stepped up to my rental car, a four door Pontiac Bonneville. Before beginning on my quest, I headed downtown and decided to stop at a Waffle House restaurant. I pulled into the parking lot and went inside, where I took a window seat to watch the traffic zooming along Grand River Avenue. I kept my eyes peeled but there was nothing noteworthy. I ordered the breakfast special and coffee. I looked around. It was a weekday so the place wasn't crowded and I could really take in the people around me. Again, there was nothing worth noting.

Forty-five minutes later, I finished my meal of pork chops and eggs. It was pretty good. Actually, I think I was just hungry; my eating habits lately had gone to shit. The waiter, a tall, slim, prematurely balding man, brought me the bill. I nodded kindly and left a five spot on the table. I went to the counter and handed the cashier my bill. She was a cute little thing with sparkling blue eyes that crinkled up when she smiled. I reached back to grab my wallet, however, she didn't allow me the chance to pull it out.

"It seems your bill has been taken care of, sir," she smiled.

Softly, I said, "Come again?"

"Your bill has been paid, sir," she replied promptly.

"What the hell do you mean" —my tone sharpened into a lash— "my bill has been paid?" I didn't give her a chance to respond. "I just came in here—by myself! Nobody should have been paying my bill?"

"I'm sorry, sir," she explained calmly with shifting eyes, "but your bill has been satisfied."

For a moment I studied the cashier. Then I said sourly, almost bitterly, as though I were incapable of saying the words, "By who? Who paid my bill, please?"

The cashier threw a glance over her shoulder, out the window. "Some woman. She came in about a half hour ago and said she wanted to use the restroom. When she came out she gave me a fifty and said this was for the darling gentleman sitting by the window dressed in the attire you have on, then she left."

My knees threatened to fail me. I could feel my strength to stand running out of me like water from a broken jug. *It was her!* I shuddered. *The woman was here!* I halted the upward spiral of my shock and looked at the cashier. I managed a smile. "Did this woman say anything else? Did she say anything in particular, like why she paid the bill?" I continued so that I wouldn't stop, so the cashier wouldn't realize how much I'd been affected. "Did she say anything at all? Or better yet, can you describe her, what she had on, her clothes, maybe the car she drove—anything?" In spite of the smile on my face I found myself snapping my fingers in impatient demand.

"No, not really," she started, almost mildly, "she just poked her head in and out. I do remember her being pretty, even with her hat and sunglasses." She shrugged her shoulders. "That's pretty much it. I'm sorry I can't be more helpful, sir."

"No…it's okay," I said as if she weren't even there. "Really, it is." I nodded my head and left the restaurant. I made my way to my car. My pace was unhurried and steady; to all the world I was simply a man strolling to his car, but inwardly, I was a man whose insides were contorted with rage. It was eating me up alive. My skin was crawling with it. Though I hadn't a clue as to how this woman looked, I could see her, *feel* her…she was in my head; I heard her premeditated goading reverberating in my ears, her sarcasm as thick as blood, *You can't escape me Terry…I'm too smart for you.*

I slid into my car and threw my head back. As I sat there the blood froze around my heart and a look of hatred filled my face. I looked up to see a post-it note stuck on my outside passenger window. Though the words were turned backwards I still managed to read them: *Can't wait to be with you.* "You crazy bitch," I whispered between clenched jaws, aiming my rage into her unseen face. A sensation of indescribable loathing rose in my throat, choking me. I was close to detonating!

At that very moment I knew, without a doubt, I could kill somebody.

As her high performance vehicle cut down the freeway she scarcely remembered or care about half of what Terry Allens had said. The other night had been just a minor misunderstanding, their first lovers' spat, and hopefully the complimentary breakfast would patch things up. No, this wasn't what had her mind boggled. What enchanted her was the man, Terry Allens himself. Everything about him. The rich whisper of his deep voice, the passionate glow she'd recalled in his brown eyes, the intensity of his movements when he walked, confident, filling out his jeans nicely. Everything about the man bespoke raw sexuality; his body oozed it from its pores.

As she gripped the steering wheel, she suddenly ached to feel his intense gaze fixed on her, with a passion of another sort. She wanted him rooted deeply within her. But it was a futile wish—at least for now she smiled. She wasn't dumb. She realized that, for the moment, Terry Allens was scarcely aware of her presence as a person, let alone as a real woman. However all that was about to change, but it would take a little time. She wanted things to be right. And besides, their love was worth it.

And tonight, after relaxing in a warm, bubble-scented bath, she would call him and make him realize she was *all* woman, more than he could ever hope for...and then some, the embodiment of a perfect rose. Every man's dream: a beautiful, sensuous, alluring woman, with a soft, delicate, curvaceous body, one that bordered on being sinful, with an opening as narrow as the eye of a needle. A woman with full, succulent lips. Smooth, unblemished, radiant skin. Long shapely legs—she had it all, and she would present her flawlessness to him, when the time was right. Then and only then. Terry Allens would have to be patient. She wasn't worried about him walking away, though. No. That wasn't even a concern. She knew he would hold out for her. But as she thought about him and that massive bulge she'd caught in his pants, the question was, could she hold out for *him?*

There was no kidding herself. She wanted him, badly.

And because of this desire there was a serious build up of dampness between her legs, and her mouth hung open as if she were waiting for his lips and tongue to come crashing down on hers. She suddenly clamped her lips together. Her legs were next. The convulsive move caused her to hiss sharply, "Terry!" as the car reached speeds well over ninety miles per hour. She twitched and rocked in her seat, trying to soothe the burning in her crotch, as her car hurtled with the velocity of a rocket. But she appeared oblivious to the high speed of travel, and wasn't watching what she was doing, where she was going. In her frenzied mind, there was no need to watch; her hands and feet knew their skills. Her mind was preoccupied with something else, something much more demanding and pleasurable: the vision of Terry Allens…grinning wonderfully at her.

The image cast a trance.

For a brief moment like the touch of a dream, she saw everything. His smile was so prominent and reassuring. He wanted her also. She nodded back, in full compliance. Then, all around her, things changed, the whole day shifted, time stood still. He was calling to her, sweet and low, again and again, sweeter, lower. "Oh, yes, sweet baby," she squealed back, "I hear you calling me!" She was about to enter into another resounding wail when she noticed her car veering sharply to the left, about to graze the cement medium. With wild flying hands she gripped the wheel and pulled roughly to the right and the car responded instantly, straightening out like the point of an arrow. People from all sides screamed and cursed her, a few flipping her the bird.

She'd caught the dirty looks, the rude finger gestures, the blaring, angry horns of the motorists. She did nothing, however. There was no harsh reaction on her part at all. There was nothing but her smile, and she did this lovingly. There wasn't anything that could dampen her spirits. Everything was going her way. Even the sky overhead showed its approval, with a perfect and breathtaking blue nirvana. The sky, her feelings—everything—it was all so wild, so good, so fucking gratifying—just like her man, Terry Allens! She could have cried out, even louder than before; but the raspness of her breath and the dampness between her legs made her realize it was time to get home, where she could do something about her condition—release some of her pinned-up pressure, by whatever means necessary.

Until the time came when her man could step in and take over...and do her body *right!* She smiled; it was an expression of longing and anticipation. The moment was going to happen. And judging by the luminous gleam in her eye and the saucy tilt to her head, she knew she wouldn't have long to wait.

Chapter 15

My brows knotted in perplexity as I clutched the phone. "So why didn't you come join me for breakfast? You just paid my bill and vanished. Heck, you could have at least said hello or something."

"It just wasn't the right moment," she murmured with a silent ache. "Besides, I looked a mess. I want you to see me when I'm at my best."

My face twisted as my thoughts raced. I didn't want to blow anything here. "No wine before it's time, huh?"

"Exactly."

"Okay, I can respect that. So, what's on tonight's agenda? What do you want to talk about?"

"You."

I pushed my supper away untasted. I picked up a glass of wine and took a sip then set the glass on the night stand. "Me again? I must be your favorite subject."

"You are," she hummed.

I picked at a roll from my plate which sat on the bed. I rolled bits of the dough into pellets and tossed them at the small waste basket ten feet from where my bed stood. The mood in the room was as dark as the night outside my window. But I had to keep myself upbeat. "So what do you want to know?"

At that, her voice became alive with an awakening light. I pictured her face suddenly becoming more vivid or brilliant as she whispered provocatively, "How *do* you like your eggs in the morning, baby?"

I chuckled. "Scrambled lightly, with a sprinkle of American cheese. Why, can you cook?"

She paused. After apparently scrutinizing my question, she said, "Not really, cooking has never been my forte." Her voice became strained. "But that doesn't mean I won't try—I can learn. I mean, don't let that be a driving factor between us, or anything."

I was quick to respond. "It won't. Besides, I can do the cooking. I'm not too bad around the kitchen."

"You can cook, too!" she said surprisingly. "*Damn,* baby, what can't you do?"

Once more, I chuckled. Behind my anger for this woman, and my concentration to figure her out, and my determined belief that she was a psychotic basket case, I was beginning to feel something for her. Call it pity, compassion. But I guess I could be misleading myself; the woman was *all* dangerous.

"Well, when you live alone you gotta make do," I smiled. "So, what's your favorite dish?"

She giggled. "Turkey and dressing with collard greens and mac-and-cheese and buttery rolls with thin slices of honeybaked ham with candied yams…"

"Whoa!" I cut in. "I said a dish—you're giving me a banquet. I take it you're a pretty good eater, huh?"

"Yeah, I have to admit, I can put it away. But I wear it very well. I'm very conscious of my body. I believe you should treat your body with the utmost respect, and I do. I work out four times a week."

"You belong to a gym?"

"No. Too many distractions. Guys hitting on me all the time, trying to get next to me. When I work out I like complete concentration. I try to be very focused, intent on what I need to do to accomplish my goals. I'll let nothing keep me from achieving what I'm after. I'm a relentless, hard-driven person. You know what I'm saying here, Terry?"

"Yes I do." Although I gnawed at an outrage that was starting to taste like acid, I refused to say anything negative. "That's a great quality to have. So many people have a tendency to give up on their goals."

"Well, not me. I go after things with a vengeance."

"Like me?" I couldn't help myself; I began grinding my teeth.

"Yes," she replied, and gave me in what sounded like treasonous information, "I knew I had to pull you away from that sordid life. That's not the way a person of your stature should live. No way. You don't need to degrade yourself by fucking strays like some whore. You're above that shit. Just the thought of you laying up with these strange, uncaring people made my skin crawl. From the moment I laid eyes on you I knew I had to take you away from that life. I knew I couldn't let you go on sinking further into that cancerous hole."

Seemingly more than satisfied with her words, she then added inside of a sigh, "Don't you feel so much better now that I have liberated you from this bondage, Terry?"

Unfortunately I couldn't reply. I couldn't do anything but bring forth a strained expression, and I guess my delayed reaction flooded her with more testimony.

"It's okay, Terry," she whispered lightly, "I know what you're going through, baby. But you don't have to worry about a thing. You don't have to worry your beautiful little head about anything else, not anymore. I've given you a new life, a second chance, where you won't be judged on your past life. I have set you free, my sweet prince."

I sighed, and tried sincerely to make myself thankful. "You did this for me, baby? You freed me? Were you really the one who removed the shackles of burden from my life? Was it really you, Darling?"

"Yes, baby," she wept, "it was I, and I'll do anything for you, anything, just tell me what you want me to do."

I thought on her request, made a few quick arbitrary decisions, then said, "These shackles...how...how did you remove them?"

At first she appeared to be struggling with herself. Then she said, "In the beginning, after we had met, I started following you, learning your schedule. Then I began my crusade to snatch you from your whorish world."

My throat closed, and I swallowed hard to open it. "You went to my church, releasing me from Sister Charles and all the others, didn't you?"

"Yes," she confessed. "I did what was needed, I needed to separate you from everybody, good or bad. I needed to give you a clean slate."

I winced, feeling myself losing it. "You mean destroy my name, don't you?"

"Call it what you will, if it will soothe your troubled mind, baby. Cause in my heart, I did nothing wrong."

My cool was dying rapidly. "You also followed me and Vera Armstrong, didn't you?"

There was silence. "Yes, I was there...each and every time you were with her." Her voice dropped dramatically. "It was hard, and it hurt me to the core, like a son-of-a-bitch. You have no idea of what I had to go through. Your tiny little mind couldn't begin to conceive the excruciating torment I had to endure. But I'm going to tell you. I think you need to hear this, Terry. Would you like to hear it? Would you like to know what I had to go through, what I had to endure? Huh, Terry? I mean, do you *really* want to know? Well, I'm going to tell you whether you want to hear it or not. Now you listen to me...I had to sit there and watch while you two *fucked* like dogs in heat in some fuckin' automobile. Yes, Terry," her voice thick with poison, "I saw it all. I saw you fuckin' this bitch in the front seat of her car. How could you do something like that, you sick bastard!"

I went silent, at a loss for words.

"How could you!" she repeated, insisted.

In response, my face became brighter and brighter until it was burning. I drew a deep breath and calmed myself, however. "The moment just happened," I let out in a sigh.

"But why?" she breathed in wonder. "How could you do something like that? How? *How?*"

"I just did, all right? Why are you making such a big fuss over this particular time? You know what I do for a living? Nothing like this should even shock you."

For some reason she didn't find this answer sufficient. After a moment, she said bitterly, "You love this bitch, don't you, Terry? You want her over me, *don't you?*"

I raised up from the bed and was quick to answer. "No. Why would you say something like that?"

"I saw the way you two were hugging outside the restaurant," she whispered, aching. "The way you looked at her. I know the look, you bastard, I wasn't born yesterday."

I raised my free hand to my face. "She's...she's just a client—nothing else, you hear me?"

"Really now?" She tried to sound casual, but didn't succeed. "Just a client, you say, huh?"

I stiffened. "That's right. Just a client. Besides, you've made sure that I wouldn't see her again, did you not?" I paced the room.

This appeared to please her; some of the bite had dropped from her tone. "Yeah, I did, didn't I? You should have seen the look on Mel Armstrong's face when I presented those pictures to him. But you know what? That son-of-a-bitch didn't even appear to be upset. Instead the dirty so-and-so tried to hit on me. Can you believe that shit?"

I closed my eyes. I turned and retreated to my bed, relieved that her mind had gone in another direction. When I sat down, my features relaxed, as if I had avoided a deadly altercation. "Yes, I can believe that," I agreed. "Mel Armstrong is a womanizer, a rich and powerful man who has to have everything tipped in his favor."

"Exactly. But he's no different from anybody else. We all want things tipped in our favor, and to tell it, there's nothing wrong with that."

"I guess you're right." After a moment I chuckled, "So the famous Mel Armstrong came on to you, huh? He must have really liked what he saw?"

"I'm sure he did," she laughed. "The look in his eyes said it all. He—" At once she fell silent. For nearly half a minute she said nothing. My shoulders hunched as if I were huddling over a pain in my chest. Something was wrong. I didn't move. Slowly, I rose to my feet and braced a hand on the wall.

"Hey," I said, concern in my voice, "you okay? You're still there, aren't you?"

She spoke quietly—so quietly that she sounded unreachable. "Yes, I'm here. Listen, baby, I've got to go. We can pick this up some other time, all right?"

With that, I heard the line being slowly disconnected. I stared blankly. Something was wrong. Something serious. The knot around my heart pulled tighter. Unable to keep my distress at bay, I hung up the phone and decided to get some air. I grabbed my keys and headed out the door. *Something was wrong*, I kept hearing myself saying, over and over, as I started up my rental car. I checked my Rolex. It was a long shot but I decided I would try to call Vera at her home. Hopefully she would be there, alone. If she was maybe I could even see her. This, too, was a risk.

But somehow, deep in my mind, I knew I wouldn't be followed. No, not tonight.

And that had me worried and slightly stunned. To the point I was nearly trembling.

The faraway quality in the mysterious woman's voice, her hesitation, the abruptness in her departure. Something was wrong.

Terribly wrong.

Tony's was a hangout for jocks and hardhats. Just a block away from Will's plant on East Eight Mile, it was a place where you could put down bets on any sporting event you could think of, including high-ticketed football squares. You could also get a blowjob if you wanted one; there was always one or two good-looking women who were more than willing to accommodate, for a price, mind you.

Tony himself tended bar and was always in the place. It made sense; he owned the building and lived upstairs. I had heard that Tony was gay, and that on certain days when the bar closed for the night, a few of his Village People-lookin' buddies would drop by and have a good old time prancing and dancing with each other, but I didn't know whether or not this was true. It probably was. But it made me no never mind, as long as Tony stayed on his side of the tracks, we were cool.

Tony was tending bar tonight, smiling and talking shit with one of the customers. I grinned. The dude was a throwback to the Super Fly era, long processed hair, wide flaring sideburns nearly connecting to his mustache, the walk, the mannerism, and all the seventies jargon to go along with it: out of sight, I can dig it, I'm hip, I *ain't* hip, right on, soul brother! Power to the people! Down with Whitey! Tony held on to it all, fiercely. And the brother still wore Swedish knits!

When Will and I climbed onto the stools, Tony put both hands flat on the bar. "My brothers," he said. "What's it gonna be?"

"I'll have a Bud," I said. "Make it a light."

"I'll have the same," Will nodded.

Tony glanced at me and Will with an upraised brow. "You two goin' run up a tab tonight?"

"No, I've got a lot to do, plus I'm driving," I said.

"And I've got to go back to work in about fifteen minutes," Will shrugged, seemingly disappointed.

Tony nodded, gave both of us a leering look, then walked away. Will nudged me with his shoulder. "I think Tony has the hots for you, cuz."

"Shit, the dude was looking at you," I smiled. "He likes the strong loud type."

Will raised up his palms. "Well, the dude can just keep on steppin', ain't nothin' happenin' here." A pile of plastic-wrapped toothpicks was at his left hand. He grabbed one, tore the plastic, rested the splinter on a ridge of bare gum, and glanced around.

I chuckled and shook my head. Then I also glanced around. There were peanut shells and sawdust everywhere, and the air was musty with the odors of stale beer and cigarette smoke. Pictures of old-time sport legends hung on the walls, among them a number of Tony's childhood heroes, guys like Muhammad Ali and Hank Aaron and Dave Bing, and going back, Sugar Ray Robinson and the brown bomber, Joe Louis. The place was nearly deserted; only a few other customers in the bar, arguing on how Barry Sanders had fucked up by quitting so early in his career and not giving the Lions a shot at shit.

Except for the regular women, the blowers, I never saw any other women in here, although one time a few months back a group of dykes had decided to make Tony's their hangout, and for obvious reasons Tony didn't like that. He discouraged their presence time after time with watered-down drinks and bad service, and they had protested against his place for discrimination and demanded equal rights. Tony told them he didn't give a shit, they could come in any fucking time they wanted. Bull dog snatch-lickers were always welcome, he said. They soon got the message and left him alone.

As I looked around, in my own world, my eyes nevertheless whizzing by two skinny, ragged specimens slouched in a corner with long-necks in hand, I thought of Vera. I couldn't get a hold of her. *Where was she?* I wondered. I hoped that Mel Armstrong hadn't put his hands on her again. I really hoped not. After leaving the bar tonight, I decided, I'd page her once more, then call it a night.

I turned my head to see Tony putting two beers in front me and Will, and walk away. I raised my glass. "To better days."

"Much better," Will said. He tossed his head back and downed his beer then wiped the foam from his lips. Afterwards, he released a gusty sigh of pleasure and placed his empty glass on the bar.

I took a couple of swallows from mine, still thinking of Vera. I could have kicked myself for ever letting her leave my apartment, seemingly my life.

Will nodded to Tony for a refill. As Tony went about refilling the glass, Will looked over at me. "This shit is really getting to you, huh, cuz?"

My gaze was straight ahead, fixed on the image of two men in the back bar mirror. "Yeah, a little, especially Vera."

Will tapped my shoulder. "The Armstrong lady?"

I nodded.

Will shifted on the stool. "You love this girl, don't you, man?"

I looked at him squarely. "Yeah, cousin, I do. I really do. I can't seem to get her out of my head. She's always there, you know."

With that, Will said with a touch of his deep sarcasm, "Aw Naw! Say it ain't so! This cannot be happenin'! My cousin, Mister Ass Waxer himself, has been ensnared! Damn, man, she must have a cape dangling from her coochie for you to be like this."

I nodded. His estimate was accurate.

Removing the toothpick from his mouth, Will howled, "This is too much! You got a picture of her. Man, I got to see *her*! She must be slammin'!"

"Only the surveillance photos," I shrugged, "that's about it."

"Sorry, cuz," Will replied, as though he had wounded me unjustly, "I didn't mean to say it like that."

"Well, don't let it happen again" —I glanced at Will as I continued, and he saw both humor and sorrow in my face— "or I'll go postal on your ass." A smile quirked my lips as I sipped my beer.

Will lowered his head to the floor and blew out the toothpick. Afterward he grinned then hunched over with his elbows on the bar. "So, you think this psycho woman has somethin' up her sleeve, huh?"

Almost without thinking, I said, "I really do. I just don't know what. When she hung up on me tonight she definitely seemed out of it, like something in her had clicked." My eyes narrowed. "The woman is plotting."

"You don't think she's plottin' against your girl, do you?"

Hearing those words I flung my head back as if I'd been slapped across the face, and my eyes flared. I didn't want to answer. The mentioning of something so terrifying was unthinkable. I knew I had to deal with it, however, and I'd muster the courage to do just that. Slowly, my voice under rigid control, I said, "She'd better not be. I couldn't take it. It's bad enough I have to worry about Vera's old man going up side her head, but to have to worry about some crazy woman going after her, too. It's just too much for the mind to deal with."

"I hear you, man," Will agreed. "So what's your next move?"

I stared straight ahead. "I don't know. I really couldn't tell you."

"Thought about goin' to the cops?"

My temples were beginning to ache. "No, not just yet. Besides, what's to report? Outside of a few guns shots and a threatening letter, which anyone could have typed, what do I have? Nothing. I don't have jack-shit."

At that Will went silent. Tony appeared and placed Will's beer in front of him, gave him a direct, obliging glance, then walked away.

"Tony definitely has a thing for you, cousin," I chuckled, grateful for a little humor.

Will, a little pissed, seized the mug by the handle and downed the beer in several gulps. He set it down with a thump. "That's my cue to leave...for good." He chuckled, then said, "Seriously, cuz, I got to get in the wind, my lunch break is almost over with. Listen, why don't you stop by Thursday around three-thirty. I'm takin' the day off to take Angela to see that new Denzel flick. We can kick it for a minute before I snatch her up."

"That sounds like a winner," I nodded.

"Cool." Pocketing more toothpicks, he turned and headed for the door, then stopped. He turned around. "Make sure you bring the photos, okay, cuz? I want to see what this Vera looks like." He grinned devilishly and ambled out the door.

I smiled, and shook my head. The brother had stiffed me again on the tab. Sometime I think he's a bit smoother than me. Exhaling sharply, I finished up my beer and laid a twenty on the bar. I looked around, disgusted. Sitting across the room, I spotted one of the regular blowers in a cheesy-looking outfit. She had her hand on some dude's knee and was looking into his eyes as she talked, obviously setting him up for some kind of sexual gratification. Then, to the left of them, there was a dark-haired man sitting at a table drinking a beer and pushing something around the table with his finger.

Once more I shook my head. It was time to leave this dump. For me to sit here and guzzle beers without Will, would somehow make me feel like a loser. And that was the last thing I wanted to feel like.

I rose from the stool and headed for the door. That's when a big, burly redneck sauntered into the place. The customers' attention, especially Tony's, centered on him briefly. The guy wore a flat-brimmed cowboy hat with the front snapped down. A large square of white silk was knotted behind his neck and hung down the front of his shirt. Strapped over a pair of crisp new Levi's was a large belt buckle embroidered with a Harley-Davidson emblem. He had a beige leather jacket with fringed tassels on the sleeves, and with each stride his boots jingled musically. He smiled at Tony and Tony blushed.

I knew what time it was.

All of a sudden, like cattle on a drive, the clump of booted feet accompanied the opening of the front door, heralding the arrival of more cowboys, in all sizes, shapes and colors. Again the customers' attention swung to inspect the rush. I stole a subtle glance in Tony's direction. He was beaming like a blushing bride. *It was going to be one of those nights!* I could hear him squealing. He turned immediately with a whiskey bottle tucked in the crook of his arm with fingers clutching a trio of glasses. He plunked the glasses on the bar, uncapped the whiskey bottle, and poured a measure into each glass, then started passing them out.

I was definitely out of there. I walked straight to the door, acknowledging *no one* while making my move. I grabbed the handle to leave when suddenly I felt my pager vibrating on my hip. I looked down to check the message. It read: "155"

At once my heart leaped!

It was Vera! She was at home!

Taken completely by surprise, I raced out the door and ran to my rental car. I slid inside and with frantic hands, I dialed Vera on my cell-phone. She picked up almost instantly. "Hello."

"Vera," I said, nervous as hell. "It's me, Terry."

There was a pause, then she announced sweetly, "Hi, Terry, I didn't catch you at a bad time, did I?"

For a second my mind went blank. My mouth had wadded up and I couldn't utter a single word. Her voice sounded so damn *good*—so good that I could actually see her face before me as I held the phone tightly with both hands—as if I were actually holding her. Then, in a tone soft with surprise, as though I had just received a revelation, I said, "Vera, baby, I've missed you so much. How have you been? You been okay? He hasn't...hurt you again, has he?"

"No, I'm fine, Terry," she breathed joyously. "How have you been? You been okay?"

Still seeing her image in front of me, I smiled, "I'm good. Just missing the hell out of you, that's all. When can I see you? I need to hold you." I felt my face brighten with hope.

In a voice scarcely louder than a whisper, she said, "We can't."

"Why?" I pushed.

There was hesitation. "Terry, you have to understand, I'm trying to make my marriage work."

Slowly, my brightened face dimmed. "That's bullshit, Vera, and you know it. I don't know why you do this to yourself. You don't owe that bastard a damn thing."

"Yes, I do," she retorted quickly. "He's my husband, and no matter what you think of him, I belong by his side."

To myself, I chewed out a long, scathing curse. She was right. But I definitely wasn't going to admit it. "So where is your husband now?" My voice sounded a bit accusatory.

She cleared her throat. "He had to step out, something to do with his business he said."

"I'll bet." I switched the phone to my other ear. "Vera, listen to me, I know you feel some sort of obligation to this man but..."

"There are no buts, Terry," she interjected smoothly, without raising her voice a decimal, "I do have an obligation, whether you want to believe it or not."

Again, I knew her to be right, but once again on my part I wasn't about to admit it. Instead, I hunched forward in my seat, and said, "I've given it up, Vera...everything. I'm no longer in the life, for a better choice of words. I've got my head together and found out what I really want."

"And what is that, Terry?"

I detected a glint of impatience in her voice, as though what I was about to say was something to be said on a whim, as if I really hadn't a clue as to what I wanted to do. And this made my heart clench up. Still, I had to speak my mind, for my sake, if nothing else. "I want you, Vera. You and nobody else."

"This all sounds so touching, Terry, it really does," she commented indignantly. "But there's a little problem here, don't you think?"

"You can leave him," I shot back quickly, "we could go away, start a new life. I'll take care of you, Vera."

"Listen to how you sound, Terry," she said dryly. "You sound like a wishful little boy without a clue to what's being said. Your mind is so filled with illusions of grandeur that you can't see the impossibility of what you're saying." She stopped, then said painfully, "I'm married, and as long as I am, we can never be. I hope you can respect my decision on this, but if you cannot, I'm sorry. This is the way it has to be."

I thought on Vera's words. She had made up her mind, because she wanted to do what was right. She didn't wish to be in her situation but she was. Her marriage made no sense—but her sense of obligation did. I had witnessed this predicament so many times in my life, where a woman stayed with her man regardless of how he treated her, no matter how much shit he'd dump on her, yet, she would stay, pain and all, only because she would feel the need to stay, some sort of warped dedication to her man. It wouldn't have matter to her if the son-of-a-bitch had had horns and a tail, or if he walked on cloven hooves and reeked of brimstone and sulfur!

There was that powerful *something* about a woman's dedication which drew her like a magnet to her man.

I didn't want to see Vera like this, she deserved so much better. And as long as I *was* a part of her life, I would make every effort to free her. For her sake, as well as for mine. But at the moment I had to accept her wishes and not push her. Yet I was too raged—and too hurt—by her devotion to this bastard; I wasn't able to see past her dedication. I guess, I was blind to the one fact she saw clearly: Mel Armstrong was the man in her life...the only man.

But I didn't want to think about this—or about anything, for that matter. Instead, at least for now, I would go with the moment, take advantage of the precious time I had with Vera, even if it was only a telephone conversation.

So for the next hour or so, we talked and laughed and cried, until she said she had to go. It was one of the most painful times in my life, saying goodbye to Vera.

Sitting sleek in a new white cashmere bathrobe in my apartment, nursing my fourth vodka of the evening in front of a crackling fire which blazed in the white marble hearth, oblivious to the world around me, I was in a daze, thinking about Vera, and about my life. On the stereo, Sade's *War of the Hearts* played softly in the background. I had the selection on 'repeat', so this was the ninth time I'd heard it tonight. At the moment I didn't want to hear anything else. I was cool with it, vodka and Sade, it was the perfect prescription for the mood I was in.

I stared at the roaring blaze. There were many phantom faces flickering in front of me, people in whom I had once coupled with, where I had created the illusion of insatiable passion and doled out torments of pleasure—nurses, judges, lawyers, real estate tycoons, corporate heads—prominent people from all walks of life—people who were once the mainstay of my worth, now just ghosts of my former past.

In the minutes that passed I amused myself with accounts of my first entourage of clients. There weren't many to speak of, maybe three or four, at the most—five. However, with charms that liquefied, gentleness that thrilled, and with skills that shattered the imagination—the momentum soon shifted to the stars! I had dozens of them! I never thought—in my *wildest* dreams—I could amass such a following; I didn't think it at all possible. But I had, and it was great! I was soon smoldered in bright lights and neon glitter—I had it all! With no shadows of guilt and remorse lurking in the corners to cast a pall over me. Shit, I was making mad money! Screwing like there was no tomorrow and taking my ends straight to the bank! What could be better!

I sighed heavily. Yes, there was money and there was pleasure, and a few good kicks thrown in there as well. But there was also anguish and torment, none of the ache I had expected. I mean, I just didn't know I'd end up feeling like this.

I took another sip of vodka, welcoming the lava-burn in my throat. I shook my head.

The horrors of my wasted life, of shriveled emotions, swept over me like a storm. I felt washed up, used. Here I was twenty-six years old and feeling this way, like I was already out looking for some plot of land to call my final resting place. I knew I shouldn't be thinking like this but I couldn't help myself, and to tell you the truth, with Sade in your ear and drinking vodka, it was really all I could do. I felt empty, with no purpose, yet, even if I wanted to do something productive in life, I hadn't a clue on what to do. For that matter, what *could* I do? I wasn't skilled at anything. There weren't any college degrees hanging on my walls. My hands were buttery soft. So what was I going to do? Become a fashion model, maybe? I'd probably have to fuck my way to the top before I could make some decent money, and if I did that I'd might as well go back into the life.

I laughed bitterly to myself and poured another drink.

I stared at the flames. Two days had passed since I'd last talked to Vera. I still recall the sweetness of her voice as she explained why we could never be. Though her words were spoken firm and quietly, I couldn't help but detect a profound undercurrent of yearning in her tone. But what could I have said to change her mind? The girl had made herself clear: as long as she was married we could never be—case closed. My heart sank as I sipped on my drink then abruptly, my features knotted. *What the hell am I doing?* I asked myself. *Am I rolling over and playing dead? Look at me, it's only seven o'clock in the evening and here I am getting hammered! Like some fucking loser at Tony's! And I'm drinking vodka for goodness sakes! I hate this shit!*

With that, I threw my hands up in a hard gesture of appeal. No way, no how, was I going out like this. If Vera and I couldn't be—so be it! Hell, I tried! It was time to move on, find greener pastures. I could start anew, and if the road before me was steep and barren and hard and vicious—so what! I would exert all my powers to overcome these obstacles and then plunge forward, and if that meant slinging my big dick in the process—so be it, goddammit! Feeling an upswelling of triumph and promise, I thrust my arms into the air. I closed my eyes, my mind embracing a strong feeling of peace and calm.

That's when it happened.

It came in short, two second intervals, a dark foreboding of coming disaster, shattering my joyous mood instantly, rudely, almost maliciously.

The sensation that I was about to get the shock of my life made everything distinct and slow as I turned my head around. I stared at it. I could hear it clearly—too clearly; in fact, it was a sound that I had come to hate.

Not ten feet from where I was sitting, it sat there, on a cherrywood and marble pedestal, beckoning me from the sofa.

It was the sound of my telephone ringing.

Chapter 16

I stood up and discovered I was much drunker than I had realized. Walking was not going to be easy. I summoned all of my abilities and negotiated my way toward the ringing phone. I snatched it up then flopped in the chair. "Yeah, who is it?"

"Good evening, Terry," the voice announced softly. "And how are you tonight, baby?"

In response, I settled back in the chair. I found myself smiling. Apparently the presence of alcohol in my system made things easier, making me impervious to the sound of her voice; but there was still a subtle rage simmering inside me. "I'm doing quite nicely," I said in an conversational tone, "how in the hell have you been? I haven't heard from you in two days. What's up, you don't find me attractive anymore?"

Her reply came back quick and true—fiercely. "Oh God, *yes*, I still find you attractive! Baby, you're a woman's *best* dream!"

"Then where you been, girl?" The concern made my voice rough. "I thought me and you were suppose to be an item?"

Without hesitation, she replied, "We are, I mean, we will be. I...I just had to take care of a minor problem, that's all, and now I'm back, okay?"

I moistened my lips. "What kind of problem?"

"Just a little somethin'-somethin' I had to do." She let out a giggle, which sounded ominously hysterical. And she had trouble making it stop.

In spite of the alcohol, my eyes went bright and extreme. "What in heaven's name have you done, Darling?" I asked, raising up in my seat.

In an effort to distract me, she asked, "Have you missed me, baby?"

Her question made me chuckle. With a frustrating effort I put aside my anxiety and then settled back. "I look forward every night to hearing your lovely voice, it's so soothing."

"Thank you, baby," she quipped. "Your voice is soothing, too. Nice and deep—*all* man."

My reply was clearly intended as sarcasm, but this loony woman accepted it as some sort of compliment. "So, what do we talk about tonight?" I sighed tiredly. "Do we talk about how your day was, or how my day was, or how you been following me? What? Tell me, what's on tonight's agenda? So we can get this thing started and get it over with."

Almost immediately her tone tightened. "Talk to me like I'm your woman, goddammit! Not like some fuckin' client, you hear me! You treat me like a queen!"

I smiled and raised my eyebrows in mock surprise. "Ooo, I must have struck a nerve, didn't I?"

With that she gave a chilling, menacing chuckle. "Oh, I get it, you done got your drink on, right? Or are you full of weed? Which one is it? Which one of these has got you swellin' up so big and bad, baby? Throwin' your chest out, and shit? Well, let me tell you something, baby-doll, I don't need artificial stimulants to make myself intimidating." She chuckled harder and then said very softly, almost intimately, "You have no idea who you're fucking with, do you?"

Unfazed I smiled, then in an urging whispered, I said, "No, actually, I don't. Why don't you tell me?"

"A smart and cunning woman who holds all the cards on your ass, that's who," she affirmed vehemently. "I thought we had an understanding on this?"

In reaction, alarm flushed through my body. Her words definitely unnerved me but I didn't dwell on it. Instead, I tried another angle. "I understand all of this, Darling, believe me, I do. But I'm so in the dark about you. Can't you see my side of things? You won't let me see you, you're so secretive, and you can be so evasive at times. Now how am I suppose to get a clear understanding on you for some kind of relationship?"

That, at least, was a question she couldn't vehemently reply on. I took this opportunity and dug deeper. "Why don't you tell me about yourself? Your hobbies? Where you work? Things you do in your spare time?"

Slowly, after drawing a deep breath, she said, "I love tending my rose bushes in the spring and summer..."

I smiled, but it was a different kind of smile, like the affectionate and faintly condescending one you would give to a kid brother or sister. "Roses, you say? Any particular kind?"

"Red and pink roses, the kind that bursts with brilliant, vibrant colors!" she proclaimed loudly. "I like to be surrounded by hundreds and hundreds of them—their petals flinging outward at me!"

My expression twisted, and I took a quick breath to steady myself. I peered at the phone strangely, uncertain how to take this woman. At times she could be so innocent and child-like, like a tiny girl that was about to explode with a burst of exuberance, with a desire to shout or sing. She was all these things. Yet, there was something dark and menacing which kept her at bay, keeping her from shouting and singing. I hadn't a clue to the reason or reasons, I just knew she needed psychiatric help. So rather than attempting to pick through her mind, I, instead, tried to encourage her outpour of affection. "Do you have a rose garden where you live?" I asked softly.

There was silence. When she didn't respond, I asked once more, "Darling, since you like roses, do you have any in your garden?"

With unexpected sorrow, she said stoically, "Yes, but they're all dead. They've all turned brown and withered and soon the extinguished petals will fall to the ground and start decomposing. It's very sad, isn't it, Terry? How things that were once so pretty can turn so ugly and waste away?"

"Yes, I guess it is," I said, thinking about her words, trying to hear what she was *actually* saying. It was important—I knew it was important. I cursed myself for having so much alcohol in my system; it was my chance to really find out what this woman was about, and here I was with fog on the brain. I fought through my haze, however and said, "The roses will be back in the spring, like they have been for centuries. There's no need for sorrow when you understand this."

Her voice came back in a croak as she said miserably, "You're so right, Terry. I guess I'm crying over something that I have no control over, huh? It's like fretting over the sun burning out in the next million years...there's nothing you can do about it, and you won't be around when it happens, so why worry?"

Her sudden perception on things moved me, and I nodded. "I think on this one you might be right."

She hummed agreement, then she said something that took me totally by surprise. "Can I describe what kind of man I believe you are, Terry? I promise I won't say anything offensive toward you?"

"Er, yeah...go right ahead." I stared blankly, still uncertain how to take her.

At that, she took a deep breath and said she'd do the best she could from what little she had known of me. "First of all, as you may already know, you are an extremely handsome man, in every aspect. I'm talking your build, height, weight, intelligence, things of that matter, you understand. You're very kind and docile, have a great sense of humor, and you can pretty much get along with anybody, but there's another side of you. You detest people who are mean or disrespectful, or those individuals who are loud and boisterous, braggers, if you will. You despise lazy, unmotivated people. You find all of these people deplorable. But nevertheless, in spite of your distaste, you still act cordial and considerate toward them." She paused for a second then went on, "You love your mother dearly, and you're very protective of her. Though she's a lot older than you and has lived a very good life, you would still die for her. Am I right so far?"

"Yes," I said mildly. "Please, go on." I chewed the insides of my cheeks.

She drew a sharp breath and continued, "At times, even with your extraordinary looks, you can be immensely vain. You need people to look at you, to gawk over you. When you walk into a crowded room you expect every eye in the place to be on you, and most of the time they are, but if they weren't you'd feel a sense of rejection, of hurt. You *need* their approval, their praises. You feed off that. When you climb into bed with these other people you feel nothing for them. You only feel proud and triumphant, that somebody needs you for something, if only for that moment, if only for that purpose. Sometimes, at night, you toss and turn, and you feel dirty. You hate your life, cause you know deep down that you're better than this, that you deserve better than this. You know with your gifted looks and talents that you should be doing something on a much higher scale...only you haven't a clue on what." Her voice fell to a whisper.

"Did I describe you correctly, Terry? Did I hit the nail on the head on a few things?"

When she'd finished my face was as rigid as stone. My throat closed and I doubled over almost in pain. The woman's words were so direct, so exact; it made me draw a different sketch of her—of how her mind worked. I swore under my breath, torn between wanting to praise and choke this woman. I shook my head then rested my forehead in my palm. "What do you want from me, lady?" I strained out. "Please, tell me. What do you want?"

She paused, letting me weep silently, then she said in the same soft, heart-wrenching tone she'd had earlier, "For now, all I want from you is for you to get a goodnight's sleep. I'll talk to you tomorrow, Terry. You have a good night."

There was a click and soon after I heard a dial tone. I held my vacant gaze until I faltered and looked down. Then I raised my head, trying my best to handle this thing like a man struggling not to let what he heard stun him. It was hard. I began to sweat. The room seemed uncomfortably warm. I looked over at the flames flickering mildly, gradually losing its brilliance and strength, as if dying. The flames made me think of my life. I swallowed hard, then, almost inaudibly, I brought the receiver to my mouth and whispered, "You have a goodnight, too, Darling."

Afterwards, slowly, as if drained of all strength, I hung up the phone.

Chapter 17

A clock gonged off-key from somewhere in the living room, then silence, the passing empty seconds measured by water clinking in the sink. As my grogginess slowly dispersed, the first thing I noticed were my legs arched crookedly on the sofa. The second thing that entered my consciousness after drifting off and waking back up, was the ringing of the telephone, relentless and annoying. I glanced out the window and saw that the sun had just begun to seep through the curtains. I grunted and rose to my feet, surprised that my head was clear after what I'd done to the bottle of vodka. Nevertheless my mouth tasted like shit as I walked over to the phone and answered it.

"Good morning, Terry," came a voice from the other end, a slight crackle of static on the line because it was a cellular call.

"Who is this?" I asked, smacking the nasty taste in my mouth.

"It's your soon-to-be woman, baby."

"Who?" I asked again, blinking my eyes and scratching myself uncharacteristically.

"It's your Darling, you crass bastard! Who in the hell do you think it is!" she shot back. As swiftly as a flick of an eyelid she nestled her rage, and said sympathetically, "Aw, poor baby, you must be just waking up. I'm so sorry for the early call but I just couldn't contain myself. So tell me, love of my life, have you seen it yet?"

My eyes went wide, and my change of mood and manner was so abrupt that my face became flushed. "Have I seen what?" I murmured harshly.

"The little gift I left on your doorstep, silly."

At once, my expression was distant and troubled. "No, I haven't been out today. What is it?"

"Go see, sleepy head," she giggled. "You'll be *so* proud of me. In the meantime, I've got to run, but I'll call you this evening around seven o' clock, all right, baby?"

"Okay." I was helpless to say anything else. Whatever strength I had in me was already committed to standing.

"I'll talk to you tonight then, baby. Hey, maybe we can engage in a little phone sex to celebrate, how does that sound? I mean, you will do me the honor, won't you?"

I wet my lips. "I will."

With that, there came a wet, slobbering kiss over the phone followed by a light giggle, then I heard the disconnection. I hung up the phone and glanced at the front door. I wondered what the hell could this crazy-ass woman have left for me? Did I really want to know? No. But I knew I had to see what it was. I walked over to the door and peered through the peephole. There was nothing. I disengaged the locks and slowly opened the door. Again, there was nothing. I looked down and saw a newspaper rolled tightly with a red ribbon around it. A rush of distress came over me as I stood there. Swallowing the lump in my throat, I looked around then picked up the newspaper. I stepped back inside and closed the door, quickly engaging the locks.

I turned and took a seat on the sofa. For a moment I did nothing. I just held the rolled newspaper in my hands. Exhausted and dreading what I had to do, I decided to get it over with. Rather than untie the silky ribbon from the newspaper I slid it off. I flipped the newspaper right-side up.

The headline was bold enough to be read from a block away:

WEALTHY AUTOMOTIVE ENTREPENUER MEL ARMSTRONG FOUND MURDERED—POLICE CALL MURDER MALICIOUSLY BRUTAL

Chapter 18

Detroit's Riverfront Plaza was thronged with people, as was most afternoons when the weather was pleasant. At one o'clock the air was a little cool, but it was still Indian summer, mild for October and with only a hint of the cold blasts that would rake the city a few weeks from now. I sat on a bench with Will, just up the walkway from the Detroit River. We were looking at the surveillance photos.

I had told Will about Mel Armstrong, and who I thought brought about his untimely demise, and he could only whistle in astonishment. He bought most of what I'd said, but I could detect a little skepticism in his expression, about it being the same woman. However, in any event, he definitely felt it was time to involve the authorities. I'd agreed, but told him not just yet, that I needed to have something concrete before I went that route. For all I know, considering my involvement with Vera, the police might very well label me as the number one suspect. No. I'd wait, see what I could bring out of this situation.

But I knew one thing for sure: the woman I was dealing with *was not* to be taken lightly.

Will was glancing over the five surveillance photos then turned to me. "I got to tell you, cuz, that Vera Armstrong is definitely a fine-lookin' honey, I'll give you that."

After a pause I said, "Yeah, that she is, cousin…that she is. One fine-lookin' honey." So that I wouldn't reveal the hurt in my face, I looked away.

Awkwardly, Will gestured for me to look at him. "Listen, cuz," he said, cutting right to the chase, "for the time being you'd better forget Vera. What you ought to be doin' is trying to figure out what to do about this psycho woman, cause if it is her, you could end up just like this Mel Armstrong dude." Then he added, abandoning the pretense that I was on the right track about it being the same woman, "But I got to tell you, man, I just don't believe it was her. I mean, it just sounds a bit too farfetched, way out of her league. I know this woman fired a few shots into the air, but killin' somebody—we're

159

talkin' cold-blooded murder here, you know what I sayin'? We both know a woman can lose her mind over a nigga, but this? This is a stretch, cuz. Think about it."

I did, and said nothing. My heart was beating too fast for me to acknowledge anything. No matter what anybody said I *knew* it was the woman; she was a straight-up killer. And she was killing for the sake of love, or what she believed was love. It was at that moment when my mind began to stray. How could she just walk up and murder a big man like Mel Armstrong? The police said his throat had been sliced from ear to ear, the body still propped in the driver seat.

That's when it hit me! Something I'd remembered kicking around in my head from the other night!

I turned to Will with wild, dazed eyes. "Don't you see—this woman gave these photos to Mel Armstrong—he was the only person who could have identified her! And she *knew* this! That would explain why she suddenly ended our conversation the other night— *she realized her error!* She somehow got a hold of Mel Armstrong and set up a meeting—somewhere secluded. That's why the car was found in an empty, dimly-lit parking lot! Get it?" I followed Will's eyes with mine. I knew at the moment I looked like a lunatic. But I didn't care—I had to make him see!

Will hesitated then stared back at me. He had no way of knowing if what I had said was the literal truth or not, but he accepted it anyway. "So what you're saying here is that, this psycho woman lured homeboy away from peering eyes and took him out? Is that what you're saying? Are you sure, cuz?"

I nodded, and felt the makings of a sly smile pinching a corner of my mouth; but as it did so my gaze slipped into the distance, and I knew my face carried a faraway cast. "Vera had paged me the same night of the murder. She said Mel had gotten an important 'business call', and left the house abruptly. I'm telling you, that 'call' was from this woman. She probably told Mel she had some other information to share, and he went out into the night to meet her…"

"And got his throat slit," Will softly finished, nodding his head. "I'm feelin' you, cuz. I think you got something going here. But what can we do? We don't know who this woman is? She knows who we are but we don't know shit about her. She just lurks in the shadows, stirrin' up shit. Hell, for that matter, this whacked-out bitch could be watchin' us at this very moment."

At that, we both looked around. They were people, lots of them, of all ages and colors, young and old, black, white, Hispanic, Arab. Many were paired off, men and women with arms around each other, strolling more slowly than other pedestrians. Some of the couples were of one sex, both partners male or both female. Younger kids whizzed by on roller blades and those new metal-type scooters, talking shit as they went. There were pigeons waddling along, paying little attention to the humans around them as they pecked for food. Near the water fountain display, there was a young brother stepping coolly with a boom box hoisted over his shoulders, like they once did in the late seventies and early eighties. The radio was huge, gleaming with chrome and covered with knobs and dials, its speakers pouring out a barrage of rap licks. Jay-Z? Busta? Dr. Dre? Will and I wasn't sure.

I suddenly realized I was tired. I'd been up every since I had gotten that horrific call from the mysterious woman. But it was more than that; my sleeping habits had been shot to hell in the last two weeks or so. But what else could I expect? I asked myself. Sleep did not come easy when you were being stalked by a crazy, unbalanced psychopath. And by the look of things, I could add murderer to the list.

I looked around and felt it was time to leave. There were a few things I wanted to do before calling an end to my day. Plus I knew Will had to get ready for work. With that thought in mind I *knew* it was time to leave. The last thing I wanted was for him to be rushing to work, especially in the traffic he had to deal with.

I was about to rise from the bench when Will pulled me back down. I noticed a strange, perplexed look on his face. "Hey, cuz, check this out," he frowned. He handed me one of the surveillance photos. I glanced over the photo and then shrugged my shoulders. It was no big deal, just a faraway shot of Vera and I hugging outside the restaurant. I gave it back to him.

"I don't see anything, man," I said, seemingly without a care, anchoring my elbows over the bench. There were other things on my mind, more important things. Besides, the photos were too painful to look at. Will took the photo, glanced over it once more, then handed it back to me.

"Look at it again, cuz," he said. "This time *really* look at it."

I turned and aimed a stern glare at him. I then articulated each word with hard-edged consonants and blunt vowels, so that I could make myself perfectly clear, "Man, I have seen those damn photos over a hundred times. There ain't nothing in there you…"

"Look at it, dammit!" Will's voice cut like a whip. "Stop runnin' your mouth and look at the damn photo—*closely!*"

My face tightened as I stared at Will. The expression in his face caught and held me. Slowly, I pried my gaze from his face and stared at the photo.

"Really look at it, cuz," Will urged, in a voice I had never heard before.

I did. But in the moments that followed I saw nothing. Telling myself to be patient, I shifted my eyes up and down the photo, taking note of everything, studying each object with care. I looked up and rubbed my eyes, then turned my attention back to the images in the photo, this time giving special heedfulness.

That's when I saw it.

It was in the far background, five or six feet behind me and Vera as we hugged. It was a reflection of a car coming off the window of the restaurant. There was a woman in the car, the driver window was down; her elbow was resting on the ledge of the door. I couldn't make out her face, there was something obscuring it. I soon made out what it was. I swallowed hard, and thought my heart would heave from out of my chest. I had to hunch over. "Yes," I gasped between my teeth. "I see it."

Will moved closer and peered over my shoulder, checking out the photo from my point of view. Then he said in a voice hardly louder than a whisper, which nevertheless sounded to me like it could be heard from a mile away, "It's a camera." He slapped my shoulder and murmured direly, "That's your psycho woman, cuz. And the bitch is pushin' a convertible XK8 Jaguar. I know that type of car anywhere. Looks like a brand new one, too."

"You're right." I shivered, and for some reason, I noticed that my hands were clutching the photo so tightly that the edges were curling up. At first I thought it was because of elation, feeling I had finally found something to go on. Then I realized I was being overtaken by a simmering anger. It became so strong that it took a few seconds for me to straighten my fingers. When I finally did, I looked over at Will, knowing that something strange was happening in my face, feeling my face hardening; my usual calm was giving way to an explosive rage.

The expression with which I met Will wasn't belligerent, but it was tight and wary, and I still hadn't lost the urge to explode.

For his part, Will had nothing to say. The look in his face said it all. He, too, was pissed and feeling a sense of fury.

Finally, I rose to my feet, ready to move. My manner invited Will to do the same. I looked at him directly, eye to eye, and stated defiantly, "I've got some runs to make, cousin."

"Where to?" he asked, narrowing his eyes.

"Over to the Shear Ritz Hair Salon."

He shook his head. "I don't follow you."

I smiled, though it wasn't warm. "That's where psycho woman likes to get her hair done at. I'm heading home and slip into another change of clothes. Then I'm going to tip out the back way, flag me down a taxi, and see if I can spot her car at this shop."

Will nodded. "I feel you, man. Tell you what, I can meet you at..."

"No!" I was immediately incensed. "I go alone on this one! I mean it, man!"

"Fuck that!" Will insisted. "Ain't no way in hell I'm lettin' you go out like that!"

Making my voice sound as if it had been forged out of iron and extremity, I countered, "This is non-negotiable, cousin. I go solo. You got to trust me on this one. This is the one time where I can get things done better on my own." My tone slapped down any rebuttal.

Will absorbed my words then nodded. "You might be right. But you call me if you need me." His jaw jutted ominously. "You still got my piece?"

"Yeah." I patted my side.

He sighed, seemingly helpless. "All right, cuz, you watch your back, you hear me?"

"I hear you." I gave him a quick embrace then reared back. "I'll give you a call tomorrow morning around eleven."

"Hell no," he snapped. "You call me when I get off work. I don't care how late you think it is, got it?"

"Got it." I then looked at Will's face. He seemed to be in mixed moods—a bit unsteady about letting me go solo, perhaps—but full of good will, trusting that I would handle myself properly. We parted ways and I headed back to my rental car. This time my walk wasn't stiff and rigid, but instead, cool and soulful. I felt good. And for the first time in a long time, I looked like I wanted to applaud.

It was time to bring this matter to a close.

Hopefully a safe one.

The sky outside my window was a perfect midnight blue studded with thousands of bright white stars. The scene could have been a photograph for a postcard. I sat on the sofa in my living room, admiring the night. The useless notations I had written down earlier that day laid crumpled on the coffee table, next to the surveillance photos, which were spread out in disarray. All that afternoon and into the early evening, I had kept an eye on the hair salon, while laboring at compiling notes into a solid core of material for me to go on. I came up with nothing. I couldn't even come up with a skeleton outline on which I could fashion my meager findings and work them into something. I had zip. All I knew about this woman, other than she was a straight-up nut, was that she loved red and pink roses, purple was her favorite color, she got her hair done at a salon called Shear Ritz—which she apparently wasn't at this afternoon—and she drove a convertible Jaguar.

Which puzzled me.

I had the strange feeling I had seen a car like hers at one time or another. The photo was in black and white so I couldn't be sure of the car's color, but I was pretty sure of the car. But what good was that? So I had some clue as to what kind of car this crazy woman drove? Where was that going to get me? I shrugged my shoulders. I guess it was a start, at least. Besides, it wasn't a total wash, if I felt I were being followed at least I would know what kind of car to look out for. *Right?* I frowned, trying to convince myself.

I propped both my feet on the sofa, watching the great night sky as I gave my mind a break. After a long and emotional draining day with only three hours sleep, I was exhausted. Now came the hard part—waiting for the phone to ring. The quiet in the room began to intimidate me a bit. I looked around and that's when I saw it. The bone-colored telephone. The stylish Tiffany lamp in the corner of the living room threw a soft spotlight on it as both sat on the pedestal. The phone appeared almost as if it were my opponent, sitting across the ring, waiting to signal the start of another round.

My eyes slanted. *And then I'd come out swinging!*

I stared at the phone, telling myself that I was ready, but knowing all the while I was nervous as hell. Each round with this woman was another venture into unknown perils. And as time went by I could feel it creeping closer.

"Get yourself together, man. Stop with the butterflies already. Handle your business," I whispered. In the moments to follow I willed myself into action. I knew what I had to do. I had to win the total trust and confidence of this woman, bring her out into the open—I had to say, sing, shout, hum—gambol like a damn monkey if I had to—whatever it took to set up a meeting with her, face to face.

I had to break her.

I was pretty sure I could do it.

Every person had a breaking point. Nobody was infallible, no matter how well-qualified they appeared. Periodically, errors occurred in people: pressure mounts and they crack, they tire, their will weakens, or they buckle under close scrutiny, and cease to operate efficiently and malfunction, sometimes to the point of sending a bullet through their brain. I had to find out which one of these faults pertained to her, so I could work it to my advantage.

I settled back on the sofa. I crossed my legs.

I was ready.

I parted the blinds and gazed into the night. Ten minutes had gone by when the inevitable happened. Seemingly from out of nowhere my phone began to ring, springing out like a predator—communicating the force and fury like a shout across a distance. A cold fist clutched at my stomach and twisted it hard. Nevertheless, I walked over to the phone and picked it up defiantly.

It was showtime.

"Hello, Terry Allens speaking, and might this be Darling?" I inquired in a deep, masculine tone.

"It is," a voice came back lovingly and appreciative. "And how is my baby tonight?"

"Oh, I'm doing just fine, Darling. How about yourself?"

"Splendid," she whispered with heavy sultriness. "Never better, and at the moment I feel *so* relaxed, baby." Afterward she moaned lightly.

"You sound relaxed," I said, expanding upon the moment. "I detect a twinge of mellowness in your voice. And judging by the sound of it you must be a little horny." Even though she couldn't see me, I flashed a knowing, flirtatious smile. It was time to put my 'servicing degree' to good use by warming up her, freeing any inhibitions that might be binding her. "So tell me, Darling, is there a little tingle to your kitty tonight?"

"It might be," she moaned long and sexy. "Why, you going to help out me with my little problem?"

"Only if you help me out with mine," I said.

"Hmm, so you're a little hot yourself, too, huh?"

"Very."

"Are you hard?"

"I'm getting there. What about you? Are you moist?"

"Yes," she gasped. "Very moist, baby."

"Well, you're going to get a lot more moist before the night is over with," I advised after hearing her gasp. "This I can guarantee. I'm going to get you off like you have never gotten off before. Is this okay with you, Darling? Would you mind if I got you off real good?"

"Oh, yes," she whispered. "I need you to get me off, baby. I'm burning up."

"Okay then," I beckoned softly in her ear, "let's do this."

In the next hour or so, I gave her something different, designed specially for her. My voice was low and deep, as I whispered and moaned lustfully, telling her how I would apply slippery kisses to her breasts, the back of her neck, the inside of her thighs, up and down her moist opening, licking her skillfully and wonderfully, getting her more than ready to accept my entry, which would be long, deep and fulfilling. And she responded, forcefully, eagerly, saying she'd accept my manhood willingly, and that she would meet my movements thrust for thrust, until we were both thoroughly satisfied, how afterwards she would lick me dry.

We went on and on, and finally, after doling out everything I could to accomplish my goal, she appeared to be sated. Afterwards, we talked a little more, about nothing, actually. Then all of a sudden, to my surprise, as we were about to end our conversation, she said a wonderful and assuring calm had come over her, that she felt so comfortable with me, so at ease, that she really trusted me. It was at that moment when I heard what I'd been waiting for so long to hear. Her request almost threw me for a loop. In fact, my face was marred by a mixture of alarm and apprehension. I had trouble holding myself still.

Whispering softly, in a voice that was firm with the conclusion of a positive decision backing her, she said she could take it no longer. That the pain and anguish and longing had become to strong for her to bear. She said it was time...time for us to meet...face to face.

My heart pummeling in my chest, I listened closely while she issued out the ground rules for our meeting. As she did there was no kidding myself...I was frightened to the bone.

"You did what?" repeated Will, his voice like the shout of a breaking board.

I cleared my throat. "Like I said...I'm going to meet this woman."

"Have you lost your freaking mind, cuz?" he protested strongly. "You're actually going to meet face to face with this whacked-out woman? Have you taken leave of your senses, man?"

"I know what I'm doing," I said.

"Oh, I'm sure you do," he said thickly. "You're going to walk right up to this woman, get with her somewhere nice and quiet so she can carve her initials in your neck, right?"

For a second my eyes narrowed, gauging Will's words. Then I said, "You know me better than that, man."

"Oh, do I now!" he gruffed. "Well, I don't! You're being set up, cuz, can't you see that?"

"Maybe," I murmured plainly, "maybe not. But it's a chance I'm willing to take. I'm tired of this cat-and-mouse shit, man. Can't you see what this woman has done to me, to my life?" My fist tightened on the phone as my anger rose. "This woman has literally turned my world upside down—she's up in my business and then has the gall to spread it all over town! She follows me around! She has me under surveillance and even takes pictures of me and Vera—causing Vera to get her ass kicked by her old man—whom she eventually kills, mind you! She keeps me under lock and key like I'm a damn prisoner! She shoots at you and Angela and threatens to put a bullet in the back of *your* head, which by now we know she's *very* capable of—and to top it all off, she has the balls to sit with my mother and have tea and cookies! You see why I have to meet this woman! Do you see why! Do you..." My voice trailed off but I brought it back stronger than ever. "I've got to end this madness, man! Meet it head on!"

Will paused then said grimly, "I feel you, cuz. I suppose a man can only take so much before he decides to put an end to it."

"And I have had my fill," I muttered through my teeth. "Believe me, I have."

Will sighed. "So when are you two scheduled to hook-up?"

"This Saturday. She's going to call me that evening with the place and time."

"She's a clever one, ain't she?"

"That she is," I rasped venomously. "She's allowing no slip-ups, no chance for me to beat her to the punch, at anything."

"So tell me, cuz, am I part of this one?"

Will had asked this in a tone which projected a hard intensity that didn't leave room for negotiating—that he'd thought through the dangers of what was involved, probably more clearly than I had. I smiled bleakly. "What if I said no."

"Then I'd say go fuck yourself."

"Then I'd say you're in." I felt good about having Will covering my back, and although my pulse was heavy in my throat with readiness, I still felt somewhat apprehensive. I didn't want anything to happen to Will. I couldn't take it. I took a deep breath, got a grip on my courage, and said, "I'll get with you the moment I hear from her."

"I'll be waiting for your call," Will stated firmly. "And remember, cuz, don't get your nuts in a sling and do this thing without me, I mean it, man."

"I won't," I reassured him. "Now get some sleep, I know you're tired after just getting in from work."

"Tired?" he chuckled. "Man, Angela's butt-naked in the shower. Do you really think I'm about to catch some zees with her lookin' like that? Maybe later, but not now. In a few minutes I'm about to knock the lining outta that box, cuz. So I'll get with you soon—and remember, keep me up on the happs."

"I will." I hung up the phone and rolled over on my back. I stared up at my bedroom ceiling, thinking about Saturday night, on how it seemed as if something bad were going to happen, that things weren't going to go as smoothly as I'd hoped. I couldn't let myself think in this manner, however. *Nothing bad was going to happen!* I told myself.

I closed my eyes and my mind drifted to Vera. Desperately, I wanted to call her, console her in her time of need. But I knew the best thing for me to do was to stay away. It wouldn't be right for me to be around her, not just yet. And although I should be leaping into the air with joy because of the death of her husband, I didn't. I couldn't. I hated the man, but I would never wish something like that on him. I pulled roughly on my face and thought Vera must be devastated. I wish I could comfort her, take her in my arms and hold her tightly, whisper in her ear that I'd be there for her—one hundred and ten percent. But again I told myself this was not possible. Not now. Maybe one day.

Maybe.

I stared at the ceiling. I soon had a mental image of Vera and I. We were attending some high society event, the kind which required evening gowns and tuxedos, a black tie affair. Yes, that's what it was. The room was stunning, with exquisite furnishings, a white marble floor, soaring ceilings, and large oversized chandeliers, with hundreds and hundreds of twinkling bulbs. The place was nothing short of magnificent, as were the attendees, men handsomely attired, women looking exceptional with their dangerously expensive diamond appointments. Everyone in the place exemplifying the epitome of class, the social elite—*creme da la creme!* As the night progressed it seemed as if the entire event had hit its peak, and nobody couldn't get any better than they were.

Until Vera and I walked in...announced through the sounds of hornpipes and tabors, flutes and bells.

That's when every head turned, and all eyes were focused...on us.

And although I was looking very dashing and debonair in my vibrant white tuxedo, it was Vera who had everyone captivated and speechless, in a black evening gown which clung to her body like a glove. The curvaceous swirls of her figure made the gown dip and wind like a long mountainous road. Her arm was laced with mine, supported and secure. With a curt nod, I gestured for her to proceed with me to the head of a long, beautifully decorated table. Her cheeks aflame, Vera complied, walking in perfect unison with me.

All around us, people greeted us by name, and we replied in a tone of friendly salutation, following the parted path provided by the people surrounding us. The rushes and sweet herbs strewn over the floor rustled softly underfoot, as I led Vera through the star-struck crowd.

After approaching the table, I held a chair for Vera, then seated her properly, taking a chair directly by her side. We dined, then danced the evening away. And as I held Vera in my arms I was enthralled by her beauty, unable to really take it all in. Not only was she a baffling mixture of something exotic and seemingly forbidden, she was a breathtaking photograph brought to life, a precious alchemy that I had never seen before, and was grateful to have and to hold. The gala soon ended, and Vera and I retired to our suite, for a night of unbridled passion…kissing…hugging…loving each other…

The vision faded and I shook my head, scowling. All at once I relapsed into normalcy, to today, realizing I was just in the throes of a passing fantasy. But somewhere in my head I heard a voice, they were words being spoken, a subtle reminder of hope, calling out to my heart in feathered whispers and changing everything. *Maybe there was a chance for me and Vera.*

I stared at the ceiling, feeling sleep slowly overtaking my body. I thought of Vera, and of her husband, Mel Armstrong. He was gone from her life. As my eyes grew heavier and heavier I had to admit to myself, while Vera and everyone close to her husband felt pain and were most likely grieving heavily, I, on the other hand, felt pleasure, like an opening had finally been made for me to take advantage of, to exploit, which was wrong. But I couldn't help what I felt. I was happy the son-of-a-bitch was gone…which was something I knew I would have to pray over.

It wasn't right to think this way.

Still, I smiled, *Maybe I could finally win Vera's heart.*

Maybe.

I soon felt myself drifting off, with thoughts of Vera swirling in my head; a ghost of her smile haunted the corners of my mouth as my eyes finally closed.

I could have her I smiled once more.

Maybe...

Chapter 19

It was three-thirty in the morning when Regina crept into her kitchen. Her kids were asleep so it was safe she figured. Her stash was on a top shelf in one of the cupboards, in a wicker basket. Derrick had left it there, making sure her supply stayed well-stocked. For him it was insurance, because as long as his woman kept her nose powdered, he'd have her where he wanted.

Standing on her toes, Regina reached into the basket and took out a plastic sack, which was filled with tiny vials of cocaine, a small fortune. She removed one of the vials and tapped out two lines on the kitchen counter, telling herself that she would soon quit. Kick it altogether, or at least cut her intake. She got a short straw from the bag and snorted each of the lines into her nostrils. Almost immediately as she threw her head back, her eyes glazed, as a delectable warmth spread through her body, and a moment later she felt light enough to float into the air. She closed her eyes and shook her head. *The high was so good* she smiled. *And if high was good, higher could be so much better.*

She reached back into the bag and took another hit, and the effect was startling. As if by magic, she became instantly attuned with her inner self. She was so much in control, had so much power, she could do anything. And so hot that the mere thought of Derrick's body lying in her bed was maddening to her. She put away her stash and returned to the bedroom. She pulled off her robe and climbed into bed. She put her arms around Derrick and kissed him long and hungrily on the mouth. He stirred, and then his lips opened. She slid a hand between his legs and gripped him tightly. Bringing her mouth down to his chest, she kissed and licked his nipples, and then she crawled on top of him, straddling his now erect penis. She moaned as she moved slowly downward, her insides pounding, so hot and excited that she could hardly breathe.

It lasted for what seemed like hours, her passion whisking her along in a delirium of pleasure. She caressed and kissed and sucked, her body shivering, orgasm after orgasm overtaking her in waves.

Derrick gave a loud, garbled rasp of satisfaction, and that added even more to the intensity of what she was experiencing.

But when it was over, she realized their lovemaking had only consumed a few minutes. Her body damp with perspiration, she rolled over and stared up at the dark ceiling, depression already descending over her like a black cloud.

"You happy now!" Vera was drunk. But it was not the kind of drunk that messes up a person's mind and tongue so that they can neither think or speak coherently. I figured she was drunk because she had to be. There was no other alternative.

It was half an hour before noon and I'd been alternately sitting and pacing in my living room, trying to figure out how I was going to handle myself this coming Saturday, which was only two days away. Vera had called me in an accusing, drunken state. I wasn't about to get into a debating match with her. That was the worse thing I could do. I just wanted to be there for her. So basically, all I could do was sit there and take the unwarranted beating, which she dispensed relentlessly.

"You got your wish, didn't you, Terry?" she continued cleverly. "You're glad he's gone, aren't you?"

"No, Vera," I rejected softly, "I'm not happy or glad or elated, in any form or fashion. I am truly sorry this has happened. Why can't you believe this?"

"Yeah, you're truly sorry, all right. I'll *bet* you are!" she snapped harshly. "You think because my husband is gone you can just *slide right in*, don't you? Well, don't even think about it! You hear me, you nickel-slick nigga! Nothing's changed—not a goddamn thing! We will never be! Got it! Not in a million years! At least not in my lifetime! Besides, I wouldn't want your gigolo, perverted, laying-up-with-men ass, anyway! You hear me! *I don't want you, Terry Allens!"*

I shrunk a little at her tone, all hope that we could mend the rift between us shriveling beneath her contempt. Through the crush I was experiencing in my heart, I managed to say, "I'm sorry you feel this way about me, Vera. And again, I am truly sorry about the death of your husband. If there's anything…"

"I don't need your piss-ass apologies," she uttered in a guttural voice, like the bite of a chain saw. "And I don't need a damn thing from you, you get what I'm saying here? Not a damn thing!"

Unable to say anything at this point, I went silent, still holding the phone to my ear. Vera was hurting deeply. The man in her life had been taken away unexpectedly, in a very cruel and brutal manner. She was alone now. Her sense of security had been stripped from her like a blanket, leaving her cold and exposed. As a result, she was bitter; she didn't know where to turn, what to do, who to call on. She was also vulnerable because of a difficult family situation. She had no brothers or sisters. Both her parents were in bad shape. Her father was an *ugly* drunk, and at sixty-one, was suffering from cirrhosis of the liver. Lung cancer had had a mean grip on her mother.

It seemed as if Vera was being hit from nearly every possible angle, in every possible way. And because of this she had to lash out, and as always, it seemed I was to be the one she'd come to. But I wasn't just a person for her to vent her damaged emotions onto, instead, I was the only one she could *really* talk to, give her heart to. I knew this all too clearly, so I didn't mind being her scapegoat.

I would be there for Vera no matter what the reason.

But at the moment I was hurt. The one person *I* wanted in my life was slicing me into ribbons. I shook my head, as the assault rained down harder.

"Vera, I know you're grieving," I said quickly, finding an opening, "and I also know you blame me in some way for all this mess. But I didn't do anything...*we* didn't do anything. Your husband's life was taken by someone who is cruel and heartless. And this someone is still walking around out there. Now please, tell me, have you heard anything on this?"

She calmed her anger and sniffed. "No. Not a damn thing, Terry." At once, she nearly bit my head off. "Why? Was it you? Did you kill my husband? So it could be convenient for you and I to sneak off to your little fantasy world?"

I sighed inwardly. Vera escaped betraying her soft and vulnerable side. Apparently she was still pissed at me—*at us*—for the things we had done.

"Well, will you keep me informed on things?" I asked sincerely, overlooking her previous statement. I knew she wasn't in her right frame of mind.

"Why should I?" She let out a sigh of disgust.

"Because I want to know, is that asking too much here?" Pain and hurt made my tone a note of harshness. "I still care about you no matter what you think of me, Vera. For goodness sake, why don't you cut me some slack?"

At that, she paused. Slowly, she said, "Get this through your thick skull, Terry Allens, I don't need you to care about me. I don't want your sympathy, your apologies, your condolences—I don't want shit from you or anybody else! I just—" All of a sudden she stopped, and the abrupt silence chilled me to the bone. I thought for sure something bad had happened. In the moment to come I'd been right in my thinking, for Vera's voice had now dropped dramatically. "This is the last time you and I are to talk, Terry. I mean this…I don't ever want to hear from you again…*ever*. You have done nothing but ruin my life. And I dread the day I ever met you. I should have walked away that day—"

Once again she stopped, I guess to compose herself. Then she went on in a seething whisper, the sullen edge of her temper surfacing more, "Don't you ever call me, don't you ever page me, don't write me, don't come by, don't try to run into me on the streets somewhere, don't do *anything*. Do I make myself clear? I don't want you in my life ever again."

"I love you, Vera," I whispered after her. "If this is the last time I have to talk with you then I felt that needed to be said. I'd like to say just a few more things then I'll be out of your life…if I may?" I moistened my lips and swallowed hard.

She hesitated then said, "Go ahead. I'm listening." Her voice carried a hollow sound like an echo.

I took a seat on the sofa. *This was it* I told myself. *The moment of truth.* I had to make my words count. The woman I loved was about to walk out of my life. But I wasn't about to beg. No. Not me. Not that I felt begging was beneath me or anything, I just felt sure of what was in my heart, and I was going to speak from my heart, and if what I was about to say wasn't good enough for Vera, than I guess me and Vera were never meant to be.

Though I felt as if I were standing on the lip of a well of darkness, I cleared my throat and decided to let the chips fall where they may. "Vera" —my voice was practically a whisper— "from the moment I first laid eyes on you I knew you were undoubtedly the only woman for me. I can't begin to tell you what I experienced and what I still experience when I'm around you. It's like a hazy fog in and around my head, with bells and whistles chiming loudly and then softly, in and out. It's a daily thing with you, and there's not a second that doesn't go by without you in it. Even as I speak to you, the world as I once knew it is fastly crumbling around me. My life is one big mess, and getting worse by the minute, but the thought of losing you, well, that would make things even more devastating. But let me get you straight on one thing here: I'm not here to try to win you over or anything like that...I'm just telling you how I feel. And you know deep in *your* heart...I did...still do...and always will have, a place in *my* heart...for you." I took a deep breath and finished by saying, "I love you, Vera. You mean the world to me."

With that off my chest, my conscious cleared, I clenched my teeth, and slowly, I did something I thought I never would do or have the desire to do...with my heart thumping madly in my chest, and sweat streaking my temples, I hung up the phone.

Chapter 20

When I walked into Regina's house, two cops were in the living room talking with her boyfriend, Derrick Collins. Regina stood by his side. She looked bad. There were cuts and bruises all over her face, and the front of her blouse was red with droplets of blood. The cops were attempting to get a statement from her, but Derrick kept intervening saying her injuries were the results due to some kind of fall, that it was just a result of a misplaced step.

One of the cops, a firmly-built brother who carried a military disposition, studied Regina's appearance. "Was Mister Derrick Collins the cause of your injuries, Miss Cook?" he asked Regina.

She shot a frightened look at Derrick then over to me as I approached closer. "I…I don't know," she rambled distantly, not sure of what to say. "I believe it was just a mistake, sir."

The cop cut his eyes at Derrick. There was a deep, implicating expression on his face. "Mister Collins, did you or did you not lay a hand on this woman?"

Surprised and appearing appalled, Derrick threw up his hands. "Naw, Mister Officer, sir, I ain't did nothin' to this girl. She just took a tumble off her front porch chasin' after one of her kids."

Standing off to the side I cut an eye over at Derrick, and he caught it. No matter how much shit he shoved at the cops he knew I wasn't buying any of it. He tried to give me a menacing look—and failed completely. In fact, when he saw that I wasn't backing down he feigned playfulness, trying to brush off the entire situation as though he had just lost his temper, and that this was just a minor mishap, nothing really to get bent out of shape over. But I knew better. When Regina had called me she was nothing short of hysterical.

Not buying much of it themselves, the two cops nevertheless took a preliminary incident report and the matter was resolved.

As the cops left through the front door I turned to Regina and took her by the hand. "Hey, girl, you okay?"

At first she couldn't answer that. She appeared too ashamed. Softly, as if she were apologizing, she said, "Yes, thank you, Terry. I'm…I'm okay."

"Yeah, pretty nigga," Derrick cut in rudely, "my girl's all right, so you can get to steppin'. I got a grip on things up in here."

I looked over at Derrick; my eyes burned. "Let me tell you something, Derrick, and you'd better listen good cause I'm only going to say this once: if you ever lay a hand on Regina again, I'll make you wish you never had. Do I make myself understood?" I stared at him without blinking an eye, and then slowly, I eased back the folds of my jacket so that he could take note of the nine-millimeter tucked in my waistband. I knew most likely he was also strapped, but at the moment I did what I had to do to make my point felt. Derrick swallowed and met my direct gaze, as if gauging me and the probability of me using the gun. I could tell from his expression he knew I would, without hesitation.

I guess I had come just close enough to the threat to unnerve him. He clenched his teeth tight, stretched a thin smile, and refused to think about it. He threw Regina a stern gaze and grunted, "We'll talk later, baby." He gave me a leering glance then turned and headed out the door. Regina started after him but I took her gently by the arm.

"Let him go," I said firmly. "He needs time to cool off." I released her arm and kissed her hand gallantly at the knuckles. "It's going to be okay. Now, let's get you all patched up."

She looked at me frightened but grateful. "You think he'll be back? He's my man, you know. We argue and stuff, but I don't want him to just walk out of my life." With that, tears began welling in her eyes. "Are you sure he'll be back?"

"Yeah," I smiled, "he will. You can bet on it."

"Would you ask him, Terry?" she pleaded, clutching me by the shoulders. "To be sure? Before he leaves? Please?"

I stared at Regina, into her eyes. I knew what she was feeling, having just been through the same identical thing. It could be a real bitch letting the one you care for walk out your life. So with an effort, I kissed Regina on the cheek and headed out the door to catch Derrick. He was just opening the door to his Range Rover.

"Yo, Derrick!" I shouted, making my way across the lawn. I walked around his vehicle and stepped up to him, non-intimidating.

"Look, man, things got a little hairy in there. I apologize for coming on you like that. It's just that when Regina called me and said you and her were fighting, *hey*, I lost it. I called the cops and headed right over to check things out myself. You've got to understand, Regina is like a sister to me and I care about her deeply. I hope you can relate to what I saying here. And I hope there's no hard feelings between us." Then, for Regina's sake *only*, I extended my hand to show my remorse.

Derrick looked at me with a murderous scowl. He obviously had no interest in shaking my hand. Instead he traced me from head to toe. Then he said with a touch of sincerity to his voice, "Okay, pretty nigga, I accept your apology." With those words, he reached inside his jacket and pulled out a black .357 magnum. He pointed the barrel directly between my eyes. The expression on his face was ghastly as he smiled, "I could really mess your face up, pretty nigga, you know that?"

My heart pummeled in my chest. For a period of time as quick and intense as the crisis before me, I said, "Yeah, man, I suppose you could."

His tone tightened. "The fuck you mean, *you suppose*? I could, pretty nigga—there's no doubt about it! Besides," looking around smiling, "who's gonna stop me? Certainly not your punk-ass?" He laughed off-key and pressed the barrel further into my face.

I swallowed hard to clear my throat. When I spoke, my voice was carefully neutral, distinct but yielding. "At the moment, no one, I guess. You hold all the cards, man." Though I remained cool, anxiety twisted the insides of my body.

As if he were reading my emotions, Derrick chuckled and slowly withdrew the gun from my face. He slid it back underneath his jacket. He smiled and turned to get into his Range Rover. Without dropping his smile, he said in a relaxed, conversational tone, "Now let me tell *you* somethin', pretty nigga. Call it a word from the wise: any time you advertise your shit, be prepared to use it." He started up his vehicle. "I ain't no sucker-ass nigga, you hear me? The next time you even *think* about pullin' your shit on me you damn well better use it—and if you do you had better take me out. Cause if you don't...well, we're cool now so we don't even need to go there, do we, pretty nigga?"

Feeling chastised as well as pissed off, I was tempted to retort. But I wouldn't. I wasn't dumb. There was danger all around when dealing with this fool, and whatever I said would most likely have consequences, and at this point in my life it was the last thing I needed. Carefully, I replied, "We got an understanding."

At that, Derrick nodded his head decisively. "I thought we would." He put his vehicle in gear, and just because it appeared as if he had the upper hand on things he had to say something, had to get one last jab at me. "You stay pretty, pretty nigga, and leave the gangsta shit to the gangstas." He winked an eye at me, at the same time blowing me a kiss. Afterwards he laughed, started coughing, and spat on the ground. Then he looked at me, and I at him. There was no doubt we disliked each other immensely.

I stood there unimpressed as he slowly pulled away, laughing. I shook my head and believe it or not, *I* laughed. Derrick was living in a world of his own, where players and pimps and expensive cars and whores and fast money—where all the gangster trappings ruled. But the brother hadn't a clue to what the real world was all about. I chuckled to myself and headed back to check in on Regina. Suddenly I stopped. It was at that moment when a thought crossed my mind. I felt myself being a little hypocritical.

Who was I to judge Derrick for living in a fantasy world? Was I any different? Wasn't I just in a world like that myself? The trappings differed from Derrick's, but nevertheless, it was still my world, was it not?

Once again, as I stood on the sidewalk, I thought about my life, *my former life*, vehemently, as if for the last time. But I quickly blocked the thoughts from coming. Now was not the time I told myself. Maybe later when the time was right, when I had time to ponder on it from different angles, to give it final closure. For now, I'd comfort Regina and help her with her wounds, both mentally and physically. And then maybe, in turn, she could help me with mine.

Chapter 21

The afternoon sun was strong as I stepped through the door of my apartment carrying an arm full of groceries. I sat the bag on the floor and picked up the phone but heard only the dial tone. Perhaps I needed to wait for it to ring. I put the receiver back. Nothing happened. I felt foolish just standing there staring at the phone, but I was afraid to leave. Maybe my mother was trying to reach me. Perhaps Will had called...or maybe even Vera. Maybe she wanted to talk about something—anything. Wouldn't it be great if we'd managed to straighten things out and at least remained as friends?

Suddenly, I felt something hard pressing against my heart, and reminded myself it was Friday. The next day I was to hear from Darling. For some odd reason, I checked my Rolex; three-twenty. How long would it be before she called? I wondered. I shook my head and sighed heavily. I turned and began putting away the groceries. My pace was hurried and uncoordinated as I placed items in the refrigerator, in the cupboards, and under the sink. I noticed that my mind was working as fast as I moved.

I knew it was a product of stress.

It was one-ten in the morning, nearly closing time at Club Taboo. The area was quiet and there were no people hanging around out front, due to the chill in the air. Even the valets chose to remain in their booths until the crowd began filing out of the club.

She lurked in the shadows.

She knew he would be out here.

This was his favorite hangout, where he peddled his drugs. She spotted him sitting in his vehicle. *You dirty bastard!* she sneered, with a determined look in her eyes, making her way in the shadows to his vehicle parked a block away from the club entrance. As she slid through the darkness her hand was closed around the ivory handle of a switch blade. She carried the knife in the pocket of her quarter-length overcoat, never in her purse, where getting it out would take longer. She took it out now, holding it close to her shapely leg so it wouldn't show. There was a look of decided venom on her face. It was a dangerous undertaking, but she couldn't pull back from it.

Not after what he'd done.

She slid through her shadowed surroundings until she was met by a swirling wind. It whipped at the hem of her overcoat and tunneled under it, lifting the material and threatening to send it flying about her face. Hurriedly she battled the billowing overcoat. The wind soon swept on down the street, its force dwindling. With nimble fingers she buttoned up her overcoat.

She drew a deep breath.

She was ready.

It was now or never.

Stepping over to the dark green vehicle where the crude, perverted man sat in the driver seat smoking a joint, she went into motion, tapping on the window. The man turned. He frowned then powered down his window. He hunched over and leaned out the window. "Girl, what the hell—"

The woman had reached up, lunged forward, then slammed the blade into the man's chest with a quick upward thrust, driving seven inches of cold steel all the way to the ivory handle. The man's mouth popped open. His eyes bulged in his head. Gurgling something low and wet in his throat he looked down, and realized what had happened.

Realized that the woman had killed him. And was stunned by this.

His eyes swung up again, and he fixed her with an astonished look. His lips quivered. "What the hell..."

The woman cursed, "You fucking pig!" Then, with her mouth coming together in a hard, taut line, a muscle flexing in her jaw and cheek, she pulled the knife from his chest, and when she did, blood spurted in a scarlet gush from the wound. He began bucking wildly. Then slowly, he leaned forward, clutching his chest, and from there his head collapsed on the steering wheel, sending out a loud, blaring blast into the night. The woman knew she had to hurry. She pulled the sluggish body back into the seat, then she retracted the blade. Stuffing the knife back into the pocket of her overcoat, she looked around nervously. Hopefully the valets had ignored the sound of the horn.

She quickly stepped away from the vehicle. She looked around with shifting eyes then began a brisk pace to her car parked a little ways down. In her rush she was almost clipped by a passing car leaving the parking lot. She stopped dead in her tracks and saw the driver shaking his fist and swearing, but nothing came out of it. She was thankful; her overcoat was dotted with blood. Without any further hesitation she hurried to her car, got inside, and seconds later, disappeared into the dark night.

Chapter 22

It was Saturday night.

A double line of gleaming limousines were parked in front of Pozanno's. There were Cadillacs, Lincolns, a Mercedes, and a Rolls, even a Hummer, the chauffeurs slumped behind their steering wheels, waiting for their owners to finish dinner. The practice had caused a traffic jam on this block every Saturday night since the restaurant's inception five years ago, but no cop in his right mind would tell one of the drivers to move. No, there were too many important figures to contend with, too many headaches or worst, repercussions. So things were just left as they were.

The line outside Pozanno's stretched for what seemed to be blocks and blocks. Fortunately reservations had already been made in my name so I didn't have to wait. Countless pairs of envious eyes were on me as I cut through the line and walked inside the Italian restaurant, and to my amazement, the place was much bigger than it appeared from the outside. The dining area was large and lavishly furnished, with gleaming fixtures everywhere, and the tables were beautifully adorned with sterling silverware which sat upon perfectly ironed and starched white tablecloths. Dressed in a crisp white dress shirt and a silk red and blue tie under a dark gray European-cut suit, I stepped up and waited until the maitre' d checked my reservations.

My body was so rigid with confusion and anxiety and so intense with apprehension that I barely heard the maitre' d beckoning me to follow him. I did, and glided effortlessly through the laughs and smiles of people around me, detaching myself from the joyous atmosphere. This was not a joyous occasion for me, and I wasn't about to pretend it was. I was soon seated at a table near the back of the restaurant. I didn't mind, the view was pretty good. I requested a wine list but instead of receiving one, a silver wine cooler with ice and a bottle of Chardonnay was brought to my table. I looked up at the waiter with a puzzled expression. The waiter read my look and gestured to a small white card propped underneath the silver cooler. I picked up the card, and the words, "Thank you for coming, I hope to be your dessert" were printed neatly on it.

How touching, I seethed.

I suddenly felt angry blood surge to my temples at the thought of this woman. Yet I was only too aware that I needed to keep my cool. The last thing I wanted was to scare her off. The waiter opened the bottle expertly and poured a little into a fluted glass, then set the glass in front of me. He then gave me a curt nod and disappeared. I sat back in my seat and crossed my legs, staring at the bottle, then the glass. I thought, *Maybe I'd have a taste of it, then again, maybe not.* I was nervous and a bit edgy, not quite comfortable with myself, so I reached out to the glass and took a tiny sip. It was good, nevertheless, I couldn't help but wonder if the wine had been laced with some kind of toxicant.

I set the glass down and looked around. There were women—beautiful, polished, bright, and seemingly well-educated. I caught a few flirting blatantly with me; a few others were stealing glances in my direction, striking poses that were too nonchalant to be natural. All in all, the gazes felt like a pair of invisible hands moving over me as I sat there, and as I leaned back in my seat I suddenly found myself feeling like the world's most eligible bachelor. It was a little unnerving and a bit scary, but exciting, too. However, as alluring and attractive as I found these women to be, I was also realistic enough to know that I couldn't allow myself to be swayed. So while I appeared to enjoy their flattery and attention, I continued my scan of the room. I soon spotted a former client, Alvin Harris. He was with his sister, whose name at the moment escapes me. They were seated near the front of the restaurant, off to the side.

To my dismay, Alvin Harris also spotted me, and gestured to his sister to look over her left shoulder. She smiled brightly and both waved at me. I nodded my head, praying that they would stay where they were. I didn't need their distractions, or anybody else's, for that matter. However, they saw differently and beckoned me over to their table. I raised my palms up and shook my head. I wasn't about to leave my seat, not for anybody. I guess they wanted to talk; both of them rose from the table and walked over to mine. I cursed like a madman under my breath, and with great reluctance, rose to my feet.

"Terry Allens!" Alvin Harris exclaimed as he strode toward me, extending his hand.

I met his firm handshake. "Hello, Mister Harris," I smiled. "And how are you this evening, sir?"

"Fine, just fine, Terry," he beamed. He swept a hand to his side. "You remember my sister Denise, don't you?"

I looked over to her. She was simply stunning. She had on a dark green, form-fitting Chanel outfit, which did wonders for her bright and captivating face. I took her hand and shook it gently. I couldn't help but notice the gold Cartier Panther wristwatch and bracelet on her arm. "Yes, I remember you, Denise. And might I say, you're looking quite the picture of perfection this evening."

She smiled bashfully. "Thank you kindly for the compliment, Mister Allens. You're looking quite handsome yourself. You really stand out in a crowd."

I nodded graciously and then turned my attention to Alvin Harris. "You guys leaving...coming...?"

"We were just finishing up dinner." He turned to his sister and kissed her cheek. "Today is Denise's birthday. After our meal I was going to treat her to a night on the town."

I bobbed my head in approval. "Sounds great." I turned to Denise and took her by the hand once more, this time kissing it softly. "Happy Birthday, Denise," I congratulated her. "May you have many, many more, and may you stay as beautiful and as lovely as you are now."

She blushed and said in her light southern tone, while fanning herself with her free hand, "Well, thank you again, Mister Allens. If you keep this up, you're going to have me turning as red as a beet."

Alvin Harris nodded agreement then said, "Why don't we all have a quick glass of champagne? To celebrate Denise's birthday?" He reached inside his suit jacket pocket and held up a .35mm camera. "Then maybe we can all take a group picture."

I was startled by the directness of his words. Yet, I had to admit, with his powerful stature and with the way his impeccably burnt-orange suit fitted him to the tee, not to mention the unquestioned authority in his voice, it was easy to comply. He was a man to be admired and respected. We all sat down together and Alvin Harris did the honors and ordered a bottle of chilled Pouilly-Fuisse. He said it was much better tasting than Dom Perignon, also saying it was a tad cheaper. "You don't remain wealthy by squandering your money," he'd added inside of a light chuckle.

The three of us went on about nothing as we sipped our champagne, which was excellent, undoubtedly the best I'd ever had. During our conversation I'd explained that I was waiting for my date, who at the current moment, was running a bit late. Though I was absorbed with my company I still managed to keep a sharp eye on the people around me, hoping to locate the mysterious woman, frowning at times when I thought I'd spotted her.

Alvin Harris noticed my frustration and said, "Looks like you've been stood up, old boy."

I nodded with a weak smile on my face. "Yes, it seems that way, doesn't it?"

He leaned back in his seat. With his manicured fingers, he ran a stroke of thoughts up and down his glass. He picked up his glass and as he raised it to his lips, he whispered in his heavy tone, "I've missed you, Terry. Why haven't you returned my calls?" He took a sip of his drink and peered at me over the rim of his glass.

Perhaps to shake off an uncomfortable situation, Alvin Harris' sister rose from her seat, and smiled, "I think I'll go powder my nose, and give two gentlemen a chance to talk. I'll be back in about five minutes or so."

Alvin Harris and I rose to our feet while she headed off toward the bathrooms. We took our seats and I immediately poured myself another glass of champagne. Talking with this man about something so touchy wasn't going to be easy. Alvin Harris leaned back in his seat and started exactly where he left off.

"So, Terry, why haven't you called?" He brought a balled fist to his mouth and cleared his throat.

I took a sip of champagne and shifted in my seat. "I'm no longer 'in the life', Mister Harris. I apologize for not getting back to you and informing you of my decision."

His mouth tightened instantly, and he tapped a fingernail against his glass. He seemed disappointed, however, he didn't allow himself to brood over something he felt he had no control over. "May I ask why?"

"I'm just tired of it," I commented just before sipping my drink. "I can't begin to tell you how tiring and unrewarding it was, how severely it played on my mind."

With that, he reached over and touched my hand. "Why don't you try me? I'd like to hear about it."

I pulled my hand away, then swallowed, feeling my stomach turning watery. I didn't want this man to touch me, no matter how rich and powerful he was. I fought through my uneasiness as well as my queasiness, and said, "You don't want me to go there, Mister Harris, it's not a very pretty picture."

He grinned, his curiosity deepening. "On the contrary, I do. And call me Alvin, Terry."

For a moment I laughed. Then I stopped when I saw that the man was dead serious. I leaned across the table. "It's not the kind of thing I like to talk about."

"I didn't think it was," he expressed quickly. "So, you going to tell me or what?" He glanced at his Rolex, which was a notch or two better than mine. He looked up at me with an upraised eyebrow. "If you recall, we don't have much time here, remember? Denise is giving us five minutes, and the girl is not only pretty but very prompt."

I stared at him, into his eyes. There was a certain look of sincerity. The man really wanted to know about the inner workings of my former life, the unpleasant, darker side. I nodded, then took a sip of champagne to wet my palate. "Okay, Alvin, but let me say this right off, my involvement with you had nothing to do with me opting out of the business. It was a combination of things."

"I understand this," he said. "Very clearly."

I cleared my throat and fell into a short trance. I guess to gather and sort through my words. When I'd figured I had, I began, "The clients of my former life, at least for the most part, were decent people. But there were some real doozies out there that I chose to deal with. People who looked and acted sophisticated, but when you got them behind closed doors, their weird fetishes sprung out at you like a striking snake. Sometimes it was unbelievable. Some of my male clients wanted me to dress up like a woman, in bra and panties, with my genitalia hanging out over the waist of the panties, as if they weren't sure of what they really wanted. And then there were the

S&M freaks, people who wanted me to wear leather and spike shoes, with five and six-inch heels that made me feel like I was walking on stilts. And for the love of money, I'd swallow my pride and put those things on, stumbling, afraid I'd fall and bust my ass."

"You never did, did you?" Alvin Harris inquired with a voice that suggested a smile.

I chuckled and shook my head. "No, fortunately for me I managed to stay on my feet." After a pause, I added with a joyous gasp, "Well, actually, to keep it real, one time I did—face-forward right into a wall!"

Alvin Harris smiled, then his eyes met mines. They were focused, not judgmental at all, but instead, direct and kind, soothing, like an old friend. And at the moment I felt as if I were finally getting some things off my chest that I always wanted to, as though this was the chance I'd been hoping for—a chance to relieve my troubled mind. I could finally express the things I had not shared with anyone.

Especially about the men.

I smiled almost appreciatively as I took another sip of champagne. I could tell by the look in Alvin Harris's eyes that he knew the things I was about to say centered around my male clients. I sat the glass down and immediately refilled it, as well as the glass of my new-found therapist. I took a deep breath and continued, "I made a lot of money compromising myself, right from the very beginning. Most of the men I encountered in my travels were quite dull, with the typical guy wanting to have a drink or two with me or sometimes dinner while I listened to whatever bullshit he was doling out. The majority of these clients would go on about how women didn't appreciate them, and that they were actually studs, their own self-imposed assumption I figured, because of their tremendous sex drive and knowledge of pleasing a woman and most of all, their staying power. I'd listen to their bullshit and then we'd get it on, and after a few minutes of huffing and puffing, it'd be all over. Which told me the real deal. The whole ordeal with these type of men made me sick to the stomach. Actually, to tell you the honest truth, *all* the men made me somewhat sick to the stomach."

"I see," murmured Alvin Harris, as if he were clinging to every word. "Please, go on."

Instead of continuing, I went silent for a moment while I relapsed into my deeper past, the more ugly, disgusting side. Again, things I had never discussed before. And as I started, words seemed to tumble headlong after each other, "Then there were the real nutcases, the real freaks of freaks. The rich clients. They were the shy ones when you first met them. And instead of bragging and boasting about their money or their careers or their possessions, they wanted you to be their partner in acting out fantasies, some of them so fucking weird, it made you wonder how in the hell had they ever thought shit like that up. They were *deplorable* things."

I shuddered, and found my eyes welling up. "A lot of those sick bastards wanted to play toilet games...where they wanted to watch me urinate, or either have me urinate on them. At first it seemed relatively harmless, pissing on them, and the money was extraordinary. The first time I urinated on a man, the rich bastard gave me three thousand dollars. At rates like that, I was more than happy to let loose on one of those pigs. That is until one day I'd reached my limit. One guy had told me before hand to take a good laxative, that he wanted to try something new..." I shook my head. "...I never did that kind of mess again...*never.*"

I wiped my eyes then smoothed a hand down my face. "Another popular request was for severe chastising, where guys would want to have me whack them on their bare asses while I called them every name in the book, and they'd jack themselves off." I took another sip of my drink and my mouth tightened as I grimaced. "But in spite of all these vile-ass things, even with the women, I kept doing them...just to feel the need to be accepted by someone." My eyes narrowed. "But not anymore, it's all over. I'll never stoop to that level again, not for any amount of money..." I looked at Alvin Harris and gave him a drilling glare. "...not for anyone."

I knew my voice had surfaced as being savage, and at the moment I didn't give a shit. I'd meant what I said: I was through with it all.

With that, Alvin Harris slumped in his seat, propping his elbows on the arms of his chair and supporting his head with arched thumbs. He peered at me with what I perceived as pure admiration. He then sat up and reached into his inner suit jacket pocket and handed me one of his business cards. "When you decide what you want to do with your life, give me a call."

I glanced over the card and said, "I thought I made myself clear, Mister Harris. I am no longer in the life." I sounded angry.

For a while, Alvin Harris said nothing. Then he sighed. "I understand, Terry. But I also understand if you are no longer 'in the life', as you put it, you may need to seek some sort of employment...or maybe just someone to talk to. In either case, I can be there for you, Terry. It's your choice."

I stared at Alvin Harris. I still felt anger coursing through my body, but all of a sudden, I regained my self-control. Without any transition of emotions, I said, "Thank you...Alvin." I placed the card in my inner suit pocket. "I'll be sure to call if the need arises...in either case." He nodded and gave me a warm, kind, understanding smile, but above all: genuine. The man would be there for me. I stood up and extended my hand, and he rose to his feet, taking my hand, shaking it firm and strong. We shared a brief moment of admiration and respect for each other as we stood there with my hand gripping his.

Then all of a sudden, coming from around the corner as if on cue, Alvin's sister stepped up to the table. She seemed eager and raring to get her evening started. I noticed that her face had been refreshed and to tell it, the girl was all and out *fine*.

"Well," she breathed anxiously, "I hope you two men have had a good talk, cause it's my birthday and I'm ready to celebrate." She nudged Alvin Harris in the shoulder. "You ready, bro?"

For a moment, he studied her. Then he said sourly, almost bitterly, as though he were disappointed, "Yeah, I guess we'd better get moving, sis." He reached into an eel-skin wallet and after laying two one hundred dollar bills on the table, he immediately became upbeat. "I know where there's a little out-of-way club where you and I can get our swirl on." He started to leave then turned and smiled graciously at me. "I almost forgot, would you be so kind as to take a group picture with us, Terry?"

I shrugged my shoulders. "Sure, no problem."

With that, Alvin Harris flagged down a passing waiter and got him to snap the picture. Afterward he turned to me. "Have a pleasant evening, Terry. Sorry about your date not showing up."

"It's okay," I replied promptly. "The evening wasn't a total washout, after all." I shook his hand once more, and for a moment he didn't seem to realize what he had given me. Then he smiled that special smile of his, and that's when I knew he had. I turned my attention to his sister. "Well, girl, you have a terrific night, you hear me? Birthdays only come once a year, so make the best of it."

At that she became excited, and squealed with her southern tonality bursting through, "I will, I will, this I can promise you. And I hope your night will be satisfying also, Terry. You have a goodnight." In a rush, she took her brother by the arm and led him through the crowd and out of the door.

I sat back down at the table. I checked my Rolex. It was getting late. The night was a bust. Well, not totally I felt. As a whole, I reflected with clarity as I poured myself a final glass of champagne, I felt as if I had been rescued. My mind had been eased, my heart was beating more like a man who had a purpose in life, and above all, I was happy with myself. *Yes,* I smiled, thinking on everything that recently transpired, *I had been definitely rescued...if only for the moment.*

For the next fifteen minutes or so, feeling the way I was, I joined in the joyous atmosphere surrounding me.

I sat at the breakfast table in Will's kitchen while Will rummaged through the refrigerator. "Hah, there it is," he exclaimed devilishly, "there's that corn beef sandwich I had the other day." He craned his head underneath his outstretched arms. "You want some, man?"

I shook my head. "No thanks. You go right ahead. That's a little too heavy on the stomach this late at night."

Will removed the sandwich along with a liter of Pepsi from the refrigerator. "Well, this brother is about to grub. I'm hungry as hell." He hooked a toe under the rung of a chair and sat down at the table where he began to peel away the aluminum foil from the sandwich.

I looked at him questioningly. "You ain't going to heat the shit up?"

"No way. The bread will turn all hard and crusty in the microwave." He lapped the sauces from his fingers.

I chuckled. "I don't see how you do it."

It's easy," he smiled, "just eat it. Besides, *cuz,* I didn't get a chance to eat dinner. You had me sittin' out there in the cold watchin' that damn restaurant. And what happens—the chick stands you up!" With that, he angled the sandwich and lit into it savagely.

Will's word left me groping for an explanation. I couldn't figure out what had happened. Unless she came in and saw me with Alvin Harris and his sister. That might have spooked her into turning away. I shrugged my shoulders then checked the time; it was almost one o'clock in the morning. I was tired and knew Will had to be the same. I rose from the table and smiled my relief and gratitude at him. The brother really did have my back. I patted him on the shoulder. "I'm about to get into the wind, man. I'll make sure to give you a call if anything comes up."

He nodded with an arched smile and a mouthful of corn beef. "Okay, man," he garbled around his food, "and next time, *you're* goin' wait in the fuckin' car."

"It's a deal, man." I gave him a mock salute and headed out the side door. I got into my rental car, thinking I would turn it back in first thing in the morning, and drove home. I threw my keys on the counter and flopped down on the sofa. I stretched out, however, somewhere in my mind, a thought came over me. I rose from the sofa and decided to check my voice mail. I picked up the phone and entered my code. I had eight messages.

The first six were former clients requesting my service. I chuckled then went on to the next one: it was Darling, saying she was terribly sorry for how the evening had ended up, and how she was going to make it up to me. I frowned, but held down my anger as I checked my last and final message. It was Regina. She was hysterical, crying uncontrollably, at times speaking totally incoherent. At one point she had finally settled down, at least to a point where I could make out what she was trying to say, and what she did managed to say made my heart stammer.

Through sobs and agonizing wails, she told me that Derrick Collins had been found murdered in his Range Rover, that his chest had been sliced open.

My mouth immediately went dry. For nearly a minute I stared blankly at nothing, which could have been attributed to shock or rage. *Could it have been her?* I wondered. *Watching me other day when I had confronted Derrick? When he pulled a gun on me?* Finally, when I came out of my trance, I heard a voice in my head, the tone emerged faint and thin and said distinctively, *I did it for us, baby...it was me...your Darling...your precious little Darling...*

Chapter 23

Even though it was three o'clock in the morning, taxis and trucks still crawled around us, irate drivers shouting and blowing horns. The light rain wasn't helping matters, either. And to add to the frustration, the street was heavy with steam coming up from the sewer grates and carrying all the pervasive stink of the city.

The building I wanted was two blocks down. As I came to a red light, I glanced over at Regina. She was so pale I thought, and her body was tight and rigid as a rolled carpet. Dressed in a light overcoat and wearing a plastic rain scarf over her head, she looked so lost. I reached out and placed my hand over hers. She'd hardly noticed my touch. I sighed and slowly withdrew my hand. The light turned green and I proceeded through the intersection. A moment later I pulled up to the City Morgue, which was faced with reddish-colored brick, giving it an air of solidity. I found a parking space and pulled in. I shut the car down and when I did, a silence fell over the interior.

This was it I felt. *Probably the hardest thing the girl would have to do.* The police could not find a next of kin. So they had turned to Regina. And now she was being asked to perform a horrific task. She had to identify the body of her boyfriend. I'd asked her earlier if she'd wanted me to accompany her but she had declined, saying this was something she wanted to do by her herself.

"You ready, girl?" I asked in a light whisper.

She looked at me with a tight mouth. "Yeah, I'm ready."

"You sure you don't want me to go with you?"

"No." Her tone was pleasant. "I'm okay with this." She reached a hand to my face and stroked it softly. "Really, I am."

I nodded then stepped out of the car to open her door. At first, she seemed hesitant, as if waiting execution, then slowly, moving as though rigor mortis was setting in, she slid out from the car. Giving me a weak smile, she said, "How do I look?"

"Beautiful," I replied, flipping up the collars of her overcoat against the rain.

She pulled back and I could see her face wilting. She placed her hands to my shoulders and said almost dutifully, "I've got to go, Terry. I got to do this. While…while I still can, you know?"

I took her hand. "I understand, and you take all the time you need, girl. I'll be out here waiting for you when you're done."

In response, she smiled. Then she turned and headed toward the building entrance. I watched as she disappeared through the sliding glass doors. I shook my head and then got back into my rental. I made a noise between my teeth that echoed inside the interior. I then felt my rage escalating, and though I sat back with my arms folded tightly, giving the impression that I could wring the throat of this mysterious woman, I found myself drifting into another direction. And in the moments to come, I could actually feel myself relaxing.

In fact, as time pressed on, the feeling of calmness was so strong I found myself smiling, as if the predicament I was going through was finally coming to an end.

I could only hope there wouldn't be anymore bloodshed.

But somehow, even with the tranquil feeling I was experiencing, I knew the capacity for disaster was just around the corner…probably watching me.

It was Sunday evening. I sat on the sofa quite still in my living room, sure that the slow passage of time was only my anxiety stretching the minutes into hours. Then I became aware of the mantel clock going off around me, then the telephone, which throbbed my nerves. I knew it was her.

I reached over and picked it up, and answered in a tired, haggard voice, "Yeah, who is it?"

"Good evening, baby," the voice emerged, sounding deep and sultry.

"Well, hello, Darling" —my tone wasn't exactly warm— "and how are you tonight?"

"Oh, I'm fine, and you, baby?"

"Oh, just dandy, just fine and dandy."

"You miss me?"

To my surprise, I didn't cringe. I felt ready to deal with this woman, feeling if I had already tripped her up once, I could do it again. "Of course, I miss you. And shame on you. I thought we were suppose to see each other last night?"

"Something came up. I do apologize, though. It was very rude on my part. I...I have no excuse for standing you up. Again, I apologize."

"Apology accepted. So tell me, what happened last night that was so demanding that you couldn't meet me?"

"Company came by unexpectedly, and sort of sprung a little surprise on me."

"Oh, I see," I commented in a conversational way, sounding a bit crushed, "your company is a little more important than you and I getting together, huh?"

"That's not true, baby!" she replied pleadingly. She took a deep breath to steady herself. "It's just that something came up that I had no control over, okay? Can we move on here?"

I started to protest, just for the hell of it, but changed my mind. "So, are we going to reschedule or what?"

"But of course," she giggled. "What day do you want to meet?"

I was shocked. "What? Did I hear you right? Are you letting *me* decide the date?"

She chuckled. "Only the day, baby. I'm not that stupid."

I chuckled myself, thinking she was so right. I shifted on the sofa. "What about tomorrow?"

"Not good. Besides, who parties on a Monday night?"

"So, you like to party, eh?"

"Oh, *yeah!* Hard and all night long, baby! Just like I want you to do me in bed—*hard and all night long! Shit, yeah!*"

"Mmm, sounds nice. Where do you usually go?"

"Last night I went to Oasis," she swooned. "We had a good old time."

"We?" I sat up on the sofa.

"Yeah...a friend of mine."

"Was it a guy?"

"And you know *this*, baby!" she retorted with a loud giggle. "I don't hang out with women, they're too conniving. All they want to do is steal your man."

"So, you and this guy you were with, you guys kickin' it?"

She giggled once more, only softer. "You mean, are we fucking?"

"Yeah, for a better choice of words."

"Heavens, no!" she laughed. "It's not the kind of relationship."

"Oh, I see, you and this guy are just buddy-buddy?"

"Yeah, we are. He's helped me through some very...difficult times. When I wasn't in the right frame of mind, so to say."

I leaned back on the sofa. "Care to talk about it?"

"No." Her tone was harsh.

"All right," I agreed, sounding sympathetic, "I didn't mean to open old wounds."

"And that's exactly what it is...*old* wounds...things that happened in the past."

"Listen," I suggested cheerfully, "you sound a bit upset. Why don't you pour yourself a glass of wine or something? I can wait until you do."

"No, I'm fine, and thank you for being so considerate."

"Hey, it's what I'm here for." I rolled my eyes in my head.

"Thank you again." She hesitated then said in a tone of kind mirth, "I'm proud of you, Terry."

"Proud of me? For what?" I had a hard time keeping my confusion under control. "What did I do?"

"You've proved yourself worthy in a couple of ways. You've been keeping your word, and you handled your business professionally."

Her response was complex; I had a difficult time following her. "Care to elaborate?"

"Let's just say, you've been a good boy. A very good boy. And I'm very impressed. I couldn't have done better."

For some reason, her response brought a strain to my face. Slowly, I made the tight lines on my face relax. I shook my head. "You're just one big mystery after another, aren't you, Darling?"

"Yes, I guess you can say that." She chuckled lightly. "Yes, that's what I am, Terry...one big, delightful mystery...waiting for you to come and get me."

My heart twisted. "When will that be?"

"Whenever you set a decent day, silly boy."

I thought on it. "What about this Thursday?"

She paused then said, "Now that'll work for me. I'll call you with the time, okay?"

"Sure. That sounds great."

With that, her voice dipped low and saucy, "Now that we've gotten that out of the way, tell me something, baby, what the hell are you wearing?"

A pained smile made my mouth crooked. *Not this shit again* I heard myself saying. The woman had a one-track mind. I decided to have myself a little fun. "At the moment I wearing my old tattered bathrobe, my flannel pajamas, and my thick sweat socks."

"Why in the hell do you have all that crap on?" she protested.

"I'm cold," I whined pitifully. "I think I'm coming down with something." I brought a balled fist to my mouth and coughed to heightened the effects.

"Oh," she said dryly, in misery and disappointment. "Well, listen, you take care of that thing before Thursday, okay? I don't want you all germy when I see you. Look, I've got to run now, I'll be talking to you later. You have a goodnight—and take care of that bug, you hear me?" She hung up and shortly afterwards, I heard a dial tone.

I laughed inwardly. The woman didn't have much time to adjust to the situation; the mere mention of me having a cold turned her off instantly. I hung the phone up and as I did, I wished the conversation hadn't ended so abruptly. There were so many things I wanted to ask this loony woman. Derrick Collins being number one on my list. But I figured she would tell me, eventually. But there was something else I wanted to find out from her: what did she mean when she'd said, "I'm proud of you."

What in the hell did I do? I wondered.

For the life of me I couldn't figure it out.

And that scared the hell out of me.

Early the next morning, having tossed and turned through a few hours of spotty, restless sleep, I woke up with the kind of headache that could make a die-hard alcoholic swear off drinking. Internal pressure seemed to be prying the bones of my skull apart, and my brain felt bruised. In addition, I felt listless, and my stomach gave the impression that it was sloshing something wet and heavy from side to side. I brought a hand to my forehead. *Hell, maybe I WAS really sick?*

As I climbed out of my bed, I didn't think so. I mean, I was as hungry as a bear. I went into the bathroom and took a long piss, closing my eyes and hoping my aim was good. It was. I rinsed my hands then brushed my teeth. I decided to take a shave. I grabbed a can of shaving cream from the medicine cabinet and worked up a faceful of lather. Seeing my image in the mirror startled me a bit, as I suddenly realized how haggard I'd become, how much my appearance had changed since the mysterious woman's entrance into my life. However, I wasn't worried. I still looked damn good. Still, later today, I'd head over to the barber shop and get my hair edged up, but for now removing the remnants of five o'clock shadow would have to do.

As I shaved, I thought about the day ahead of me and my hand tensed. A drop of crimson appeared on my chin, bright against the white leather, and I cursed as I saw it. I dabbed the cut with a damp hand towel then stuck a scrap of toilet tissue on it and then went on shaving, still thinking about the day ahead of me. That's when it hit me. I had nothing to do. Not a damn thing. I went through my list of possibilities: *Will was probably dead sleep and in all likelihood through for the day until it was time for him to go to work. Regina was most likely grieving and to tell you the truth, I couldn't deal with that kind of thing, at least not today, anyway.*

Unconsciously I rubbed my chin, really engrossed in my thinking, and getting lather over the tips of my fingers. *Today was Monday so my mother was probably taking her stroll with Mister Carter and wouldn't be back until late afternoon. So what was I to do?* I thought about calling Vera, but quickly decided against it. I didn't feel like picking up any more new clothes—I'd probably never wear all the ones I had, and I didn't feel like kicking it with the few good friends I had left. And I definitely didn't feel like working out at the gym.

Sort of in a trance, I stared in the mirror. *Mister Terry Allens,* I then smiled, *you, my friend, have got to get yourself a life!* I continued removing the stubble from my face and came to the painful conclusion that there was nothing to my existence. It seemed that, like a Boeing 747 approaching Metro Airport, my life, since I'd stopped *living in the life*, was going into a "holding pattern". Although I knew I had the talent as well as the desire to do something else with my life, it seemed as if I didn't know how to make that all-important transition into the "real world".

Rinsing the hand-razor, I began to worry about my future. I was twenty-six and wasn't part of anything concrete, normal stuff like pension plans, paid vacations, 401k's, things of that nature. And that's what I wanted. To be a part of society on a much higher, productive scale. To hold down a real meaningful, rewarding, good-paying job.

Which posed a problem.

My past could somehow resurface at my workplace and haunt me big time, causing further anguish in my life. I could almost see it now, the many scurrilous jokes and rumors being circulated at my expense, eventually all of them dutifully reported to my superiors. And then, when I would be addressed about these accusations, one of two things would most likely happen: I'd be terminated or find myself banging the people around me. And I didn't want to experience either of these things; it would mean failure, no matter how many different ways you sliced it.

So what was a brother to do? I wondered.

I pulled roughly on my face. Maybe I should have waited a little longer before opting out of the life? I smiled as it hit me, an old saying my mother used to tell me, "Don't throw out dirty water until you've found clean!" *She was right* I chuckled. *Hell, for that matter, she always is.* But I knew even if I were free of this mysterious woman, I wouldn't return to my old ways. I wanted to go forward, not backward. I wanted to try something new, using my brains this time.

The thought of trying something new made me think of Alvin Harris and his offer of employment. I wondered if this was just a ploy to get me to stroke him on the sly, or was the man really being sincere as he came across the other night. I thought about it and felt he was. I mean, if the man wanted to be beat down, I'm sure I wasn't the only stud available at his disposal. I shook my head and then rinsed my face. I stared into the mirror. Other than the minor cut on my chin, it was a pretty decent shave, and I had to admit, I looked good, still vibrant and youthful. It was at that moment when I decided I would give Alvin Harris' offer a shot. I went over to my dresser and picked up his business card. I gave him a call and he said for me to come to his office around three o' clock this afternoon.

As I hung up the phone I found a huge, beaming smile scrawled on my face. No matter how professional Alvin Harris came across, the man still made it clear, even though it was done ever-so-subtly, that he wanted another roll in the hay. And because of this, as I stripped out of my silk boxers, I felt invincible, and a tad bit cocky. It was that old feeling coming on. I couldn't help it. I suddenly felt with my looks, and the jimmie swinging back and forth between my legs as I climbed into the shower, I could do just about anything...have just about anybody, man or woman...if I so desired.

The building was one of the smaller ones on South Woodward Avenue, but nevertheless, it was still exceptional, black glass and modern, exuding class and tradition, not to mention, money. Wearing a dark brown London Fog top coat over a tan two-piece suit, I stepped through the thick glass doors. There was a security/information station in the middle of the lobby. I told the attendant, a stocky man swelling around the chest and shoulders, who I was and the reason for my visit. Afterwards he picked up his phone and spoke into it. I noticed he was wearing a sand-colored jacket and a green tie. I remembered the same outfit on another security attendant when I had first went to see Alvin Harris at his home; evidently he decorated his staff at his place of business, as well. But I noticed this guy didn't have a gun or even a club, for that matter. I guess there wasn't a real need for either.

When the attendant put the phone down, he said, "Mister Harris will see you now. Take the elevator to the ninth floor, if you will, please. When you get come to the ninth floor, walk straight until you reach the reception area. From that point, Mister Harris' secretary will instruct you from there."

I looked at the attendant and smiled. "The man is guarded tighter than the president."

The attendant smiled back, though tightly. "We like to think he is, anyway."

I nodded kindly and took the elevator to the ninth floor. The doors opened and I walked in the direction the attendant had given me, which was the only way for me to go, down a short hallway. My footwear made no sound in the ankle-deep gray carpeting as I made my way to the reception area. I opened the door and went inside.

Alvin Harris and a woman, small and dark with horn-rimmed glasses and dressed impeccably, who I assumed was his secretary, were standing at the windows, carrying on an animated discussion. At least Alvin Harris was animated; the woman seemed serious, wearing a preoccupied frown, hanging onto his every word. In either case both appeared to be engrossed in the discussion. They didn't notice me. I cleared my throat and that's when both turned. Their eyes became fixed on me, and I had to admit I felt a bit intimidated, standing there as if I'd been slugged in the stomach. Alvin Harris smiled hard and introduced me to his secretary. Her eyes narrowed, not liking my presence, but uncertain how to take me. I could have sworn I'd seen a muscle cording along her jaw. After the brief introductions, Alvin Harris gestured me inside his office.

I nodded then walked pass his secretary, who threw me a glare that could have split a wooden log. Apparently I was treading on her turf. I stepped inside the office and looked around. The office was laid to the bone, from the thick, heavy furniture, to the automated Venetian blinds, down to the white-piled carpet—even the computer off to the side was laid, trimmed in what looked like real wood grain, situated inside a custom built wall unit. The office was huge and spacious, and because it was on the top and final floor, the ceiling soared, with paintings of all shapes and sizes lining the walls. A few I could recognize, but the majority of them were beyond me, looking as if some maniac had gone loco and heaved buckets of paint on the canvas. But regardless of how the paintings looked, I knew for a fact they cost a fortune; the man who sat in this office didn't appear to be the kind of individual who skimped when it came to the furnishings.

Hiking up the trousers to his dove-gray suit, which fitted him to a tee, Alvin Harris took a seat at his enormous desk and settled back in a well-padded leather chair. "Have a seat, Terry. I'm really delighted to see you."

I removed my top coat and took a seat in a wide winged-back chair in front of the desk. As I did, a quickness of tension came over me; but my distress receded. I figured the man was just glad to help me out, and nothing else. "Thank you for seeing me on such short notice, Mister Harris," I said while shifting in the chair. "I know you're a very busy man."

He smiled and held it. "No problem, none at all. In fact," he went on smoothly, "things have been a little slow around here, especially when you consider it's Monday, the busiest day of the week for my business."

"Why is that?" I asked, crossing my legs.

He studied me for a moment, as if gauging my question and rating it. I guess I must have scored high because his words broke like a dam, "My business consists of mainly real estate, both residential and commercial. The majority of my prospecting clients do their scouting over the weekend so on Monday my staff is really on the move, answering telephones, showing property, closing deals. More than half of my net worth comes from a Monday's transaction."

"I see." I hunched forward in my seat. "The real estate business, as a whole, is it as profitable as the experts claim it is?"

"Very much so," he said in an incisive voice, his jaw jutting. "You can make a lot of money in the business, a whole lot, but on the other hand you can lose the shirt off your back. There are a lot of driving factors which can determine this: the market, the economy, interest rates, your available inventory, all these things are key factors in the real estate game. But a smart and well-trained agent can usually overcome all of these pitfalls, and make a ton of money in commissions."

"Is that right?" I sucked in my cheeks, giving serious consideration to what I'd just heard.

Alvin Harris must have caught the drifting expression on my face. He tapped a fingernail on the half-inch glass top which covered the entire surface of his desk. He raised an eyebrow and said, "You could do extremely well in this business, Terry. With your looks and charisma, not to mention that killer smile of yours, and a little bit of training and P.R. behind you, you could be very well off in about three years or so. I'm talking middle to upper six-digit figures here."

With that, I stared at him, at a loss for words. Then I said, "You really think I could do this?"

Slowly, he leaned forward and nodded his head; his eyes met and held mine. "Yes, I do. I think you are eminently qualified, and because of this, I would like for you to be part of my winning team."

He settled back in his chair and laced his fingers together. "What do you say, Mister Allens? Ready to make a living the honest way?"

I found myself gazing at Alvin Harris as though his face was on fire. The boldness and the possibilities of what he proposed threw me for a loop. At the moment I was trying to fight for a way that made my voice sound unaffected. The man was no joke, that much was for sure. The visit to his home told me that.

"I can have you in the next training session at the first of the month," he put in promptly, "and after a standard probationary period, I can turn you loose on the world, even set you up with some of my key agents who could show you the ins and outs, the loopholes, if you will. The rest, however, is up to you." Finishing, he watched me closely, sensing anticipation within me, a whetted enthusiasm, a will in me that was bursting at the seams.

And he was right.

I did feel this—all of it.

I sat up in my seat and said calmly, "All right, Mister Harris, since you believe in me so strongly, how can I say no. Besides, I'd be a fool not to accept your offer. And I'm willing to give it a try." I caught myself. "What I meant to say was, I'll give it my *best* shot."

Slapping his palms on the desk, he beamed, "Excellent move on your part, Terry! You'll see, you're going to make your mark on the world!"

I rose to my feet and extended my hand. "I hope so, Mister Harris, I really would like that."

He shook my hand firmly, as usual, and then said privately, "Keep your nose clean and make the company some money and I can turn you on to some pretty important players out there, Terry. People who have ties in nearly any and everything. I'm talking bank presidents, restaurant owners, jewelers, furniture and clothing retailers, automotive dealership owners, you name it. Hell, I just turned a sweet deal on a foreign number a couple of months ago from one of the automobile dealers I'm connected with—practically stole it for a song and a dance over lunch. I ended up giving it to Denise. Hell, I didn't really need it—but the offer was so good I couldn't turn it down. See what I'm talking about? This is the kind of things you can have at your disposal."

I smiled hard, almost uncontrollably. It all sounded so great; I'd love to have that kind of advantage. "Thank you very much, Mister Harris," I said, extending my hand and shaking his once more. "I won't let you down, sir."

"I'm sure you won't." At that he paused, and looked dead into my eyes. "Let me say this for the record, Terry. This offer comes with no strings attached. My relationship with you will be a purely professional one. You do well in the field, you make the company a lot of money, I'm happy. You don't—you're out. Plain and simple. I'm a fair man, Terry. I'll willing to work with you but not for you, understand what I'm saying here?"

I slanted my eyes to show seriousness. "I do, and I can respect your position on things. And let me say this for the record, Mister Harris: I intend to do the very best I can."

"I'm sure you will, Terry. I have no doubts." He walked around the desk. "I'll have my secretary give you a call and maybe have you come in next week so you can go over our benefit package as well as our incentive program. I'm sure you'll find both pleasing to the palate."

"Sounds like a winner." I checked my Rolex for the time. "Listen, I won't keep you any longer, Mister Harris, I know you have things to tend to." I shook his hand a final time and headed for the door.

As I reached for the brass handle Alvin Harris stopped me in lighthearted voice. He then walked around his desk and removed a yellow Kodak mailer envelope from his desk drawer. He pulled a stack of pictures from the envelope, saying that these had been taken the other night with his .35mm camera. He handed me the pictures. I thumbed through them. A lot of the shots were of him and his sister. The shots were nice; I complimented him on the exceptional job he and his camera had done. There was also a shot of me in one of the photos. It was the group shot with me standing with Alvin Harris and his sister while at Pozanno's. Again I complimented him on the pictures and surprisingly, he gave me one, the group shot.

Thanking him one last time, I placed the photo inside my overcoat pocket and left the office. Twenty minutes later I was back behind my Benz-o—cutting down the expressway and feeling great! In spite of the negative shit happening in my life, I was beginning to see a positive side of things. And despite the mysterious woman who lurked in the shadows of my mind, I felt a great sense of relief. I felt my life turning around!

Feeling this surge of immense pleasure coursing through my veins, I decided to stop by my mother's place. At times like this, there's no better place I could think of that I wanted to be. But first, since my mother loved pizza, I'd stop at her favorite pizza joint and get her the fattest, greasiest pizza they could make—with all the toppings! With all the Pepsi the beautiful woman could guzzle, too! I thought about seeing my mother and this did nothing but make me even more elated. Me and Moms were going to have a good old time—throwing down on pizza and guzzling pop! What could be better!

I tromped on the accelerator, exceeding the speed limit by nearly twenty miles, zooming by the mild traffic at breakneck speed. *Let a trooper even dare and try to stop me!* I grinned. *He'd never catch me, and if he did—who gives a shit!*

At this moment I was feeling great. Today, I'd found a little bit of peace...especially with my inner self...and there was no better feeling in the world.

I drove even faster.

The pizza had everything on it: pepperoni, mushrooms, Italian sausage, onions, peppers, and some other stuff I didn't recognize. I handed my mother a thick slice and picked up a stringy slice for myself and bit into it, finding it hot and delicious.

"Ground beef," my mother said, smacking her mouth, "you forgot to get ground beef."

"I didn't forget, Mom," I smiled. "I just figured you'd want something to fuss about."

We sat in my mother's kitchen and it was nice. It had been a while since I had really sat down and ate with her. She was truly special I thought, looking at her as she wiped her mouth, sitting in her pink and white duster. She was always there for me, and now that she had lost a step or two, I'd be there for her, thinking it was time for her to prop her feet up and let me do all the work.

She deserved it.

I chuckled to myself as I watched her. The little five-foot, round-faced woman could drive me crazy at times, running me here and there whenever a whim hit her, always nagging me about settling down and marrying a beautiful black woman, and giving her lots of grand kids. *Lots* of them. She would mention this so many times, I had to think she was serious.

Normally when she started in on me about me settling down and getting married, I would curb her mercenary tactics by ribbing her back, teasing her good-naturedly about Mister Carter being her secret love interest. She'd laugh and tell me she had no desires for that old man, saying he was too settled for her wild ways. She was a real character at times, and I really loved her, cherished the ground she walked on. She was my hero and mentor, my everything…my Black Pearl.

"So, did you and Mister Carter walk today?" I asked before taking another bite of pizza.

"Yeah," she said, glancing over the pizza and wiggling her fingers, searching for the perfect slice, "I took him for his daily stroll. As usual, I got him out to get some fresh air and let him do his business."

I shook my head. "You make him sound as though he were a pet or something."

She glanced into the air with a sly smirk on her mouth. "I guess, in a way, he is, an old Saint Bernard, drooping eyes and all." With that, she turned her attention back to more important matters—food.

I stared at her, loving everything about her. "You need some money, Mom?" I asked.

She shook her head. "But I'll tell you what I would like, if you wouldn't mind?"

I rolled my eyes. "What is it this time, Mom? Run to the post office? Get your groceries? Buy you some new furniture?"

"No, it's none of those things," she said, her voice thick with sarcasm, "I just need you to pick up something from the restaurant for me tomorrow."

"And what is it *this* time?" I propped both my elbows on the table and rested my chin in my palms. "Chicken? A subway sub-sandwich? A catfish dinner? Another pizza? Some new and improved burger?"

"What's that suppose to mean, boy?" she whispered, cutting her eyes at me and trying to suppress a smile.

"Nothing," I grinned, rearing back with my palms in the air. "I didn't mean nothing."

"Okay," she snapped, "don't let me have to exalt my authority around here." Her eyes then went wild as she hunched forward. "Tomorrow, if you can, I want you to pick up the new mozzarella deluxe at Arby's—it's a ham and cheese sandwich dipped in egg batter and deep-fried."

"I see." I gave her a long, leering look. "Sounds fattening, Mom."

"Of course, it's fattening," she retorted, "it can't be good if it's not fattening! It's probably loaded with earth-shaking calories! And I bet after one bite—*boom*, it appears on your hips and butt seconds later." Her eyes danced back and forth in her head. "I want one, Terry! As a matter of fact—right now!" She then went into her pitiful act, wilting her brown eyes at me. "Can you go get me one, baby? Please? For your old gray-haired mother?"

Sucking my teeth loudly, I just stared at her, then I closed my eyes and shook my head. *The woman was a pro* I thought. I shrugged my shoulders and rose from the chair. "Okay, Mom," I sighed tiredly. "You need anything else while I'm out?"

"No, baby," she smiled sweetly. "That's all."

I threw her a kiss and turned to grab my top coat. As I jostled the coat in my arms something fell to the floor. It was the group picture Alvin Harris had given me.

Like radar, my mother honed in on the picture and squealed, "Ooo, lemme see. Is it a picture of your girlfriend?"

"No, it's just a shot of me and a couple of friends I'd met this past Saturday night, nothing big." I wiped the picture off on my pant leg and gave it to her.

Eagerly, she glanced over the picture. "Oh, look at my baby," she chanted pleasingly. "You look so handsome and sharp in your suit." She looked up at me. "Who's the other guy in this picture, he's very handsome, too? Not as handsome as you are, but he's still quite handsome, though."

After shrugging my top coat in place, I walked over to my mother and peered over her shoulder. "That, my beautiful and demanding mother, is Alvin Harris. He's quite an icon in the real estate world, and that's his sister standing next to him."

At that, my mother nodded her head knowingly. "Yeah, I've seen her before. That's the census taker that came to my apartment a few weeks ago."

Almost immediately I felt an internal chill, and my heart stopped. Then it began to beat in my throat as though it would erupt from my chest. I looked at my mother as if she had uttered something obscene, and found myself gaping almost right through her. I took a deep breath. "Who...who did you say this woman was, Mom?"

She looked up at me lovingly. "That's the census woman, baby. You know, I told you about her stopping by and having tea and cookies with me, don't you remember?" She smiled and looked so innocent, the picture of calm.

In contrast, I flung my head back as if someone had slapped my face raw, and my eyes flared. Slowly, my voice under rigid control, I said, "Are you sure it's her, Mom? I mean, are you dead sure it's her?"

She glanced over the picture and then turned back to me. "I'm positive, baby. That's her. She's really beautiful, isn't she?" She looked at me closely. Slightly unraveled she brought a palm to my face. "Terry, baby, you okay? Suddenly you don't look so well." Sensing that something was definitely wrong, she took my pulse and felt my forehead. "You feeling all right?"

I didn't want to answer. Speaking would reveal the tumultuous emotions going on in my body, in my head. With all the sincerity I could muster I kissed my mother on the cheek. Inhaling and letting the air out, I said, "I've got to go, Mom. Listen, I'll...I'll pick up your sandwich tomorrow, okay?"

She looked at me strangely. "Terry, are you—"

"I'm okay, Mom." Though my dazed eyes probably stated otherwise. I could tell she wasn't buying it, either. I had to ease her mind, if nothing else. "Hey." My voice was soft, warm with affection. I gently ran a finger along the underside of her jaw to the point of her chin and lifted it a fraction. "I'm all right." With an extreme effort, I forced myself to sound good-humored and smiled, "You save me some of this pizza, okay? And save me a few of the good pieces, not the scrubby little ones, all right?" Once more I leaned over and kissed her cheek. I turned and opened the door. I gave my mother a warm smile.

It was hard to do this.

Extremely hard.

I stepped out into the hallway and closed the door. I locked it. An instant later, I tried to recollect myself as I made my way down the hallway. I had to. There were a few senior citizens who knew me by name and they smiled brightly as I approached them. Once again, I tried to smile. Now, however, I felt like a man bravely suppressing an impulse to throw up. I couldn't believe what was happening in my life.

In a state of pronounced awkwardness, despite long strides, I made my way to my car. At the same time, a trickle of foreboding sluiced down my spine. I felt my eyes growing small and hard with spite. I fumed like an enraged bull. Yet, deep down, there was fear, and it tasted like bile at the back of my throat.

Chapter 24

It was five forty-five in the afternoon, and as I paced the living room furiously, my mind was in high gear. I had paged Will and had been waiting for over an hour for his reply. I knew he was at work but I needed to talk with him—pronto! I had a plan I wanted to share with him and I wanted to share it while it was still fresh in my mind. I turned and stared at the phone. I'd give Will another fifteen minutes, I thought wearily, and then I'm giving up. I paced the floor once again.

Normally my cool would have outlasted my discomfort, but this was not the sort of thing that usually came up. *The mysterious woman was Alvin Harris' sister!* I heard myself saying over and over again. *She was a killer! A cold-blooded, sick-ass killer! First Mel Armstrong then Derrick Collins! Who was next on her list!*

At that, my body suddenly became electrified as my heart leaped in my chest. I stared wide-eyed as panic fused my feet right on the spot. *My mother!* I thought, fright making my body tremble. *She might go after her!* Then my heart leaped again. *Will! She might go after him, as well!*

In my haste, and with anxiety coursing through my veins, I hadn't given thought to the well-being of the two most precious people in my life; in the grand scheme of my planning I had almost overlooked them.

"Goddammit!" I cursed, frustrated, but determined to solve my dilemma.

In the background, the telephone began to ring. I turned for a moment and stared at it. The air around me suddenly seemed to bear down on me, making it hard for me to breathe. Then I thought, *not yet. Denise normally doesn't call this early.* I walked over to the phone and picked it up. It was Will.

"Will," I said coolly, "I hate to bug you on the job but I just had to talk to you, man. You got a minute?"

"I think I do, cuz." He laughed brusquely. "Our line just went down and judging by the look of things, we may not start up for at least a few hours. Sorry I couldn't get back to you sooner. So tell me, cuz, what's so important you had to page me at work?"

I swallowed nervously and my heart thumped wildly in my chest, and I was a bit shocked by this reaction. Nevertheless I took a deep breath and said in a voice that was crisp and all business, "I think I know who the mysterious woman is. The cards have finally tipped in my favor."

Will hesitated for a second. "Well, who the hell is it?"

My mouth tightened. "You don't know her, but believe it or not, she was at Pozanno's the other night with her brother, Alvin Harris. Her name is Denise."

"No shit," Will breathed in astonishment. "You sure it's her, man?"

I nodded, sure of myself. "Yeah. Nearly a hundred percent."

"How did you find this out? Did you spot her tailing you or something?"

Pressure in my chest made me draw a shuddering breath as I said, "No. Moms actually told me who it was."

"Your mom!" Will shot back. "What...?"

"Yeah, I know." I smoothed a palm over my face as I tried to explain, feeling anger building up inside me, "I took a picture with Denise and Alvin at the restaurant and showed it to my mother. Moms said Denise was the same woman who was at her apartment impersonating the census taker."

"You've got to be shittin', man," Will said, totally shocked.

"I wish I was." My fist bunched, and my anger rose even higher. "And check this out," I went on darkly, "remember the jaguar in the picture?"

"Yeah?" Will murmured lightly.

"I remember where I saw it...it was at Alvin Harris' house, parked in the front. The taxi dropped me off right next to it."

Will went silent then rasped, "Damn, cuz, it *is* her. It is that bitch."

My face blank, I replied, "Yeah, it is." I gripped the phone tighter. "Listen, cousin, I got a plan in my head but I need to ask a big favor of you, and I'm afraid it's a pretty big one, too."

"Shoot, I'll back you anyway I can."

Will had said this without hesitation, and that made me feel good. I felt a swelling of love and respect for the man. I cast a thoughtful glance at the receiver in my hand, sort of in a trance. I quickly got my emotions together and said, "So tell me, cousin, can you get some time away from work, like a leave of absence, maybe?"

Slowly, questionably, Will said, "Yeah, I guess I could. I mean, it'll probably be without pay."

I immediately shot back, "Don't worry about the money, cousin, I'll spot you for any time missed—plus any overtime. You know I got the ends to back what I say."

He whistled under his breath. *"Damn*, man, what you got up?"

My voice was studiously neutral. "I need you to take my mother on a vacation, some place out of state where it's nice and warm. Perhaps Florida or maybe even the Bahamas. The point is, I want it to *appear* to be a vacation, for my mother's sake, you follow me?"

"Yeah, I follow you."

I smiled then took a seat on the sofa, feeling my plan coming into play. "I'll foot the tab on everything for you, my mother and even Angela, that is if you want to bring her along. I'm talking all expenses here—airfare, hotel, spending money—*everything*. I just got some things to bring to a head and I need to know that my mother is in good hands, away from any repercussions. You know what I'm saying, cousin?"

There was a pause, then Will said, "Yeah...I feel you, man." He blew out a long sigh afterwards.

At that I clenched my teeth. Will seemed to be in agreement, but his tone appeared distracted, as if he weren't all that pleased about leaving me alone to deal with my predicament, as if he were somehow abandoning me. Trying to take the edge of the situation, I said humorously, "It'll only be for a week, so don't you even think about runnin' up a tab on me, playa." My voice then turned serious. "And while you're keeping an eye on my mother, I'll keep you abreast on everything happening back on the home-front. I'll call you every night, religiously." I crossed my fingers and hoped that Will would go for it. And I also hoped he hadn't seen what I was really trying to do: kill two birds with one stone—getting *him* as well as my mother out of the picture.

After thinking about it for a moment or two, he finally said reluctantly, "Okay. I'll do it. As long as you call me *every fuckin' night*." His voice was hard and carried its might strongly.

All I could do was smile. "It's a deal." I hunched forward on the sofa. "I know all of this is kind of sudden, but can you be ready to leave by this Thursday?"

In spite of the situation surrounding me, Will chuckled, "Shit, yeah. Man, I can be to ready to book up from this place tomorrow if you want me to. Just say the word."

I chuckled back. "Slow your roll, cousin, this Thursday is just fine. You can leave anytime you'd like. That'll give you time, my mother time, and Angela time, that is if you were planning on taking Angela?" I raised my brow. "You are planning on taking her, aren't you?"

In a low, leering voice, he said, "I guess so. I mean, it could get lonely over there. And plus, we're talkin' *a week*. And the worst thing for a brother is to be horny in the Bahamas, especially on a beautiful night, and especially when he's thinking about his woman. And the last thing I want to do is jack-off under the stars thinking about the woman I'd left behind."

I had to laugh. Will made no effort at concealing what was on his mind. "So, I take it you got the Bahamas in mind, huh?"

He laughed back. "Hey, you said it, not me. Hell, we can all go to Aruba if you're footing the bill!"

In a small chuckle, I replied, "No, the Bahamas sounds nice."

Will laughed and made a few other suggestions, then a second later, turned serious. "So what you got up, cuz?"

I paused, pulling my plan together in my head. When I finally did, I gripped the phone tighter and told Will what I'd had in mind. He'd agreed that it just might work; I was sure it would. But nevertheless, deep inside, I'd hoped like hell it wasn't going to back fire on me.

The consequences could cost me my life.

Chapter 25

On Thursday morning, Will, my mother, and Angela caught the 9:40 flight out of Metro Airport to Fort Lauderdale Florida. It was tough watching them leave, and as I drove back to my apartment, my mind was a dark swirl of imagery, a melting landscape of things around me. It was as if the world was slowly coming to an end, like the last flickering frames of an old movie reel. On top of this unpleasant, dismal mix of emotion, my stomach felt like a washer full of softballs stuck in the agitation cycle. I clutched the steering wheel and gave it a gentle squeeze. I hoped that my plan would work, and that Alvin Harris didn't cancel on meeting me this evening at his place.

This was extremely crucial in the scheme of things.

An hour later after filling my gas tank and grabbing a newspaper, I was back in my apartment. In the process of fixing myself a light breakfast of coffee and buttered toast, I couldn't help but feel how eerie and vacant the apartment seemed with my mother being out of town. *Hollowness* was a word that came to mind. The entirety of the apartment, even me, for that matter, seemed empty.

During my four and a half year stint in my place, I had grown accustomed to a certain way of living. There was a sense of warmth and belonging here. Now I was surprised to find myself wanting to leave this place as soon as the opportunity presented itself. I finished my breakfast and tried to read the newspaper, but found I couldn't. The apartment hung too heavy with despair. It felt like a wet trench coat thrown about my shoulders. I needed to get out for a while, to ease my mind and to get some fresh air, so I decided to do just that. As I turned and headed for the door, my phone began to ring.

I stared at it, feeling a strange sensation coming over me.

I walked over to the phone and picked it up.

It was Denise.

"Well, hello, Darling," I announced charmingly, "and how are you this morning?"

"What the hell do you think you're doing?" she demanded.

I was taken aback, first by the early call and then by the tone in her voice. "What do you mean?"

She drew a harsh breath. "Your mother, and your cousin, and some other bitch, where the fuck are they headed?"

For a moment, I stared straight ahead. Then with an urgency which even surprised me, I said, "They're going to a funeral. My uncle George, my mother's brother, passed away a few days ago. He died of a massive stroke." I found myself holding my breath, clamping myself rigid to restrain what I felt, praying that she would buy it.

"Is that right?" Her voice had risen to a pitch of doubtfulness. "You sure you're not trying to pull some fast shit on me, nigga?"

Unable to sustain the way I felt—even if it *were* a lie—I gripped the phone tightly, then—more abruptly than I had intended—I said, "Yes! And I wish you would show a little respect for what I'm going through! You're always talking about me being a little crass and inconsiderate, well, at the moment, I think you're the one who's doing just that! Instead of coming down on me, I'd appreciate a little compassion!" I released my grip on the phone and shifted my eyes back and forth, thinking I was really becoming good at deception in the last month or so. I held my breath as I waited nervously for a response.

Slowly, I guess taking it all in and sorting it out in her head, she said, with a note of sadness entering her voice, "I apologize, baby. Maybe I did fly off the handle a bit too soon. It's just that...we're so close to coming together, and I don't want anything to upset this, you know?"

By degrees, I released the air from my lungs. "I understand." Then I said in a verbal shrug, "And I accept your apology. Sometimes things are said unjustly in the heat of the moment." My tone was soft and reassuring.

"Thank you, Terry." She sighed heavily. "We still on for this evening?"

"Of course. You're going to call me tonight?"

"Yes. How does seven sound?"

"Great. I'll look for your call then." I'd said this in a hurried tone.

"You gotta go?"

"Yeah," I said sadly. "I've got to clear my mind...you know, with my uncle's death and all."

With that, she gave me her condolences and hung up the phone without another word. Apparently, even with her deranged mind, she had recognized that something important had happened in my life— something that required privacy. When I realized this I placed the phone back on the wall. I turned and gazed out the window, thinking today was such a beautiful day, the sun shining brightly and the colors of the trees bursting vividly. I found myself frowning, though vaguely—not as if I weren't appreciative of the day, but rather as if wondering what the night had held in store for me. I hoped that tonight would be the night when things finally came to a head, once and for all.

I was tired.

I was also pissed.

I shut my eyes and shook my head. Then slowly, unconsciously, my hands closed into a fist. *Tonight would be the night!* I heard myself shouting, protested decisively. *Tonight, dammit! Tonight would be the night!* I opened my eyes and stared out the kitchen window. *Tonight...*I nodded...*tonight would be the night...it had to be.*

I looked at the clock in the living room as the telephone began to ring. It was six fifty-nine. Shortly afterwards the clock gonged that is was straight-up seven. It was showtime I thought to myself.

I picked up the phone and then flopped out on the sofa, crossing my legs on the ankles. I brought the phone to my mouth. "Hello."

Good evening, Terry," the familiar voice announced. "And how are you doing tonight?"

I grimaced, then fell into a wry grin. "I'm fine. Just getting myself together. Got to look good, you know what I mean?"

"Yes, I do," she whispered low and sultry. "And I can really appreciate a man who looks his best for his woman-to-be, especially when it's their first date."

I took a deep breath, thinking *this was it. The time had come to play my hand. It was now or never.* Exhaling slowly, I closed my eyes and shifted on the sofa. When I figured I'd found my spot, I said boldly, "I'm not meeting with you tonight, Darling. I've made other plans, and unfortunately they don't involve you."

At that, she giggled that silly-ass giggle I had grown to hate so terribly, and it was loud and boisterous, too, full of shrill. She apparently found this notion both humorous and ludicrous. When she settled down she said, "What the hell do you mean, *you've made other plans?* We have a date, goddammit. You gave me your word."

Moistening my lips and leaning back into the folds of the sofa, I said, "On the contrary, we *had* a date. All that has been changed. It seems that I've found a more promising prospect to spend the evening with, maybe even two. So I'm afraid I'm going to have to cancel. But we can reschedule, if you'd like? How does next Thursday sound? I can pencil you in right now while that day is free?"

Slowly, she replied, "What the fuck is going on here, Terry? Who done slipped a hair up your ass, huh? What the fuck is this?"

"Nothing," I said calmly. "I just decided to go back into the life, that's all. I've grown bored with you. At first your little game was fun, but now, it's becoming mundane, drab, you know what I'm saying here? So I just decided to move on and do my thing, have myself a little fun."

Finding my words enjoyable, she laughed out loud, "Nigga, *I* decide when it's over—not you. And I'm not about to let you go back to turning tricks. No man of mine is doing that kind of shit."

"I beg to differ, little lady." I slanted my eyes. "I'm my own man. And I do what I want with who I want. And if I want to bang 'em in the bed, that's my business, got it?"

There was a moment of silence; I figured her to be wondering what the hell was going on. I could almost picture the stunned expression on her face. Then, before she knew what she was going to say, I began telling her all about how I was going deeper into the life, dwelling into some real sick, perverted shit, and this did nothing but enrage her even more as she absorbed every word I had said, most likely interpreting it as some kind of shortcoming on her part as a woman.

But there was another side to this ruse, a darker, deadlier side. I knew by doing this there would be no turning back; the fire was lit and was burning intensely. The woman wouldn't have wanted me now even if I had begged and pleaded with her on bended knees. No.

There was no chance. At this juncture, I had crossed the point of no return.

The trap had been sprung shut.

"Who is the little tramp you're seeing tonight!" she demanded. "Huh, who the fuck is it! Tell me, goddammit!"

I hesitated, allowing more flames to build in the fire. Then I said smoothly, "I have an exclusive date with Mister Alvin Harris."

"Alvin Harris—" There she faltered, and there came a long pause. Lamely, she finished, "Alvin Harris? You're choosing some hard-legged man over me, nigga?"

"Yes, I am, if you must know," I commented snottily. "We had a talk about us getting together this past Saturday night, at Pozanno's. In fact," I went on, sure I had sparked her total interest by now, "he's invited me to move in with him, and I'm thinking about accepting his generous offer."

"You're a sick bastard," she rasped through labored breathing, as if she had just run up several flights of stairs. "How dare you treat me in such a manner. How could you…" The impossibility of going any further proved to be difficult. However, she did manage to say something, and the words chilled me straight to the bone, "If you think I'm going to let you run off with some man—over *me*—you got another think coming, Terry Allens. I cut your ass into tiny strips before I'll let that shit happen. You hear me, nigga? I'll gut you like a pig, like I did Mel Armstrong." Her voice dropped dangerously low. "But I'll make you suffer even more. You know what I'm saying here, man? I told you before, nobody fucks me over on their word."

"Well, I did. So I guess you gotta do what you gotta do." Though I had said this in a calm, nonchalant way, my blood was frozen around my heart. *Had I pushed too many buttons? Too quickly? Too hard? If I had, fuck it, there was nothing I could do about it now.* I took a deep breath and said, "Look, we don't have to take it to that level. We can still be friends. I mean, we never actually had a thing going so the way I see it, nothing ventured, nothing gained, okay?"

"You smug bastard," she answered through her panting. "You think you can smooth this shit over by saying something as weak as that? Oh no, you're going to pay. I'm going to hunt you down like a dog. There won't be a place on this earth where you can hide, you hear me, goddammit—not a place in this *world!*"

With those words, said in such a tone, I had to admit to myself I was more than unnerved, and several moments had passed before I realized that my face was sheeted in sweat. Nevertheless, I had to persevere; too much was at stake. "Listen, I'm done here, Darling," I said tiredly. "I've got an appointment with Alvin Harris, and most likely I'll be staying there for a while. I've got a suitcase packed. So I'll be out of touch and away from you." I paused then added in a self-assured voice, "You won't be able to torment me, Darling...not anymore."

Tightening my mouth, I slammed the phone down hard. Afterwards I looked around, my chest heaving as if my lungs were made of cast iron. My hands shook something terribly and my eyes were bright with anger or perhaps even tears.

Nevertheless I reveled in the reaction I'd caused...or maybe I was just scared shitless. I couldn't tell which as I slowly rose from the sofa.

I smoothed a palm over my face and saw that my hand was drenched with perspiration. I turned and went into the bedroom. I had to get ready. *God be with me* I heard myself saying as I made my way. I entered the bedroom and took a seat on the bed where I shook my head. Covering my face with my hands, I said a light prayer. Then, as if somebody was prodding and poking at me in the ribs with some kind of stick, I rose from the bed and went into the bathroom. I had a date tonight...and I prayed that it would go well.

"I see," Alvin Harris said quietly and without emotion. A glass of cognac was in his hands; swirling it lightly, sitting in a thick padded chair, he looked off into the fire.

Dressed in a navy blue, doubled-breasted blazer, a beige Cardin turtleneck, and sharply-creased jeans, I sat in a heavy wicker chair and said nothing. I knew the man needed time to garnish some kind of reply. I checked my Rolex. It was eight forty-five. I looked up. For a moment I stared off around me, then my eyes flashed back to Alvin Harris.

We were sitting in the rear of his home, in the terrace room, a spacious, smartly decorated room where the light of the moon found its way through thick paneled window sections and melted over overstuffed floral-print furniture and bamboo end tables. Over the span of a half an hour, Alvin Harris and I had touched on a few aspects concerning my employment with his company, and although our conversation had went somewhat smoothly, he could tell that there was something else on my mind. I figured I'd just come clean and tell the man what was going on, hoping like hell he would buy it.

In the moments that seemed to wane by, I had did just that, and I believe he did buy it. I mean, the man didn't become unglued, upset or irate, none of that. Nor did he ask me to leave. Instead, as he sat there in a brown silk twill shirt with matching drawstring pants, I'd noticed that there was a certain expression to his face, a certain look in his eyes, an awareness to what I had said. The man *knew* something, of this much I could tell.

He stood up from his chair, I guess to refreshen his drink. "I'm afraid there may be some truth to your beliefs, Terry," he sighed, pouring himself another shot of cognac. When he was done, he turned to face me. "Denise has done something like this—"

Suddenly there was a loud boom, and one of the paneled window sections shattered, sending shards of splintered glass everywhere. I immediately dove to the floor where I had the wind knocked out of me and it took a few moments to get my senses back. When I did, I came up on one knee and looked up to where I'd last seen Alvin Harris. I could just make out the top of his knee as he laid on the floor between the chair he was standing by and the rattan coffee table. *Was he dead?* I wondered. I prayed that he wasn't. Crouching low on my hands and knees, I made my way over to him. That's when another barrage of bullets came flying into the room, shattering more window sections. I dove back to the floor and laid flat on my back, staring up at the ceiling as the teak and plaster wall just behind me disintegrated into chunks, showering me with pieces of drywall and wood.

The assault lasted only seconds; I figured it had to be some kind of automatic weapon. Easing up on my side, I swung one foot over the other and found a bit of leverage against the wall. Then, rolling over on my stomach, I reached out to the loveseat and pulled myself up. I stood up slowly, and was suddenly afraid I'd lost my gun. But no, it was still there tucked in my waistband. Taking it out, I slid the hammer back and set a live round in place. Then, with one hand against the riddled wall, the gun in the other, I started for Alvin Harris. When I reached him I saw that his shirt was soaked in blood. He moaned lightly and his throat throbbed violently. He was losing blood rapidly.

I hurried over to the telephone which sat on the bar cart and picked it up. The line was dead. My jumbled nerves running amok, I slammed the phone down. I then rushed out of the house and ran to my car parked out front, realizing that the entire area around me was now pitch black. I figured the power to the outdoor lightning had been extinguished in some form or fashion. I opened the door to retrieve my cellular phone. As I did, the interior light came on, and the moon slid out from behind the clouds almost simultaneously, putting a spotlight on me from all vantage points. Instinctively I dropped to my knees just as a slew of bullets whizzed by and pummeled my car. I covered my head and rolled to the ground. I kicked the door shut. Then the moon melted into the clouds and darkness and silence rushed back into the night.

I looked around. I had no idea where the shots had come from, so any kind of retaliation on my part would be useless.

I turned behind me, then back in front of me, slinging sweat in the process. I wiped my brow but it was no use. The more sweat I wiped the more emerged. I swallowed a huge lump in my throat as I slowly raised up to peel away my blazer. I threw it to the ground, keeping my vigilance for another assault. I didn't dare try to open the car door again to retrieve my cellular phone. It would be a dead giveaway. Instead I scanned the area. There was nothing. Nothing but blackness.

Using the blackness for cover, in a kind of scrambling roll, I stood up and ran toward what I believed was the entranceway into the subdivision. Hopefully I could get to the guard shack and summon some help or at least get some assistance for Alvin Harris. *The man was dying!* I fretted. With this laying heavily on my mind I ran hard, feeling as though my lungs would burst from my chest. I clenched the gun tightly in my right hand as I followed the main drive, grateful for the scant illumination of moonlight peering over my shoulders. I rounded a curve and saw the guard shack. It was about fifty yards away, just around a turn in the road. My shoes pounded the asphalt as

I ran closer. I came around the turn and as I did, I felt something slap hard against the back of my neck. The blow flung me forward and sideways.

I turned to brace myself for the fall, at the same time I heard a loud explosion. Then I felt the ground hit me in the back, and for an instant everything went black. When I opened my eyes all I could see was the moon and a hissing of clouds. I smelled gunpowder and realized that my gun must have gone off, and as I looked around in a frantic state, it was nowhere to be found. Instead of rising, I found myself laying there for a stunned instant, conscious of stinging sensations darting over me in a dozen places. Nothing throbbed; there was no searing pain anywhere, just the vague overall ache that comes from a hard, unexpected landing. Bracing a hand to the ground, I started to ease myself up when the sound of a car engine roaring to life drew my eyes down toward the entranceway. Because of the darkness everywhere and the blow I had sustained, my vision was obscured, but a pair of headlights cut through the black night, followed by the sound of peeling rubber.

The whine of the tires on pavement seemed to echo the inner screaming of my own nerves as I fought to maintain my senses.

I stood up and closed my eyes. A pain in the back of my neck became suddenly excruciating, and I could feel blood oozing down my back. I dabbed at the wound while staggering toward the guard shack, still cautious of the area around me. I started to feel a noticeable stiffness in my right hand and wrist, but all my fingers worked and I could rotate my wrist, which indicated there wasn't anything broken. My arm was beginning to swell, though—and sore as hell. I made it to the shack and found that the door was ajar. I pushed on the door and it stopped abruptly. A foreboding chill washed over me as I turned and scanned the darkness. I then looked up and down the road, then passed it, as if making sure I was alone. Feeling I was, I turned and peered into the shack through the narrow gap in the door and through the filtered moonlight, I could see a single, bare bulb enclosed by a wire cage, mounted on the ceiling. I slipped a hand inside and ran my fingers along the wall until I felt a switch, where I flipped it on. The tiny room instantly became flooded with light. The brightness stunned my eyes for a brief second.

Experiencing a ray of hope as well as wanting to conceal myself from a straying bullet, I pushed harder on the door. I couldn't figure out what was blocking the entrance. I finally pushed my way inside. After a short pause, doing nothing for several seconds, I leaned against the wall just right of the door. I began wondering oddly at how the wall seemed to be swaying. I felt the impact of the wall against my shoulder and realized it was I who was swaying. And worse, I couldn't seem to stop. I shook my head, trying to fling off the little tremors of darkness that had begun to swirl around the outer edges of my eyes, knowing I had to move—before I blacked out. Running on will alone, all my vast reserves of strength depleted, I grabbed the doorknob and pulled myself into motion. The door flung back out and then stopped.

What was blocking the door? I frowned. I peered around the door.

My eyes lit up and my breath left me in a rush as I saw what the problem was.

It was the guard.

His lifeless eyes glaring at the ceiling told me the story. I crept closer and hunched over the body. That's when my own body went rigid. The guard's throat had been slashed from ear to ear. A deafening silence fell over me. My eyes bucked with devastating amazement, also shock, and horror—all the reactions which could steal your breath away. I told myself to calm down, however. I quickly composed myself and spotted a black telephone mounted on the wall. I stepped over the body and picked it up, grateful when I saw the green numbers on the keypad light up. I brought the phone to my ear. There was a dial tone. I dialed frantically for assistance.

Chapter 25

In the emergency room of Grace Hospital, a crew of medics intubated Alvin Harris' trachea to keep him breathing, then slowed the bleeding from the hole in his chest with pressure dressings. Doctors administered antibiotics and started an IV of packed red cells, and after that took X-rays. From there he was wheeled into an operating room. I paced nervously in the waiting area, feeling that I'd caused most of the shit that had happened this evening. I *knew* this woman would show up at Alvin Harris' home. But I didn't know she would come at me this hard—*this soon*. I had laid the trap and she had outsmarted me.

And now there was a man in there stretched out on an operating table fighting for his life. I took a seat in one of the chairs in the room and placed my head in my palms. I leaned forward then, quietly, peacefully, almost to myself, but no less deeply, I wept.

I wept for Alvin Harris. I wept for Vera and her deceased husband, for Derrick Collins, for the dead security attendant. I even found the tears for myself, and they flowed relentlessly.

A team headed by Doctor William Shaper, a surgeon who had dealt with more than his share of gunshot wounds, spent five hours attempting to repair the damage done by the nine-millimeter slug that had passed through Alvin Harris' body. When the doctor had done all that he could, he inserted a chest tube and closed the wound. Alvin Harris was then given a round of antibiotics and sent off to intensive care.

When Doctor Shaper appeared in the waiting room and called my name, I immediately rose to my feet, waiting anxiously for a reply. The doctor, the head surgeon on duty, most likely, was a short man, and his green surgical gown was crisp and creased, as if he were readying himself for his next victim. His gray hair was matted with sweat. I also caught the fatigue in his face, and I was almost afraid to ask, but I did. "How's Mister Harris, Doctor?"

"Too early to say," he replied. "But I'll tell you this much, though, he was damn lucky. The bullet had done considerable damage but luckily none of his vital organs were injured. There were a lot of torn nerves and if he pulls through, he's going to need some type of therapy."

I approached closer. "Will he make it?"

"Don't know at this point. But he's got a fighting chance. He's fairly young, and seemed to be in good shape. But God was on his side, had the bullet deflected up instead of down...well, let's just say you and I wouldn't be here talking as hopeful as we are right now."

I smiled. "Yeah, thank God." A sense of relief like a cool breeze drifted over me.

The surgeon smiled back, then reminded me about keeping some kind of antibiotic salve on my cuts and scrapes. Afterward he shook my left hand and then disappeared through a set of doubled doors. I looked around the waiting room, feeling okay but looking like shit—my shirt was torn and draped loosely over my shoulders, and my jeans were shredded at the knees. The back of my neck was as stiff as a board and heavily bandaged where the people in the same emergency room had cleaned and dressed the gash I had sustained. I stepped out into the hallway where two detectives I had talked to earlier stood waiting for me. Flexing the fingers on my right hand that were beginning to stiffen from the swelling, my expression grim and tight-lipped, I made my way toward them. I knew what I had to do. There were statements to give, papers to sign; I was going to be put through the ringer with a barrage of questions, and then there were more statements to give. I knew the drill.

But I didn't mind.

In fact, I would give them everything they wanted, and then some.

I was tired, tired of it all. I just wanted the nightmare to end, and it appeared to be heading in that direction. But somehow, deep in the annals of my heart, I knew it wasn't quite over. No, not yet. The woman was still out there...waiting for me. And in all likelihood, her rage was building by the second.

What would be her next move? I wondered.

At five o'clock in the morning the taxi dropped me off. I paid the driver and headed up the walkway. A pair of lantern-style lights were mounted on the brick wall flanking my apartment door, illuminating the area immediately in front of it. That's when I saw it. The front door to my apartment slightly opened. I immediately glanced around. I didn't see anything. It was quiet, only the light chirping of some song birds could be heard. Instinctively, I flexed my right hand. The ice pack the nurses had given me was doing the trick; the swelling was down and the pain had faded to a dull throb. Still stiff and sore in a dozen other places, I turned back to my apartment door and walked up to it. I glanced around once more then gave it a soft push. That's when I saw that the inside of the doorjamb had been torn away from the wall. It was probably done by a crowbar I thought. Pissed off that I had lost Will's gun after taking the blow to the back of my neck, I stepped inside and flipped on the light.

I found my living room in wild disarray. The leather sofa and loveseat had been gutted savagely from one end to the next. Pictures that used to line my walls now laid on the floor, ripped to shreds. To my right, a pair of end tables were scarred and broken. My custom-made blinds had been crudely pulled from its supports and laid mangled and tattered. I walked further into the apartment and noticed faint droplets of blood everywhere. Not knowing what to expect at this point, I went into the kitchen and grabbed a long butcher knife from out the drawer. I gripped the handle firmly then went into my bedroom.

The sight held me in place.

My king-size bed, as heavy as it was, had been somehow lifted and overturned. Slashed and ripped, the mattress and box-spring slumped against the wall. The bedside lamp my mother had given me hung precariously, just inches above the floor, having been knocked off the bed table but stopped short by its cord just before hitting the floor. I exhaled hard through my nose, and although my mind screamed *get the hell out of there!* I stepped inside the room and walked over to the closet. I opened the door and found my clothes still intact, untouched, as were my shoes. As I turned and scanned the room, I noticed the presence of more blood droplets. I walked over to a blood spot and bent down. I touched it lightly and found it to be tacky.

"Bitch," I cursed hoarsely.

Standing up, I tried to ascertain what had happened to cause the spots of blood. My mind flashed to the loud boom I'd remembered hearing as I fell to the ground, as I held the gun in my hand. *The gun had discharged* I thought. *Maybe I had hit her?*

Suddenly it occurred to me that she might have somehow doubled back and followed me to the apartment and could possibly be waiting to finish me off. *But could she?* I wondered. I had no way of knowing how badly wounded she was, or if she was wounded at all, for that matter. But I knew one thing: I couldn't stay here and find out—I was a sitting duck. I turned to leave, and that's when the phone in my bedroom began to ring. I craned my head and stared at it, feeling my temples throbbing. *Who the hell was it?* I shuddered.

I started not to answer it but then I figured it might be Will, since I hadn't talked with him since early yesterday afternoon, after his flight. I walked around my overturned bed and picked up the phone. To my surprise it was Vera. "Hey, girl, how you doing?" Despite the carnage around me I found a smile on my face.

"Terry," she asked, with a slight shake to her voice, "can you come over? I...I need to see you...if it's possible. Is it?"

I frowned. "Vera, are you okay?"

"Yes, I'm fine."

I slanted my eyes. "What's the matter?"

"Nothing. Why would anything be the matter?"

"You okay? You're not in any trouble, are you?"

"No."

"You sure?"

"Yes. I'm sure."

"Then why do you sound so nervous? Your voice is shaking like a leaf."

"Is it? I didn't know it was." Her voice became firmer. "So, can you come over? Just to talk?"

I glanced around the bedroom, thinking maybe I could crash at Vera's place. But before I could respond Vera cut in with a flicker of passion in her voice, and said, "Terry, can you come and see me?"

For a moment, I hesitated. I thought I detected something else in her voice, like a plea. I shook my head and then said, "Yeah, I can come, but it'll be an hour or so, my car is down for the count. Just give me some time to clean up and call a taxi, okay?"

She paused for a moment or two. "That'll be just fine, Terry Allens." She paused once more, a little longer, then she hissed urgently, "I need to see you, so please hurry. I'll leave the front door open so you can just come on in, okay?"

I nodded and moistened my lips; every nerve in me had an edge to it. "You got it...and, Vera, don't you worry about a thing, I'll see you through this." Slowly, I let the phone slip through my fingers as I hung it up and when I did, I felt a new emotion rising inside me. It seemed to crawl up from the pit of my stomach and burn in my chest like a molten, ulcerous bubble. It was the scorching flame of hatred. I stared at the wall with gritted teeth. *The bitch was there! The bitch was there with Vera!*

I stood back from the door, letting it swing open on its own power. Absently, I wiped perspiration from my upper lip. I was definitely terrified and if I was trembling, I couldn't tell. I knew I was wrong for not calling the police, especially after what I'd just been through, but I couldn't take the chance of this woman harming Vera.

Trying to control my breathing, I peered inside, thinking a bullet could shatter my head in an instant. But nothing happened as I looked around. There was nobody there, nothing but furniture. Inching inside and closing the door quietly behind me, I shifted my field of vision, taking in all my blind spots. There were few I noted. Feeling an eerie sensation coming over me, I reached into the inner pocket of my light jacket and felt the butcher knife. I experienced a slight sense of security as I took a few steps into the foyer.

Vera's house was so huge! I thought.

Sweat stung my eyes like tiny needles as I tried to determine which way to proceed. I scanned my options: the living room to the left of me, the dining room to my right, or straight ahead down a hallway that was about fifty paces or so. I chewed my bottom lip. *Which way?* I found myself staring straight ahead. Something was telling me that was the way to go. *Trust your judgment, Terry,* a voice in my head said, *trust what you feel.* With that, I crept slowly down the hallway.

I found a voice and whispered, "Vera..." I shifted my eyes back and forth then behind me. "...Vera, are you here? It's me...Terry. Vera...?"

There was no reply.

Wiping my brow, I proceeded further down the hallway, my Reeboks hitting the hardwood floor silently. I reached the end of the hallway where I came to three steps. The steps went down and led to what was a den or some kind of recreation room. I headed on. Then my eyes were drawn to a large clock on the wall at the bottom of the steps. Its minute hand stood straight up. It was exactly six o'clock in the morning. As if on cue, the clock emitted a soft fluttering tone which affirmed this time.

At the same moment, emerging from behind me, came another announcement. It was too amply pitched and smooth to come from a man; it was the sound of a woman's voice, which came at me vile and menacing, "Good evening, Terry...or should I say, good morning. In either event, I'm glad you could make it."

My heart pounded furiously in my chest as I also heard the metallic clicking of a round being snapped into a chamber. Slowly, I turned to see who and what it was.

Chapter 26

"Hello, Denise," I said calmly, turning to face her directly. "I thought I'd find you here."

Dressed in black jeans and a black suede jacket with specks of grass clippings on them, and mud-covered tennis shoes, she stared at me with a sly smirk. Her long hair had been pulled up into a French knot. With a slow, sexy sway to her hips she took a few steps toward me then stopped. As she stood there, she was no longer the timid, innocent-looking woman I'd recalled at the restaurant and she was no less deadlier, as she raised a nine-millimeter gun and pointed the barrel straight at my face. "A quirk of fate, isn't it, Terry?" she declared. A smile edged the corners of her mouth, echoing the humor she found in the notion. "You knew I would be here and I knew you would come."

I sighed, trying to give the picture of calm, though my lungs surged and collapsed as I sucked in air through my nose. I found myself dazed by her appearance, as if she were a still photograph, frozen in time. The image of our first encounter was there in front of me, in my head, every detail in sharp focus—her warm greeting as she met me at the front door, the kind expression in her eyes, the soft gesturing accompanying her exceptional smile, the brief but pleasant exchange of words we shared—it was all there. I was stunned, and I guess my expression said more clearly than any words I could possibly believe: it was the same woman.

It was.

It really was.

Finding enough moisture in my mouth, I asked, "Where's Vera?"

"Shut the fuck up!" she protested loudly. "I'm runnin' the show around here, dammit!" She quickly threw her head back and laughed. Then just as suddenly, her face twisted into a grimace. "I told your ass you couldn't hide from me, didn't I, Terry?" She laughed, without humor.

I shrugged my shoulders and nodded my disadvantage. "Yes, and apparently you were right in assuming so. So now what?" Instead of answering she retreated; she didn't appear to even hear my words. That's when I noticed that there was an odd expression on her face, as if mentally she was somewhere else.

"Why didn't you want me, Terry?" Her face wilted and her brow creased in heavy concentration. *"Why? Why didn't you want me? Why Why?"*

I walked closer toward her and said, "I didn't know it was you, Denise, otherwise things could have been different. Why didn't you just come out and say you wanted to get together?"

She seemed to go into deep thought about that. I sensed a contradiction going on in her head between what she should have done and her actions. Finally she shook her head. "I...I don't know. I couldn't tell you."

When I saw a wariness leap in her expression, a wariness and something that looked undoubtedly like fatigue, I stepped closer.

"Slow your roll, motherfucker," she demanded with white-hot anger, her eyes dark and stormy with it. "Don't you dare take another step, you hear me? Or I'll blow that pretty face of yours clean off."

I immediately stopped dead in my tracks, panic clawing at my insides.

"That's better." She stared at me glassy-eyed and then she groaned. She brought a hand to the bottom of her stomach and clutched it tightly. I noticed blood oozing from underneath her jacket.

"You're hurt," I whispered softly.

"That I am." She groaned again, and blood continued to flow. "It seems as if you were lucky tonight. You got me right in the gut...good shot."

I shook my head. "I didn't mean to. I didn't know it was you."

"Bullshit." She stretched her mouth into a demented grin. "You knew I would show up at my brother's house," groaning softly, "that's why you said the things you did over the phone. You knew I would take the bait and come running like a dog, didn't you, Terry?"

I nodded, finding myself groping unsuccessfully for a response.

"At least you're being honest here, I'll give you that." She closed her eyes and her body swayed and rocked, as if she were about to faint. In an instant, however, she opened her eyes and became extremely focused. Her grin was back. "But now I have you looking like a dog, don't I, Terry?" She raised her other arm to support the gun. "Tell me something, Terry, are you ready to die?"

"No," I managed to say frankly. "But if I must, can you at least tell me what brought all this on?"

With that, she smiled, I guess reflecting. She gasped and let out a low grunt. Sweat had surfaced and sheeted her face like a layer of ice. She drew a quivering breath. "I was married once," she began slowly, "to a wonderful man. He was everything a woman could want…handsome, caring, attentive to my needs. But things started to change after a couple of years. I guess the whole business of living in close proximity to another person got to him. He started tipping out on me…with another man. When I confronted him about this he beat me something terrible. The man had me groveling on the floor to the point where I lost complete control of my faculties. I ended up in a coma, and I stayed that way for nearly two weeks. When I finally came around and got released from the hospital, we tried to make things work. I thought all marriages deserve some degree of second chances, but I soon realized I'd been better off as a celibate. He was back up to his old ways, back to the men—the man had *dozens* of them. I couldn't take it anymore. My physical and spiritual vitality was being sapped. I threatened to leave him…I just wanted out of the marriage, you know, nothing else, just out of it…"

She faltered as more blood oozed from her jacket. She was becoming weaker and had to support the gun firmer with one hand while clutching her stomach with the other.

Maybe I could inch toward her, I thought. A foot or so at a time. Get close enough and I'd have a chance to kick her gun hand. I kept my eyes locked on hers. "I do see the difficulties you were faced with. The man was inconsiderate in every way. So what happened, Denise? Tell me. What happened after you told him you were going to leave?"

She blinked to release a tear. "He said fine—go right ahead, but like a fool I stayed, and things turned from bad to worse. His tipping became bolder, and he started flaunting his business right in front of my face, like I didn't exist. He was always rushing to and fro, hither and thither, constantly invading my space and berating me with his actions, laughing, taunting me with endless chatter about his men…That's when I told myself that was it…no more. The man didn't even respect my privacy and peace. I grabbed a suitcase and started packing right there on the spot. And that's when it happened. He cursed me something terrible and began beating me like I was the devil himself. But this time I fought him off. I had bought myself a gun and used it on him. What a brilliant solution to my problem! I sank a fuckin' bullet right between his beady little eyes. Then I took a knife from the kitchen and slit his throat from ear to ear. Though my actions were a bit excessive it was deemed self-defense so I didn't have to go to jail. But the pressure of this was too much for me, and soon I was committed to an institution, seemingly without a moment's hesitation. Months later, I tried to hang myself, by knotting strips of bedclothes together. But as you can see I never did succeed." She shook her head, trying not to break down. "Anyway, a year later I was released, under the care of my brother. He took me into his home and helped me to get my life back on track. But I think he knew I was a basket case. I could see the look in his eyes. It was as if he was secretly convinced that there was a hidden madness deep inside me, a fettered beast just waiting to burst its chains. At times he would peer at me...afraid...waiting for me to explode."

Once again she shook her head, then she looked up with a sorrowful expression on her face. "How is he, anyway? I didn't kill him, did I?"

"No. The doctor said he may pull through. Right now everything is touch and go." With that I stared at her, feeling pity and compassion, concluding that she was just a woman with a horrific past, the stuff movies were made about. The beautiful woman standing before me with a confused and disseminated heart had once been a great person to be admired.

I stepped closer. "You've had it pretty rough, haven't you, Denise?"

She looked at me and her body swayed, as if she were about to topple over. She drew a sharp breath and managed to stay on her feet. She looked up and said in an absent murmur, "Yes. Yes, I have. I tried to move on...I even tried to date other guys, but I found myself distrusting all of them. Nothing worked. I found myself too paranoid to be involved in a relationship. I would follow them, stalking them, but I never did anything. I told Alvin about this and he helped me to cope by taking me out a lot, and talking to me. And for the most part,

I guess, it worked." She stared into my eyes and hers began to well. "That is, until I laid eyes on you, Terry. From the moment I first saw you I wanted you. I...I thought that maybe I could change you, somehow make you see that what you were doing was wrong, and that maybe you would be appreciative to what I was trying to do for you...and in return, you'd thank me...by becoming the man in my life...the only man."

Moaning lightly, she brought a hand to her head. She teetered a bit and leaned against the wall for support, steadying herself, still pointing the barrel of the gun at me. I watched her; she appeared sufficiently out of it for me to move a step closer.

She looked up, and her face grew distorted with rage. "Get back! Get the *fuck* back! Don't you think I'm too weak to pull this fuckin' trigger! I'll shoot your ass in a heartbeat!"

I took a step backward, raising both hands, palms up. "Okay, Denise, I'm sorry. Just take it easy here, okay? I'll keep my distance. I'm not going anywhere."

Her voice rung out in deep challenge. "You're not? *You're not?* That's what you think, Terry. You're about to die. First you, then that bitch Vera...then me."

The hard and heavy beat of my pulse drummed in my ears. The thought of dying—of Vera dying—was numbing, almost too painful to grasp. "We don't have to take it there, Denise. We...we can work something out."

She looked at the gun in her hand, and then at me. She was whimpering. "How, Terry? How can we possibly work something out, after all the shit you've put me through?" She reaffirmed her grip on the gun, her lips drawing back over clenched teeth. "Tell me how, Terry, *this* shit I would just love to hear."

I swallowed nervously as she became more and more dependent on the wall for support. "We can still be together, now that I know how you feel about me. We can go away...start over someplace where nobody knows about us...about our past. What'll you say, Denise? You and me? Leaving all of this behind us and starting over? We could do it. We could do it, Denise..."

She struggled to catch her breath. "You lie, Terry Allens, you lie so well. You don't want me." Her eyes rolled in her head. "You never did."

I swallowed hard. "Denise...let's leave this place, while we still can. Denise..."

The sound of her name coming from my lips, the false protestations of running away, the big promises, and the sight of me standing there—I guess all of these things combined to break through the last of her restraints. She frowned her skepticism, a hard and relentless cast to her features. Then, seemingly lost, confused, and angry, with a half-sickened look, she leveled the gun and fired. The blast was deafening as the nine-millimeter slug ripped right pass me tearing through the wall, which was only an inch away from my face. Two more blasts erupted, these bullets also missing me by mere inches. The aftershock sent her reeling backward. I saw my opportunity. In one swift motion, I leaped at her and tackled her to the floor. We both came down hard.

Before she could roll free I was on top of her, trapping her beneath the weight of my body and pinning her arms to the side. Still, she fought like a wildcat, bumping and writhing with a will like I had never seen or felt. I was breathing as hard and deep as she was. When she realized her actions were futile she tried to tip the gun toward me, but I pried the gun from her grip with a kind of controlled savagery.

"I hate you, Terry Allens!" she protested barbarously, swinging her arms madly with dazed eyes. "I hate you, you hear me!" Blood was now gushing from her wound, soaking the both of us. I pinned her back and gazed into her face, which was growing deathly pale. A lump filled my throat. I didn't have to be a physician to know that she was dying. The miracle was that she had managed to live this long.

"I hate you, Terry Allens," she still protested, though now softly, "I hate—" She shut her eyes tightly as pain shot through her body. "I...hate...you..."

For an answer I relaxed my grip and shifted over her until I was nestled by her side. I took her by the shoulders and held her in my arms. I hugged her tightly. "No, you don't hate me, Denise," I whispered, cradling her body even tighter, "and I don't hate you."

Slowly, as blood seeped from her mouth, she grunted low and hoarse, "You don't hate me?" She looked like a little, lost girl.

"No," I smiled, "no such thing. I could never bring myself to that."

Rasping harshly, she tried to rise, but could not. Melting back into my arms, she beckoned softly, "Then do…then do you love me, Terry Allens? Is that what you're trying to tell me?"

Even through her pain, I could see that there was a hopeful expression in her face, in her eyes. I brought a hand to her face and stroked it gently. "Yes…yes, Denise…I love you. Very much so."

She hummed and nodded her head, seemingly very pleased. She then looked up at me with fading eyes. "Can I ask a favor of you, Terry? Please? Before the angels come and sweep me away?" She winced. *"Please?"*

I looked at her. There was nothing anyone could do for her now, but ease her pain. The overwhelming reality that her life was flowing out of her, defying her every effort to keep it in, was maddening. I could barely contain what I felt. Tears began welling up in my eyes as my voice broke with emotion, "Yes, Denise…whatever you want…ask me."

At that, she stretched her scarlet mouth and uttered, "Can I…can I call you my Darling? Please?" She managed a gurgled chuckle. "I never had the chance to call you this…" She closed her eyes, as if trying to save her strength. She opened them slowly. "Please?" she insisted. "May I…may I call you my Darling? *Please?"*

I could only gaze at her, at such a strange request. It was all she ever wanted. Somebody to love her truly. *It was important to her,* I shuddered. *Very important.* "Yes," I gasped, my voice erupting in a sob, "yes, you may."

Exhaling in a deep sigh, she then groaned, with bubbles of red appearing between her lips, *"Merci, monsieur…merci,* my dear Darling." Almost immediately her eyes went bright with pinpoints. For a second or two, there was no change in her expression or in the intensity of her gaze. She had the look of a woman caught in the grip of something powerful and magical. A distant star that stood only yards away. Soaring side by side with a near-extinct bird. She held the expression. Then slowly, gradually, her eyes went blank, and the veiled gaze she now wore made it clear she could no longer see me.

In response, with tears streaking my cheeks, I brought a hand to her eyelids and gently closed them. I looked up. My face was tight with hurt. I shook my head and held her body for a moment or two longer. Then I shifted my body and laid her head to the floor. Through my tears I stared at her face, and the look in my own suggested regret rather than relief.

The woman had died in my arms, I sighed, my heart melting. As she laid there peacefully I thought of what she'd said, about her wanting to be surrounded by hundreds of roses. I would make sure she'd have her wish, if it was the last thing I was to do in life. I leaned back against the wall, wilted and drained.

As quiet spread throughout the house I looked around. Then suddenly, with new found strength and urgency—I jumped to my feet. "Vera!" I shouted loudly. "Oh, my God! Vera, where are you!"

Chapter 27

Having checked nearly every room in the house I'd come full circle, back to the hallway. I found myself drenched in cold sweat. *Where was she!* I fretted. I thought of something and ran to the laundry room and tried looking in there. There was nothing. From there, I checked the garage, the attic, as well as the cellar. Again, Vera was nowhere to be found. I decided to contact the police and walked into the kitchen. As I picked up the phone I looked around, clutching the receiver tightly in my hand.

Damn it, I'd been through every inch of the house and hadn't found a single clue to Vera's whereabouts. Except for the spots of blood in her bedroom, particularly by the phone, where apparently she'd been instructed to call me, there was nothing else. She was no place in the house. At that, my eyes went wide.

Or maybe she wasn't in the house!

I felt a sense of growing apprehension. Call it an instinct, or perhaps a gut feeling, but I suddenly felt sure that Vera was not in the house—but some place near! Looking over the kitchen once more, I noticed utensils and other objects on the work surface of the center island. I stepped closer and saw that there was a long knife, a vegetable parer, and a head of lettuce and several diced tomatoes. There was also chopped egg whites and an unopened bottle of Bleu Cheese dressing. Obviously Vera had been fixing herself a salad. I noticed that there was a smashed plate and some diced mushrooms on the floor. There was also blood.

Just as the blood droplets in her bedroom had, the kitchen also suggested a surprise, an unexpected interruption. Wiping my face and pulling it hard, I scanned the floor and spotted a set of keys, about five or so, on a silver ring. I picked up the keys and jostled them in my hand. There was a white tag clipped on the ring which read: storage bin. At once my heart leaped, and with lightning speed I ran from the house and headed for the outside storage shed, which was approximately thirty yards from the house, in the rear.

As I ran I saw that the ground had been kicked and disturbed, as if somebody had been dragged, or pulled. I approached the storage shed in a rush. The shed was very large, about the size of a two-car garage, and made solely out of aluminum. There was a thick Master Lock threaded through the door latch opening. I looked down and discovered that the ground was dotted with blood, some gathered into small pools. With frantic hands, I wrestled with the keys and inserted them one by one into the bottom of the lock until I heard a click. I let out a hard gasp of relief when the lock surrendered its grip.

Slowly, I pulled the lock away and opened the door, where the strong aroma of freshly-cut grass and gasoline greeted me immediately. With my eyes adjusting to the shed's shadowed gloom, I peered inside and stocked right near the opening was an array of lawn equipment: a John-Deere riding lawn mower, several weed-whackers and trimmers, electric hedgers, leaf blowers, and a couple of heavy duty fertilizer spreaders.

I flipped on a light switch and looked around, fright filling my insides.

The shed was neat and spacious. Everything in here was placed just so. I stepped further inside, taking in my surroundings. One wall was used for storage; garden tools, seemingly hundreds of them, of every kind, hung from brass hooks. The sight of these tools did nothing but unnerve me even more, turning my insides several degrees colder. *Had the woman stabbed Vera with*—I blocked the thought from my mind; it was too disturbing to think about.

"Vera," I announced, with a shaking voice. "Vera, are you in here?" Standing there for a few seconds, I kept scanning the shed. It was strange, but the feeling persisted that I'd stumbled onto Vera's whereabouts. *But where was she? People didn't simply evaporate; apparently somebody had been dragged in here? So where was she?*

My mind began playing tricks on me, filling my head with random spurts of sound from within the shed: fluttering and scratching, sudden stabs, the *ping* of something soft against something hard.

The panic of attempted escape.

I froze, fear—like any strong emotion—heightened my senses. Realizing time may very well be running out for Vera, I began rummaging through the shed, flinging everything from one side to the other, screaming her name over and over. I kept my frenzied pace until I came upon a large cedar chest. I suddenly froze on the spot. There were blood droplets everywhere. I stared wide-eyed at the tarnished handles of the chest. *Vera couldn't possibly be in there* I heard myself praying, too rigid to move. Shaking my head, I *willed* myself to move. I stooped down and grabbed the handles. Then slowly, gradually, I lifted the lid.

And found Vera.

Chapter 28

It was late October. The afternoon was beautiful; seventy-two degrees; probably the last nice day of the year, and as I drove my Benz with the top retracted, the sun beaming down and around me and the birds soaring overhead, high against the deep blue sky, I was sure it was. By it being such a glorious day, I decided to head to my favorite spot at Belle Isle Park. I hit Jefferson Avenue and in fifteen minutes, I approached the bridge. The tires began a rhythmic thumping as I crossed over. Rubbing the light stubble on my face with one hand while gripping the steering wheel with the other, I approached the other side of the bridge, and as I did, my mind drifted, to thoughts of Alvin Harris.

In the weeks that followed his tragedy, his condition had improved dramatically. The doctors had all agreed with a little more time and healing, he'd be back behind his desk. The local media had run a rash of stories covering his condition as well as the murders connected to his sister. Stories such as *WEALTHY REAL ESTATE'S SISTER MURDERER OF THREE*, and then the story spotlighted her past, and how she had suffered through a series of horrid events which eventually led to her outburst.

I tried not to read about this, or watch any television coverage concerning this matter.

It was too painful.

At the moment, my main concern was Alvin Harris, and his condition. He really did appear to be coming around; his sprits were up and he smiled a lot. As far as the physical therapy went, the man seemed determined to rebuild his damaged muscles by diligently following the program of exercises the doctors had laid out for him. One of the routines involved squeezing a tennis ball while extending his hand as high as possible, and he'd done this with ease, with a triumphant smile on his face. Other than a few precautionary measures he had to be mindful of, like not putting too much demand on his upper body, and not partaking in any strenuous exercises, at least not until he was deemed a hundred percent, he could expect to live a normal life.

And as expected, he was extremely appreciative of his outlook, as was I. But I noticed something else in Alvin Harris, in his eyes especially, when I'd stop in to see him. There was definitely something else there, just below the surface. It was a certain glow, and it would shine brighter on every visit. Though he had never said a word about this subtle illumination, I believe I knew what it was. Aside from his promising prognosis, I couldn't help but notice that he seemed relieved that the entire incident was over, as if he knew it would eventually come to a head and was finally glad it had.

And though I had never said a word about this myself, I could relate to what the man was feeling. No matter how sadly things had turned out...it was, indeed, finally over.

I visited Alvin Harris nearly everyday, sometimes Vera would accompany me, and this really helped me. Vera kept me strong. Actually, she kept me sane, and although she was still dealing with her own bumps and bruises both mentally and physically, she was always there, right by my side. But she wasn't the same Vera, and I grew steadily worried at the way she acted toward me. There was nothing in her glances, her attitude, or the remarks she made to me that suggested she was—or had ever been—anything other than a friend. She treated me exactly as she treated everyone else. No friendlier and no colder. Nevertheless, I was grateful for her being there...for me...but I wanted more than just her support. I wanted the woman. I wanted *her*.

But I couldn't see it happening.

I tried to tell myself that it was okay. That under the circumstances, it was probably best. Yet the longer it went on in my mind, the more it grated. But I knew I had to let it go. I had to come to grips...come to realize that...that ship had sailed—it had come and gone. There was no chance for Vera and I—especially after all the shit I'd caused.

No way.

Besides, a week had gone by and I hadn't heard anything from her, and this gap in time only reinforced what she'd said before: we could never be.

I soon found my favorite spot. I pulled off to the side and shut down the engine. However, instead of getting out and taking in the sights around me, I powered up my windows, leaned my head back and closed my eyes. I exhaled tiredly and laced my fingers together. I thought of my mother and Will. I thank God for these two people. They were the best of the best. I couldn't ask for better. Everything had gone smoothly and my mother hadn't suspected a thing, and if she did suspect something, she certainly didn't have a clue it was the mess that I'd been through. I didn't like deceiving my mother, my Black Pearl, but I had no other choice, because if something would have happened to her—over some shit *I* had caused—

I shook my head. No. I wouldn't allow myself to think like this. The crisis had come and gone. It was over.

I exhaled and sank deeper into my seat, thinking about nothing, or at least trying to. I just wanted to relax, and not do anything, and for nearly an hour I did just that. At times I drifted in and out of sleep. I checked the time and discovered I'd been sitting here for nearly two hours. I smiled, thinking I was going to sit here another hour or so. With that, I melted back into my seat. All of a sudden I heard a tap at my window. I opened my eyes and peered out the window.

Immediately I sat up in my seat!

OH, MY GOD! I heard myself shouting. *It was Vera!*

I smoothed a palm over my face and then opened the door. My heart was beating like an out of control bongo as I slid from the car and stood up. Slowly, wetting my lips, I closed the door and stared at Vera, nearly mesmerized.

She was simply beautiful I marveled, a vision.

Her face was beaming just so, naturally, without a stitch of makeup. Her black hair was pulled into a ponytail, held in place by two green tortoiseshell clips. She had on a white silk blouse under a light blue blazer. Her black jeans hugged her body, showing her hips to full advantage. She looked both innocent and alluring, though I knew neither of these was the look she was striving to achieve; she was just being herself...being Vera.

As I stared at her she was just that...just Vera. A great beauty...no, more than a beauty...an angel.

I stepped over to this angel and took her by the hand. I could smell the fragrant soap on her skin. "Hello, Vera." I looked into her eyes. "It's really great to see you."

She smiled, stepping closer. "And it's really great to see you, Terry," she whispered. She looked around and asked leeringly, "And what brings you out here?"

I shrugged and grinned warmly. "I can't help myself. I come here a lot. The place is so beautiful, so relaxing." I chuckled. "This used to be our place, you remember?"

Still looking around, suppressing a smile, she replied, "Yeah, I remember. I remember it well. We spent a lot of time out here, at this very spot." She turned her focus to me. "And what do you mean *used to be*, Mister Terry Allens?" With that, she stepped into my face.

In a voice like dry husk, I said, "I just thought we—"

She stopped my words with her soft lips, then slowly, she pulled back. As she did I stared into her eyes, which glittered like polished stones. I didn't know what to say; my mouth had lost its ability to open, and my heart thumped wildly. Finally, after clearing my throat, I found enough moisture in my mouth to say, "Vera, I...I didn't mean—" My voice caught; I couldn't go on. I could feel my entire face burning for her forgiveness. "I'm so sorry, Vera," I tried again, "I didn't mean to bring any grief into your life. And I'm so sorry that things turned out the way they did. I really am. If I could change it all, you know I would. I truly am sorry." I placed my hand over hers. "Can you ever find it in your heart to forgive me?"

She looked down on the ground and shuffled her feet. Then slowly, she raised her head, chewing on her bottom lip. She cradled a curved palm to my face and looked deep into my eyes, as if probing the truthfulness of my words. Then, aiming a mute acceptance at me, she said, "It's over, Terry...we both need to stop blaming each other and let it go."

I nodded as though I were in complete agreement. I gripped her hand tighter. Managing a weak smile, I said inside a deep sigh, "Well, Vera Armstrong, where do we go from here?"

Her chest heaved. Then she said with a humorous grin, "Well, if I recall, you did say something about sweeping me off my feet and taking care of me." She raised a brow. "You *do* remember saying this, don't you, Terry?"

All at once, my throat went dry. I had to swallow several times before I was able to say, "Yeah...I guess I did say something like that, huh?"

"You sure did, mister," she smiled in a teasing tone, "and I'm here to see that you keep your word."

The expression she gave me almost stole my breath away. In response, I swung a saucy look at her. "I'll gladly keep my word...on one condition."

At that, her smile twisted. "And what might that be?"

Hearing those words caused my heart to beat triple time. *This was it!* I told myself. *I had finally reached that final hurdle!* I stared into her eyes. I could only hope she would go for it. My hands started shaking like a leaf, so in a hurry to steady myself, I gripped Vera by the shoulders and brought her closer to me. I drew a deep breath, and at the moment my mouth felt as though it was packed with gluey cotton. Nevertheless I said, with the utmost sincerity in my voice, "Vera, I love you with all my heart and soul." I took her face into my hands. "You are my everything. You're my day, my night, my sun, and my moon. Vera, baby, believe me when I say *you are my everything.*" I swallowed hard and brought her face closer to mine. "But, baby, there is one thing that you are not. And it burns like hell, right down to the core." Unable to keep my distress from showing, I turned away and shook my head. It was that painful.

She looked at me, puzzled by the expression on my face, then she asked in a pleading murmur, "What is it, Terry?"

I turned and looked at her. My voice was cramped in my throat as I moistened my lips. "Vera, I need to have you in my life...but I need to have you more than just as a friend, or as a lover...Vera, baby, I need to have you as my wife." I cleared my throat then fell slowly to one knee, glaring up into her bright gray eyes. "Vera Armstrong, the most beautiful woman in the world...would you do me the honors in making me the most *happiest, luckiest* man in the world by becoming my wife?"

With a slight whimper, she raised a hand and clamped it around her mouth to keep herself still. Her eyes began to well. *Say yes,*

Vera, I uttered to myself. *There could be no other answer—say it, baby! Say it!*

In the seconds that followed she hadn't given me a reply. My brows knotted in perplexity. My face twisted as my thoughts raced. *Had I blown it?* I feared. *Had I put my foot in my mouth?* My heart began to sink like a rock. For just a second, I wanted to say, *Let's just forget what I said—hey, let's just be friends, okay? I'm fine with that—really, I am!*

Vera remained silent, and just stared at me. Her scrutiny had seemed to last a prodigious amount of time, but in reality must have been a second or two. In that little eternity, I could feel blood burning in my veins, could feel the wild slam of my heart against my rib cage, like the pound of a fist against a wooden door. *Thu-thump! Thu-thump! Thu-thump!* it hammered. I was certain Vera must be able to hear it, too. I swallowed, wondering like hell what her answer would be.

I didn't have to wait long.

A moment later, Vera's smile said it all. Through a tearful gasp, her lips shaped the word *yes*, as if she were scrambling to catch up with her voice. Then finally, as the yellow light on her face shifted from the patches of sunlight filtering down through the trees above, she'd found the words and whispered tearfully, "Yes...yes, Terry Allens, I will marry you."

Temporarily stunned by her reply, my eyes slanted, then went wide, and then I felt my heart erupt and soar like an arrow freed from a bow. Unable to suppress the excitement and joy charging through me, I jumped to my feet. With both my hands I took her by the face and kissed her lips. I pulled back and stared at her momentarily with my mouth opened. Then I let out a whoop that echoed around us. Whatever cool I had—it was gone! I was like a kid locked in a candy store—it was a dream come true!

I quickly settled down and then splaying my fingers over her slender curves, I caught her about the waist and drew her close to me, ducking my head to whisper in her ear in a lilting, controlled, sure tone, "I'm going to make you the happiest woman in the world."

She looked at me lovingly. "I'm sure you will. And I'm going to make you the happiest man, baby, just you wait and see."

I nodded, showing my exuberance plainly. "Yeah, I think we're going to be good for each other." For a long moment, we embraced, whispering in each other's ear, telling the other exactly what it was we were after, and vehemently promising to supply it. The embrace was magical, and as I held her in my arms I still recalled the memory of the first kiss between us. Once that step was taken, once that invisible line was crossed between us, two people who were destined to be together, there was no going back from it and no forgetting it. Every time I looked at her I would remember that kiss, just as she would.

Little did we know, something as simple as a kiss...

We held each other for quite some time, then slowly, Vera pulled away.

Looking up at me she smiled, then chewed her lower lip; a habit I'd grown to love. "I was wondering..." she started distantly yet directly.

I shook my head. It was difficult to speak. The way she was standing there—breathtaking, the way she was *looking* at me, as if she could plumb my very depths—was so unsettling!— "Yes?" I managed.

She took a step back and her lips curled in a smile that was pure feline amusement, as she purred in a low, sultry voice, "Well, with me not *seeing* you for such a long time...I seem to have a little problem here."

"And what might that be?" I inquired, stepping closer to her and running my knuckles up and down her cheek, which was soft to the touch.

Still smiling slyly, even a bit devilishly at this point, Vera began unbuttoning the front of her blouse as she met my arms. I looked down. Her skin was firm, smooth and inviting. I smiled and waggled my eyebrows, then, looking around first, I buried my face between her breasts.

"Ouch," she whispered. "You could use a shave, baby."

"First things first," I crooned silkily, holding her tightly and brushing my lips against her open mouth. "But we have to be careful...we don't want to be caught doing it out in public."

Vera reached down and gripped me. "It's a deal," she said, unable to mask the twitching of her lips, the merriment dancing in her gray eyes, as she did so. Standing on the tips of her toes, her tongue flickered against my lips. "But who wants to be careful?"

I looked at Vera, the love of my life, her face glowing like a jewel, as if lit from within. She had a point; you had to decide what things in life took priority. With that in mind, I scooped her up in my arms and carried her over to her Lincoln Navigator.

Chapter 29

When I walked through the doors I could see that The Mirage was going full blast. Colored spotlights played on the small stage while a troop of naked women gyrated, hips grinding and bumping, tits bouncing, the women moving in perfect sync with the driving beat of the music. In the audience, men hollered and barked, their glassy stares fixed on the writhing flesh. Clouds of tobacco smoke drifted through the beams of light as skimpily dressed waitresses moved among the tables, serving drinks and getting pinched on the ass.

I threaded my way through the crowd then found myself an open spot to stand, next to a cigarette machine. I propped an elbow on it and stared at the stage. To the boisterous crowd the women moved exceptionally well, mesmerizing their audience with their undulating flesh. But to me, compared to Regina, the women were tamed. There was no contest. The girl reigned here. I hoped I hadn't missed Regina's new number. I looked around the room hoping to spot her. After a few seconds I did.

She was sitting by herself at the bar, a barely touched drink in front of her. But as I watched her something didn't look right about her appearance. Instead of wearing her usual pre-performance outfit, she was dressed as if she were about to leave, black slacks and a gray turtleneck sweater, and a black overcoat. Outwardly, she appeared troubled. I cut through the crowd and gave her a quick peck on the cheek, then took a seat beside her.

"Hey, girl," I said, "why aren't you getting ready for your number?" I checked my Rolex. "You haven't gone through it already, have you?"

Regina looked at me and gave me a weak smile. "No." With that she took a pull from her drink.

"Well, when do you go on, girl?" I asked, rubbing my palms together. "I'm ready to see you shake that ass!"

She dismissed the notion without a glance. "I'm not. I'm thinking about quitting, Terry. I'm really getting bored with this shit." She turned to face me, her face straining as she went on, "I

251

mean, what is it with these fuckin' men, huh? Does all this simulated sexual twitching and grinding really stir them up—making their dicks throb in their pants? Or is it just that they enjoy looking at us women as their object of affection, their playthings, their little possessions to ogle and talk down to?"

I looked around, feeling her emotions, almost to the letter. I put an arm around her shoulder. "Listen, girl, you don't have to do this. You can always change jobs. Hell, look at me, who would've thought I'd be selling houses, huh? I mean, who would've thunk it?" I threw my head back and laughed. "If somebody would have approached me six months ago and told me that I'd be selling real estate property for a living, I'd be like, get the fuck outta here. But look at me, it's what I do. So you see, it's never too late to change your agenda in life."

"I'm not selling houses for a living, Terry," she said stiffly. "So don't even suggest it, okay?"

I chuckled then reached over and took a sip of her drink. "Don't worry, girl, I wasn't even about to head down that avenue. Besides, with your inflated tits, your clients wouldn't be able to concentrate anyway." I rocked her shoulder and kissed her cheek once more.

The gesture brought a warm smile to Regina's mouth. She looked at me and shook her head. "I love you, Terry Allens, you know that?"

I nodded. "I love you, too."

With that, she began sobbing low and deep. She covered her face with her hands and leaned into my body, as if trying to conceal herself.

"Hey," I said, cradling her closer, "what's going on here, girl?" She cried harder, and moaned as if in agony. "Regina," I asked, easing her back and staring into her face, which was a mess, "what's really troubling you?" I handed her a few napkins from off the bar and dried her eyes. I made her blow her nose then I wiped her remaining tears. I shifted on the stool and faced her directly. "Okay, Regina, out with it. I want you to tell me the real deal here, all right?"

Sobbing from deep in her throat she nodded. She took a sip of her drink to wet her lips. She turned to me and grasped both my hands into hers. Then, in a tone of faraway sadness, she murmured, "I've done something terrible, Terry..." Her voice caught and she took a deep breath and stared at the ceiling. "Something very, very bad."

I shook my head. "What? What is it?"

With a fierce effort, she quelled her rising sorrow. The exertion left her teary-eyed and panting, but in control. "Terry, listen to me, cause I don't know if I can ever say this again." She swallowed hard, then said, "I...I killed Derrick."

Instantly, I felt as if something had slammed me in the chest; my breath left me in a rush. There was a silence going on inside of me while I mentally reeled under the impact of what I had just heard. I shook my head dumbly. I couldn't think. But at last I had sufficiently recovered to say in an uttered voice, "Regina...it was you?"

She nodded her head, as if stricken mute.

I blinked rapidly. "But why?"

With those words Regina turned a gaze like stone on me, and a muscle shifted along her jaw. "I caught Derrick with one of his hands down the back of Damion's pants. He was masturbating with the other." She paused, having difficulty with her breathing; the pressure growing in her chest seemed to cramp her lungs. She looked at me with wilting eyes. "The dirty motherfucker had his filthy hands down my son's pants, can you believe that shit, Terry?" She turned away, seemingly laughing to herself. "I wasn't going to stand for that shit...no fuckin' way. I knew I had to kill that bastard. I mean, there's no way in hell I could overlook something like that, you know what I'm saying?"

Though I was still somewhat shocked, I had to agree. "Look, you did what you had to do," I said casually, tightening the grip on her hands, "and now it's time to move on."

"But, Terry," she said tearfully, "what I did is inexcusable."

A stillness followed her words which lasted ten seconds or so. I knew, all too well, ten seconds can seem a very long time when one is inwardly writhing with humiliation and regret, but at last I saw her torment easing up a bit.

"Yes. Yes, it is," I softly agreed. Slowly, I cupped a hand under her chin. My tone then went hard, casting hints of authority, as if I could make Regina taller under the weight of her burden. "And someday, hopefully *soon*, you can make peace with God over this. And as far as I'm concerned, this matter *only* concerns you and God." I frowned, making sure my point was felt. "God has the final, *ultimate* call on this—on everything. So you'd better recognize,

Regina, you know what I'm saying here? Don't blow this off without asking for forgiveness…don't you *dare* do this." My choice of words wasn't a warning or some well-intentioned brotherly advice. It was an order.

I then met her gaze, the look was sort of an exclusion of everything else in her life, as if the rest of her life were something I would never comment on. Regina was her own woman, she had her own mind, and if she felt she was tired of dancing, it would be her decision, hers and hers alone.

Regina smiled, agreeing with me without the use of words. Then, with an effort, she swallowed the distress that clogged her throat. I gave her hand a squeeze and she squeezed back, and it was at that moment, as I recognized the profound understanding and willingness etched in every line of her face, that the scales of her pain began to recede. Her face started to glow and her eyes brightened, and I saw that she was simply beautiful, that she was going to be okay. With a small, victorious smile, she asked quietly, "You going to stay and watch me dance?"

"That depends," I inquired, squinting my eyes, "you goin' to tear the roof of this sucka or what?"

In response, she pulled me to her and kissed me forcefully on the lips. Now smiling viciously, she said, "You just watch me!" With that she slid off the stool to go change and as she did, she bumped into an old man, obviously too old to be in the place, wearing an even older, loud, back-in-the-day-player-type outfit: red blazer, a red silk shirt open at the throat and spread wide to reveal a thick gold chain nestling in a patch of gray and black waxed chest hairs. The hair on top of his head was the same color combination, a carefully styled, mass of finger waves.

His thick lips curled in a smile. "Hey, where you goin', baby?"

Regina's tone was flat. "I'm about to do my number, *if* you must know." She swung her gaze to the women on stage, who had now reached what evidently was the high point of their act.

Having recognized Regina as the star of the place, the old man moved closer, until he was near enough for her to smell a mixture of cologne, sweat, and cigarette breath. "Listen, baby, after your number why don't you and I kick it a bit? My friends call me Sugar Ray.

Now what'll say?" With those words he stepped back, opened his blazer, and flashed a cheeky smile.

Regina looked over at me then back at the old man. "Get the hell away from me, nigga. I've got a show to do."

The man's thick lips popped open, then twisted in a snarl. "Hey, girl, you listen here—"

"I said step the hell back," Regina snapped. She pointed a finger in my direction. "Or I'll have my big brother beat the crap out of you."

The old man looked over at me. Immediately he held his palms up. "No offense, partner, I didn't know this was your—"

"Get to steppin', old dude!" Regina cut in with a smile. "Move it!"

"Okay, okay. I'm about to break." He frowned as he drew a long, slim cigar from his shirt pocket. He lit it with a match and shook out the flame before tossing the dead match into the crystal ashtray on the bar. Then he turned and melted into the mass of patrons, grumbling about the uppity bitches you could run into.

Regina blew me a kiss then disappeared in the back. I nodded then turned to finish her drink of scotch and water. As the women on stage swirled and twirled and pulsed their bodies toward their climatic end, I found myself thinking about Regina, and what she had said, about her killing Derrick, then of Denise. Suddenly, as I sat there, it all made sense. That's what Denise was so proud of me for. She thought *I* had killed Derrick. *You handled your business professionally*, I recalled her saying. But there was something else she had said she was proud of me for, and as I sat there I couldn't think of a thing.

Nothing came to mind.

I shook my head, then pushed it away altogether. *What was the use, anyway? It was over.* I took a sip of the scotch. *The shit was over.*

Fifteen minutes had passed. Then all of a sudden, all around me, the lights dimmed, and that's when Regina took the stage. The crowd roared its approval, well-pleased that things were *finally* getting started. Primed and ready Regina strutted and pranced, and as she did so, I felt a thrill as I realized the moment I'd come here for had arrived. The featured act *was* on, and when the lights hit hard on

Regina's lush body which rippled like waves in the ocean, with her long, silky black hair cradling her lovely face with large brown eyes and an alluring, wonderfully full mouth, I felt myself becoming hard as iron.

More cheers followed when Regina strode around the stage, with a look of fierce determination. *Wanton and shameful,* my mother would have called it. But I saw nothing but beauty and perfection. I suppose with age I might find this kind of thing a bit under par, but as my gaze intensed, I thought it highly unlikely, as most patrons in the place. But there was something in me that separated me from the others. I *knew* the spirited woman on stage, one who laughed and cried and raged with equal abandon. I knew the brilliant mind and personality and potential that laid inside her—beyond those full, rounded curves, and I wasn't about to let her forget any of that. Not as long as I had breath in me.

She was my girl.

For always.

As if by some mental telepathy, Regina, very slyly, threw a saucy, wet look in my direction. Then, in a blinking of an eye, she turned back to the matters at hand—entertaining the crowd. She found her zone, which required the utmost concentration, and struck a pose.

I picked up the glass and took a long swallow, draining the glass, experiencing a buzz partly inspired by the scotch but in larger part by the stunning figure on stage.

A hush fell over the crowd, the music pulsed and surged, and Regina began to dance.

Chapter 30

I was in an expansive mood. Wearing a new tuxedo, compliments of Elgin Kirtz's clothing store, which Elgin had finished for me only a few days before. With Will by my side, I strode through the lobby of the hotel to the waiting limousine, responding to the doorman's salute with a jaunty wave.

As Will and I crossed the sidewalk, the chauffeur came to attention and opened the door. Will slid in first and I followed. Once inside, I settled back on the seat, nervous as shit. But then, it was to be expected: it was a special day for me, the eleventh day of June, a bright and beautiful Saturday afternoon; it was the day I was to be married.

Yes, my time had finally come. And Will had made this point vehemently clear, joking boisterously all throughout my bachelor party, stating that the player had finally been ensnared, and that it was time for me to check in my player card—time to pass on the reigning crown. I could only smile with agreement. As drunk and plowed as we all were, Will was right. The crown belonged to somebody else. My past life was just that...past.

My life was starting anew, with the woman of my dreams. I took a deep breath, still not believing that this was all happening. In about an hour or so, Vera Armstrong would be Vera Allens. She would be my wife...for always...forever and a day.

"You ready to do this, cuz?" Will asked, punching me lightly in the shoulder as the limo pulled away.

When he said that, my heart gave a lurch—and then my bladder seemed full, as if I had just drunk a gallon of water. "Yeah," I nodded, still a little nervous. "But right now I got to take a piss."

Inside a chuckle, Will said, "Yeah, man, me, too."

I turned and looked at him. "Hey, remember when we were teenagers and how we would cruise around, and when one of us had to piss we'd pull off to the side—no matter where we were—and let loose?"

"Yeah," Will smiled, slapping his knee, "that was some wild and crazy shit."

"Well, cousin," I murmured, "I gotta piss…you gotta piss…?"

Will looked at me strangely. "Nah, man, no way. Listen to what you're sayin'. Man, you're about to get married."

I ignored his protest. *"And?* I still got to piss."

With that, Will gave it a quick consideration then shouted to the driver, "Hey, chauffeur dude, stop the car at the first secluded spot! The groom and his best man back here gotta take a whiz!" He laughed and gave me a jab with his elbow.

Pulling off Summer Avenue, the limousine came to a stop near a clump of Magnolia trees, where the land rolled, an undulating expanse of dips and swells. There were also a thick stand of holley shrubs. Will and I climbed out of the car and stepped behind a set of shrubs to empty our bladders. Laughing like old times, we finished our business, piled back into the car, and continued on for the church.

A half an hour later the limousine pulled in front of the church, a huge sprawling building with mountainous steeples and stain-glassed windows. I glanced around and noticed a long procession of cars and vans, snaking their way along the turns and curves of the street. Almost immediately, butterflies fluttered in my stomach. I was nervous, and felt as though I could piss again. I found myself shivering, but realized that it was a billow of excitement, not fear, that shimmied down my spine. Desire, not regret or second thoughts, that spread its heat throughout my body.

I was only experiencing anticipation.

I cannot remember when I had last felt so overpowered by these kind of emotions.

However, Will read my emotions as nervousness and because of this, he said, with the most tender smile I had ever seen on a man, "Let's go get you married, cuz."

I blinked at him, then blinked again, thinking of Vera, in all her glory, waiting for me. I smiled as it hit me…*something as simple as a kiss*…With that, I nodded firmly, "Yeah, I've got somebody special waiting for me."

Will and I stepped from the limousine. He turned to face me and then gave me the quick once-over, brushing my shoulders and straightening my bow-tie. I did the same for him. Then, with that done, we headed up the steps of the church. Overwhelmed, I smiled, *Yes, a special woman was waiting for me...for Terry Allens...and her name was Vera Armstrong...soon to be Vera Allens.* I nodded strongly within myself. *And I wasn't about to keep her waiting a second longer.*

Boldly, triumphantly, I stepped inside, ready to accept my bride, ready to start a new life, but above of all...*most of all*...ready to bring God into my life. HE had seen me through a storm, and literally left me unscathed—standing by my side throughout all my turmoil—bringing me relief and peace of mind...not to mention a beautiful bride.

HE said HE would never leave me. And this was *so* true. HE had kept HIS word.

HE had never left me.

And now, feeling renewed...reborn, there was nothing left for me to do...but return the favor.

About the Author

    Ray Burton lives in Nashville Tennessee. *A Day in the Life* marks his second literary venture. His long-cherished aspiration to write became a reality when he put pen to paper and created the bone chilling, highly controversial *If I Ruled the World.* Needless to say, the reviews went through the roof. For those who thirst for more, Ray has three thrillers waiting in the wings: *The Turnaround, Marked!, and Devil's Pie.* Ray is extremely diversified, and likes to keep each book separate to keep his readers guessing. For all inquiries about Ray's work, or about interviews, book signings, comments, or autographed copies, you can e-mail him at: authorRayB@netscape.net

www.ingramcontent.com/pod-product-compliance
Lightning Source LLC
Chambersburg PA
CBHW030255290526
45785CB00001B/98